Education, Occupation, and Earnings

Achievement in the Early Career

STUDIES IN POPULATION

Under The Editorship of: H. H. WINSBOROUGH

Department of Sociology
University of Wisconsin
Madison, Wisconsin

Education, Occupation, and Earnings

Achievement in the Early Career

William H. Sewell and Robert M. Hauser

Department of Sociology
University of Wisconsin
Madison, Wisconsin

WITH   Duane F. Alwin
       Dorothy M. Ellegaard
       Janet A. Fisher
       Kenneth G. Lutterman
       Vimal P. Shah

ACADEMIC PRESS   New York San Francisco London

A Subsidiary of Harcourt Brace Jovanovich, Publishers

001 5-12

ACADEMIC PRESS, INC.
111 Fifth Avenue, New York, New York 10003

United Kingdom Edition published by
ACADEMIC PRESS, INC. (LONDON) LTD.
24/28 Oval Road, London NW1

Library of Congress Cataloging in Publication Data

Sewell, William Hamilton, Date
    Education, occupation, and earnings.

    (Studies in population series)
    Bibliography: p.
    Includes index.
    1.   Success.   2.   Social status.   3.   Motivation
(Psychology)   4.   Ability.   I.   Hauser, Robert Mason,
joint author.   II.   Title.   III.   Series: Studies
in population.
HF5386.S4183   331.1'1   74-10214
ISBN 0–12–637850–9

HF
5386
.S4183
1975

To Otis Dudley Duncan

Contents

Preface

In this book, we report an extensive analysis of the achievements of a large sample of Wisconsin men during the 10 years following their high school graduation. The analysis focuses on the causes and consequences of higher education, providing new and important evidence about the effects of socioeconomic background and academic ability on post-high school education, occupational achievement, and earnings; about the role of social psychological factors on the processes of achievement; about the influence of type and quality of colleges on occupational attainment and earnings; and about the effects of military service and ability on earnings.

The Wisconsin data are of unique quality and importance because they come from a carefully designed longitudinal study which has been unusually successful in obtaining follow-up information on a very high proportion of the original sample, and because the data include information on the socioeconomic origins and the current economic standing of the young men, as well as measures of academic ability; information on educational performance, aspirations, the encouragement of parents, teachers, and friends; and information on military service and occupational achievement.

The analysis is based largely on a recursive structural equation model of achievement, which elaborates and extends the work of

Peter M. Blau and Otis Dudley Duncan (*The American Occupational Structure* (New York: Wiley), 1967), and Otis Dudley Duncan, David L. Featherman, and Beverly Duncan (*Socioeconomic Background and Achievement* (New York: Seminar Press), 1972), and of William H. Sewell, Archibald O. Haller, and Alejandro Portes ("The Educational and Early Occupational Attainment Process," *American Sociological Review*, February 1969), and William H. Sewell, Archibald O. Haller, and George W. Ohlendorf ("The Educational and Early Occupational Status Attainment Process: Replication and Revision," *American Sociological Review*, December 1970), as well as the recent work of economists of education and human capital.

Our basic model links socioeconomic background (as measured by father's and mother's education, father's occupation, and parents' income) and son's academic ability with the son's educational, occupational, and earnings achievements. We then elaborate our basic model to include, as mediators between the background and achievement variables, such social psychological factors as rank in high school class, perceived expectations of significant others, and education and occupational aspirations, in order to provide further insight into the process of socioeconomic achievement, especially in relation to educational attainment, which is basic to occupational achievement and earnings. In the final elaboration of our model, we take into account, for those who went on to college, the effects of college attended on occupation and earnings.

Wherever possible, we have made comparisons between parameter estimates in our sample and those in national samples. The evidence suggests that the basic process of socioeconomic achievement that we find operating for our sample of Wisconsin young men also holds for young men in the general population of the United States.

Although we believe that the work we describe in this book adds materially to our knowledge about socioeconomic achievement in American society, we plan to extend our longitudinal study by doing an extensive follow-up of our sample in early 1975. In this follow-up, 18 years after high school graduation, we plan to obtain for both males and females information on more recent experiences such as family formation, marital stability, migration, graduate and adult education, on-the-job training, job satisfaction, and aspirations for the future. With these data and information on current occupation and earnings, we believe that it will be possible to arrive at a more complete understanding of the socioeconomic achievement process. But, until this research is completed, we offer the analysis contained in this book to sociologists, economists, psychologists, and educators, and to the informed public as one part of a comprehensive effort to understand achievement in American society.

Acknowledgments

The analysis reported in this volume grows out of a research program on "Social and Psychological Factors in Status Attainment," which has been under the direction of William H. Sewell since its inception in 1962. The planning of the project was done while Sewell was a fellow at the Center for Advanced Study in Behavioral Sciences in 1959–1960. It was a natural outgrowth of his continuing interest in social stratification, which was first exemplified in the publication of his *The Construction and Standardization of a Scale for the Measurement of the Socioeconomic Status of Farm Families* in 1940, and numerous articles and monographs since that time. The early planning for the present volume, and some of the preliminary research on which it is based, took place in 1968–1969, while he was a Visiting Scholar at the Russell Sage Foundation. For these very special years in his professional life, he owes thanks to Ralph Tyler and to Orville G. Brim, Jr., then director and president, respectively, of these organizations.

In 1969, Robert M. Hauser joined the project just after completing his own Ph.D. on similar research at the University of Michigan, under the direction of Otis Dudley Duncan. Since joining the project, Hauser has played a principal role, not only in the research activities of the project but also in the management of the research program.

The research program has been supported continuously by grants from the National Institute of Mental Health, U.S. Public Health Service, Bethesda, Maryland (MH 06275). The specific project, which was the source of the research reported here, was supported by a Cooperative Research and Demonstration Grant under the title, "Effects of Ability, Family Background, and Education on Earnings and Careers," Social and Rehabilitation Service, Social Security Administration, Department of Health, Education, and Welfare, Washington, D.C. (Grant No. 314). This project was funded from September 1, 1966, to June 30, 1973. The present volume constitutes the final report on that project and is in fulfillment of our obligations to the Social Security Administration under the terms of the grant. Our work also has been facilitated by small grants from the Research Institute of the American College Testing Program. We wish to acknowledge the services of the Madison Academic Computing Center, which were provided by grants from the University of Wisconsin Graduate School Research Committee, and the cooperation of Harry Harder and his staff at the Wisconsin Department of Taxation in providing income tax data.

We wish to acknowledge the assistance of a number of persons, most of whose names do not appear among the authors of this report; the authorship of each of the several chapters is indicated in its first footnote. We begin by acknowledging our gratitude to our colleague and friend, J. Kenneth Little, Emeritus Professor of Education, who directed the original study of the College Plans of Wisconsin High School Seniors (1957) which has served as the starting point of our longitudinal analysis since that time. Over the years, several persons have served as programmers on our project. Their services have been invaluable in the development of the data file and in the design and modification of the complex computer programs needed in our data analysis. We are especially grateful to Richard G. Wolfe, Keith R. Billingsley, Denise Praizler, Michael L. Wiseman, Donald Hester, and Peter J. Dickinson for their creative efforts in this area. Four people have been principally responsible for the maintenance of our vast data files since the beginning of the project. They are Vimal P. Shah, Victor Jesudason, Dorothy M. Ellegaard, and Taissa S. Hauser. All of them in their turn have shown great ingenuity and responsibility in the performance of a difficult task. In addition to these responsibilities, each of these persons has also doubled as a research assistant and has helped in numerous ways, ranging from constructing tables to coauthoring manuscripts, several of which have been published. Others who have served as research assistants or associates on the project include Oluf M. Davidsen, Herschel Shosteck, J. Michael Armer, Alan M. Orenstein, Eldon L. Wegner, Alair A. Townsend, Rosanda R. Richards, Richard A. Zeller, Alejandro Portes, George W. Ohlendorf, Ruth M. Gasson, Nancy D. Carter, Duane F. Alwin, Charlotte W. Yang, and James R. Kluegel. Most of these have written theses or dissertations using project data or have been coauthors of papers, as well as helping with more routine details of the project.

Our faculty colleagues on the project over the years have been Kenneth G. Lutterman, who, in addition to contributing to two of the chapters in this volume, has played an important role in obtaining the income data from the Wisconsin Department of Taxation and the earnings information from the Social Security Administration; Ronald M. Pavalko, who was responsible for much of the work on the 1964 follow-up survey; Janet A. Fisher, who is the major author of one of the chapters in this report and who has generously counseled all members of the project staff on economic and other aspects of our analysis; Archibald O. Haller, who has coauthored several of the published papers emanating from the research program; and Paul R. Marty, of the Computing Center, who has faithfully carried out the instructions of the Social Security Administration that were worked out to safeguard the earnings data. Other colleagues who have helped us with critical comment from time to time include Beverly Duncan, Burton R. Fisher, David L. Featherman, Warren O. Hagstrom, David Mechanic, Bryant E. Kearl, Seymour Spilerman, Halliman H. Winsborough, Donald J. Treiman, Martin David, Arthur S. Goldberger, and L. Joseph Lins.

We must not fail to acknowledge the excellent secretarial services of Alice J. Thompson, Lorraine S. Borsuk, Rebekah D. Heideman, and Pat Klitzke. They have not only typed the various drafts of this manuscript, but have deciphered our scribbling, corrected our spelling, constructed tables, checked references, and read the proofs on many manuscripts for us, and have done all of this with amazingly good humor and only an occasional loss of patience.

Many clerical assistants have worked on this research, but only one, Viola M. Olson, has been with us for a long period of time. We wish to thank her for good and faithful services.

Also, we wish to acknowledge our great debt to certain members of the Social Security Administration whose cooperation has made this research possible. Ida C. Merriam, former Assistant Commissioner for Research and Statistics, originally made it possible for us to obtain the Social Security earnings information and helped us to devise a linkage system to analyze earnings data and at the same time to preserve the confidentiality of Social Security records. John Carroll, currently Assistant Commissioner for Research and Statistics, has continued the tradition of cooperation established by Dr. Merriam. Ira Rifkind and Creston Smith of the Office of Research and Statistics, and William E. Hanna, Jr., and Wayne Lough of the Bureau of Data Processing have been of unfailing assistance in the complicated task of providing earnings information. William R. Collier and Henry P. Brehm of the Office of Research and Statistics and James D. Cowhig, formerly Chief of the Cooperative Research and Demonstration Grants Branch, have demonstrated their interest and support of this research in numerous ways.

We have a rather special debt to Otis Dudley Duncan, to whom this book is dedicated, for expert consultation and encouragement over the years. We also have strong personal and intellectual ties with him—Hauser as his student at the University of Michigan, and Sewell as a close friend and professional colleague for many years beginning in 1937 when Duncan was a young student and Sewell was an Assistant Professor in Sociology at Oklahoma Agricultural and Mechanical College (now Oklahoma State University).

It goes without saying, but we must say it, that none of the persons whose help we have acknowledged (unless they are authors of chapters in this report) bears any responsibility whatsoever for any errors that may be found in these pages, nor for any opinions or implications stated therein.

1

The Socioeconomic
Achievement Process[1]

Introduction

The research reported on these pages analyzes the influence of social origins on educational attainment, occupational achievement, and earnings, with particular emphasis on earnings. Of course, it is widely recognized that many factors are implicated in an individual's social and economic achievements: such ascribed socioeconomic characteristics as parents' education, occupation, and income; racial, ethnic, and religious origins; the environments and opportunities offered by home, community, and school; and individual characteristics like abilities, aspirations, and efforts. In a sociological interpretation of the achievement process, the interesting questions are three: To what degree do an individual's achievements depend on factors other than his own ability, aspiration, and effort? What are the organizational and social psychological mechanisms of this dependence? And to what extent do ability, aspiration, and effort themselves depend on factors other than the individual's own experiences and prior achievements? [2]

[1] This chapter was prepared by William H. Sewell and Robert M. Hauser.
[2] It will be noted that our statements about the achievement process, in this chapter and elsewhere in this volume, closely parallel those of Duncan, Feather-

To state the matter differently, earnings are supposedly paid to the individual for the performance of an occupational role rather than awarded because of some extrinsic considerations. But are there other factors that can be identified as having an influence on earnings and that may help to account for the wide variation in earnings among the members of any particular cohort? What is there about the individual's social background that provides favorable or unfavorable conditions for future earnings? How do these conditions exercise their influence on earnings? Throughout the history of mankind, it has been commonly assumed that people from higher status backgrounds achieve more because they possess superior God-given capacities—due either to divine ordination or biological inheritance or both. We do not wish to enter into what has been a mainly fruitless debate on this issue, but rather, prefer to attempt to chart the complex process by which an individual's social origins influence his capacities and achievements in educational, occupational, and economic spheres.

Quite obviously, one source of variation in earnings between persons of varying social origins is the differences in individual characteristics of those persons. Those with higher status origins, as indicated by numerous studies, on the average score higher on ability and achievement tests, earn better grades in school, have higher educational and occupational aspirations, are more likely to obtain the education that will qualify them for the more demanding and high prestige occupations, and, consequently, tend to earn more money. We believe that much of the influence of social background on earnings and other socioeconomic achievements is due to the superior cognitive and motivational environment provided in the homes of higher status parents and to the advantages in schooling and job opportunities that such parents can provide for their children. But we believe, too, that ascriptive elements are at work that permit the direct transfer of occupational and economic status, whether high or low, from father to adult sons, irrespective of the sons' abilities, motivations, and educational achievements.

We believe that earnings, here defined as direct monetary reward for occupational performance, are only one of a number of

---

man, and Duncan (1972:3–16) and Blau and Duncan (1967:1–10, 163–177). Another review of the status attainment literature is found in Haller and Portes (1973).

rewards that may accrue to a person because of his performance of social roles—in this case an occupational role.[3] For this reason, we think the distribution of earnings should be interpreted in the context of the allocation of occupational roles and their related perquisites. That is, earnings are a status achievement, just as is educational attainment or occupational achievement. Moreover, earnings are to some extent dependent on occupational attainment, just as occupational attainment is to some extent dependent on educational attainment. The degree to which these achievements are interrelated, the extent to which they are connected with socioeconomic background, and the mechanisms by which socioeconomic background influences them all remain problematic. Already evidence, particularly from the work of O. D. Duncan and associates (Blau and Duncan, 1967; Duncan, Featherman, and Duncan, 1972) and William H. Sewell and associates (Sewell, Haller, and Portes, 1969; Sewell, Haller and Ohlendorf, 1970; Sewell and Hauser, 1972), has accumulated to indicate, at least tentatively, the mechanisms that are involved in the status achievement process.

Blau and Duncan (1967) in their classic study, *The American Occupational Structure* (see also Duncan, Featherman, and Duncan, 1972), were the first to elaborate the status attainment process, suggesting it as a new approach to the study of social mobility. They view status attainment as a process that develops over the life cycle of the individual and have indicated appropriate techniques for its analysis. Their approach is different from traditional social mobility analysis because it focuses on the degree to which the occupational status (or other socioeconomic achievements) of a person is dependent on that person's social origins and the degree to which it is explained or interpreted by the person's own experiences or characteristics that intervene between origin and destination statuses. The analysis is carried out by arraying the relevant variables in a block-recursive structural model of the socioeconomic life cycle.

Using data from a 1962 national sample survey of males 20 to 64 years old, Blau and Duncan (1967) estimated a causal model of status attainment beginning with the educational and occupational status of the father, followed by the son's education, the

---

[3] The operational definition of earnings used in this report is given in Chapter 2. The techniques used for measuring earnings are discussed in Appendix C.

son's first job, and the son's occupation in 1962. They estimated the dependence relationships in this model through a series of recursive equations. This provided a quantitative assessment of the antecedent conditions of socioeconomic achievement and of the relative importance of social origins and educational attainment for such later socioeconomic achievements as first job and current occupation. In their basic model, educational attainment accounted for nearly all of the effects of father's occupational status and father's education on son's occupational status in 1962. Holding constant social background statuses, education was more influential than first job in determining later occupational status. Because educational attainment was largely independent of family background, it had a large independent influence on later achievements. These general results held for the various age cohorts into which the sample was subdivided, and they indicate the crucial role that education plays in the occupational attainment process. While there are many other analyses reported in the Blau–Duncan study and in later extensions of it (Duncan, Featherman, and Duncan, 1972), these may be less important contributions to stratification research than are the approach and methodology that lie behind the basic model.[4]

---

[4] The differences between our two analyses have more to do with the differences in our sets of data than with any differences in sociological orientation. The Wisconsin data differ from the Blau–Duncan data in the following major ways: Their data are for a sample of United States males aged 20–64, while ours are for a sample of Wisconsin high school seniors of both sexes in 1957; their data are cross-sectional, while ours are longitudinal; our data include measures of individual social psychological variables, while their data do not. The latter two facts make it possible for us to stress social psychological variables in our models, whereas Duncan and his associates for the most part have had to use information from other data sets when they wished to estimate the effects of social psychological variables in their models. The Blau–Duncan data do not have parental income or respondents' earnings over a period of years, but do have first occupation and occupation later in the respondents' careers. Our data contain Social Security earnings for men employed in covered occupations for the period 1957–1967, but this is of course early in the earnings career and may not fully reflect the effects of education; our occupational attainment data are restricted to 1964, the year of the last follow-up. Featherman and Hauser (1972) are doing a replication and extension of the Blau–Duncan research in 1973, which will enable them not only to replicate the Blau–Duncan models approximately 10 years later but also to develop new models of the attainment process using additional social structural and social psychological variables.

Early Work on the Wisconsin Study

During the same period that Blau and Duncan were at work on their project (beginning in 1959), Sewell and associates at Wisconsin were engaged in a closely related study of social, economic, and psychological factors in educational and occupational aspirations and achievement. Our data, to be discussed in detail in later chapters, consist of the responses of a large probability sample of 1957 Wisconsin high school seniors to questions regarding their socioeconomic origins, educational experiences, and educational plans and occupational aspirations. These same students were followed up in 1964 to determine their post-high school educational and early occupational attainments. Still later, information on the Social Security earnings of the males in our sample was obtained by means of a complex linkage system that assures anonymity of individual information. A more complete discussion of the sample and sources of information is given in Chapter 2.

Most of the results of the work done to date on the research program, of which this project is a part, have already been published in journal articles, chapters, and monographs. These are available to those who wish to pursue them in detail. However, at the time of this report, 29 items had already appeared in print, so a brief summary of the research to date may be helpful to those who wish to know how the research reported here fits in with the earlier efforts on this project.

We began our work on the longitudinal study in the fall of 1962, five years after the original questionnaire study of the students. We were convinced, from our earlier work and that of a number of other writers, that educational and occupational aspirations are a major factor in the achievement process and that there are wide differences in the aspirations of youth from varying social, economic, and psychological backgrounds. The data from the 1957 sample, which had been gathered for other purposes by J. Kenneth Little (1958, 1959), had not been analyzed to demonstrate these differences or to furnish good clues as to the factors that may be implicated in the development of educational and occupational aspirations.[5]

[5] Little's purpose in making the original study was to obtain data relevant to planning for higher education in the state. He published two widely read reports on the original survey (Little, 1958, 1959).

We first produced several papers dealing specifically with the influence of community of residence on educational and occupational aspirations (Sewell, 1963, 1964; Sewell and Orenstein, 1965; Sewell and Haller, 1965; Sewell and Armer, 1966a). Both educational and occupational aspirations were shown to vary positively with size of community of residence, those from rural communities having far lower aspirations than those from urban communities. However, it was also clear from the data that both size of community and aspiration levels are related quite directly to the socioeconomic origins and measured intelligence of the students. Crosstabular analysis revealed that much of the difference in the aspirations of students from varying sized communities could be explained by the differences in the sex, socioeconomic status, and ability distributions of the communities, but that significant differences still remained for some specific subpopulations—e.g., high status–high ability rural boys are less likely to have high aspirations than are similarly advantaged boys from larger communities. Several possible theoretical explanations for these results were offered.

Because of our intriguing findings regarding the aspirations of the rural residents, several other analyses were done in an attempt to further explicate the results of the crosstabular analysis (Sewell and Haller, 1965; Haller and Sewell, 1967; Portes, Haller, and Sewell, 1968). One of these papers (Sewell and Haller, 1965) employs data from the project to check a number of theoretical ideas, such as those dealing with opportunity structure and self-perceptions to explain rural–urban differences in aspirations. The other articles (Haller and Sewell, 1967; Portes, Haller, and Sewell, 1968) are addressed to the differences in family background, social psychological supports, and self-conceptions of farm boys who aspire to farm, blue-collar, white-collar, and professional occupations. Using appropriate multivariate techniques, it was demonstrated that there are no significant differences between boys aspiring to farm, blue-collar, or white-collar jobs on the many variables composing the above-mentioned clusters, but that there are large differences between those having aspirations for professional positions and those aspiring to any of the lower status occupations.

Continuing with our interest in the influence of social contexts on aspirations, a rather elaborate study was made of the influence of urban neighborhood socioeconomic status on educational aspirations, using data on Milwaukee area high schools (Sewell and Armer, 1966a). There has been much practical as well as theoretical interest in the influence that neighborhoods and schools have on student aspirations. The principal claim has been that the neighborhood in which one lives or the school one attends has an important influence on one's aspiration level over and above the effects of one's family and one's ability. By means of multivariate analysis, the combined effects of these variables, as well as their independent effects, were assessed. The results indicated that the independent influence of neighborhood was disappointingly small; its added contribution to the explained variance in educational aspirations, beyond that accounted for by sex, socioeconomic status, and intelligence, was less than 2.0%. By means of crosstabular techniques the subpopulations most affected were specified, e.g., neighborhood context is associated more with the educational aspirations of girls than of boys and is strongest for girls from high socioeconomic status families. Various possible explanations for these results were offered.

The finding of the relatively small independent effect of neighborhood resulted in an interesting controversy in the *American Sociological Review* regarding the proper assessment of effects and appropriate models for causal inference (Turner, 1966; Michael, 1966; Boyle, 1966; Sewell and Armer, 1966b). Subsequently, we have completed an analysis of covariance that examined the within-school versus the between-school variance in aspirations for the Milwaukee schools and later for other samples of schools. The results indicate that most of the variance is due to differences in school populations rather than to school effects. Thus, it would seem that factors in the student's family background are probably of considerably greater importance in determining aspiration levels than are the characteristics of the school he attends or the neighborhood in which he resides. This finding has been confirmed by other writers (Coleman *et al.*, 1966; Wilson, 1969; Smith, 1972).

We then turned to an examination of the influence of significant others on educational aspirations, with primary emphasis devoted to the crucial role of parents, both as models to be emulated and in terms of the child's perception of parental expectations (Sewell and Shah, 1968a,b). Using multivariate, crosstabular, and regression analysis, we found that both father's and mother's educational attainments have strong positive effects on the aspirations of their children. The effect of father's education is generally greater, but mother's education has a slightly larger independent effect on the aspirations of daughters. When parents have discrepant educational attainment levels, the answer as to which parent's education has more effect on the child's aspirations is contingent not only on the sex of the child but also on the child's intelligence level and the level of the parent's education. However, discrepancy in parents' educational achievements is far less important in motivating children to high-level aspiration than is consistently high educational achievement of both parents. This finding, of course, casts serious doubt on the applicability of the theory of status crystallization to children's educational aspirations when discrepancy is defined in terms of the educational achievements of their parents. But it supports the notion that the model of high-level achievement of one parent, and especially of both parents, is an important factor in the child's educational aspirations.

The influence of parents' expectations on their children's future attainments has been assumed to be a powerful factor in children's educational aspirations. In our research this variable is measured by the extent to which the child perceives his parents as encouraging him to have high educational aspirations. We find large differences for both boys and girls in the percentage aspiring to a college education, depending on their perception of the degree of encouragement furnished by their parents (Sewell and Shah, 1968b). These differences persist when sex, socioeconomic status, and measured intelligence are held constant. Correlation analysis reveals that neither parental encouragement nor measured intelligence, either singly or jointly, can account for socioeconomic class differences in educational aspirations. Using regression and path analysis, we demonstrated that parental encouragement is a powerful intervening variable between the socioeconomic background and ability of the child and his educational aspirations. Parental encouragement has its strongest effects on the educational aspirations of children who score relatively high on ability tests and come from high-status families.

Once the 1964 follow-up data on the subsequent educational and occupational attainments of the members of our sample were in hand, we were able to address various central issues in social stratification. From the beginning we had been especially interested in learning more about how the child's social origins affect his educational attainment—particularly because of the crucial role that education plays in later attainments. The first major study we did after obtaining the follow-up data involved a thorough examination of the effects of socioeconomic origins on the attainment of higher education (Sewell and Shah, 1967). We assessed the influence of family socioeconomic status, controlling measured intelligence, for males and females separately on the progress of our students through the process of higher education: from college plans, to college attendance, to college graduation. This was done by a multiple crosstabulation procedure in which 16-fold tables were developed for each sex, showing, for four categories of socioeconomic status crossed by four categories of measured intelligence, the proportion of students in each cell who planned on college, attended college, and graduated from college. The results indicated that, for each sex, socioeconomic status is an important determinant at each level of attainment in the process of higher education—even when intelligence is controlled. Moreover, when only those who went to college, rather than the total cohort, are considered, socioeconomic origins still make an independent contribution to the likelihood of college graduation. For both sexes, intelligence becomes more important than socioeconomic status as progress is made through the educational system, but at no point does socioeconomic status cease to be an important determinant of who will attain the next step in the process. Path analysis was then used to provide more precise estimates of the direct and indirect effects of socioeconomic status and intelligence on the attainment of higher education. The results of this analysis clearly showed that both socioeconomic origins and ability are important determinants of higher educational attainment. Both have direct influences that are independent of their relationship to each other and to aspirations, and indirect effects through their relationship to college plans. Both direct and indirect effects of socioeconomic status are greater for girls than for boys.

Our results indicate that the most critical factor in the process of obtaining higher education is the decision to plan on and to enter college. At this point, over one-fourth of the high-ability boys (the top quarter in measured intelligence) and almost one-half of the high-ability girls drop out of the educational attainment process. Socioeconomic origins powerfully affected these decisions of high-ability youth of both sexes; just over one-half of the high-ability boys of low socioeconomic status enroll in college, in comparison with 90% of the high-status boys of equal ability; for girls, the corresponding figures are 28% and 76%. Moreover, the yield of college graduates for boys in the high-ability quarter is only 20% among those with low socioeconomic status origins, in comparison with 64% for those with high socioeconomic status backgrounds; for girls, the yields of college graduates are 14% and 51%, respectively. Even if only those who enter college are considered, socioeconomic status still exerts a powerful influence; only 38% of the high-ability boys who are low in socioeconomic status graduate in comparison with 71% of those of equal ability but high socioeconomic status. For girls, the respective figures are 50% and 67%. Similar trends hold for less able youth.

From all of this evidence it seems clear that although ability plays an important role in determining which students will be selected for higher education, socioeconomic origins never cease to be a major determinant of who shall be eliminated from the contest for higher education. It is also important to emphasize the finding that girls are disadvantaged at every stage of the educational attainment process—even when socioeconomic origins and and ability are controlled.

There are, of course, many other ways in which socioeconomic origins and sex influence the selection process in higher education. The lower socioeconomic status students and girls of all socioeconomic levels are more likely than higher status students and boys of all socioeconomic levels to attend vocational–technical schools if they continue their education after high school graduation; if they go to college, they are less likely to attend high quality colleges and universities and are more likely to drop out; if they drop out, they are less likely to return to college; and if they complete college, they are less likely to attend graduate or professional schools. These differences hold, even when we control for academic ability (Sewell and Shah, 1967; Wegner and Sewell, 1970; Sewell, 1971).

The Wisconsin Status Attainment Models

During the past several years, the major thrust of the analytic work on the project has been directed toward the development of causal models of the status attainment process. Our work with models began in the mid-1960s and was much influenced by consultations with Otis Dudley Duncan and by his writings on linear causal models (1966, 1969). Our first publication in which path analysis was used came in 1967 (Sewell and Shah, 1967); we were interested in the direct and indirect effects of socioeconomic status and measured intelligence, as mediated by educational aspirations, on the attainment of higher education. Even earlier (although the article has a later publication date), we had constructed a model in which parental encouragement was the mediating factor in interpreting the influence of socioeconomic status and ability on educational aspirations (Sewell and Shah, 1968a). Other useful models were developed but not published. All of this work led to the development of complex linear causal models to explain the educational and early occupational attainment process.[6]

From our earlier work on the project, we had identified a number of experiences that young people undergo in their formative years that have an important bearing on post-high school educational outcomes. These include level of performance in high school, whether significant others encourage or discourage high educational and occupational aspirations, and whether or not the students actually develop these aspirations. All of these experiences intervene between the social origins, academic ability, and sex characteristics of the individual and his later achievements and become the mechanism through which these background characteristics transmit their influence. In addition, these same social psychological experiences have direct and indirect effects of their own, quite independent of the youth's background characteristics.

This complex multivariate process has been the focus of much of our recent research, and we have been developing and testing linear causal models to further explicate the process of attainment. Building on the work of Blau and Duncan (1967), we have devised and published a linear recursive model that attempts to elaborate

---

[6] We have also been influenced by recent work on the economics of education and of human capital. This work, although it arises out of a different tradition, shares some common concerns with sociological research on the achievement process. Many useful articles, reviews, and compendia dealing with this literature are available, including: Mincer (1962), Schultz (1963, 1972), Becker (1964), Robinson and Vaizey (1966), Bowman (1969), Joint Economic Committee (1969), Wood and Campbell (1970), Hansen (1970), Kiker (1971), and Orwig (1971).

and explain the effects of socioeconomic origins and academic ability on educational achievements and occupational attainments as these influences are mediated by social psychological processes (Sewell, Haller, and Portes, 1969; Sewell, Haller, and Ohlendorf, 1970). This model links socioeconomic status and academic ability with educational and occupational attainment by means of such social psychological variables as academic performance in high school, the influence of significant others, and the youth's educational and occupational aspirations. The model demonstrates that socioeconomic status has no effect on performance in high school independent of academic ability, but that it has strong direct and indirect effects on significant others' influence and on educational and occupational aspirations and, through these, on educational and occupational attainments. The role of academic ability is somewhat different in that it has strong direct effects on high school performance, independent of socioeconomic status, and direct and indirect effects on significant others' influence and on educational and occupational aspirations and, through these, on educational and occupational attainments. For the boys in our sample, this model succeeds in explaining 57% of the variance in post-high school educational attainment and 40% of the variance in early occupational attainment.

Recently, we have further elaborated our model by disaggregating socioeconomic status into its component parts—parents' income, mother's education, father's education, and father's occupation—and by decomposition of significant others' influence into parental encouragement, teachers' encouragement, and peers' plans (Sewell, 1971; Hauser, 1972; Sewell and Hauser, 1972). This has enabled us to obtain estimates of the individual role of each of these variables in the status attainment process.

Organization of the Volume

Most of the analysis reported in the chapters that follow involves the extension, elaboration, and interpretation of this model as it is applied to socioeconomic attainments—particularly occupation and earnings. Chapter 2 is devoted to such methodological problems as sampling, sources, and quality of data, and the operational definition of variables. Chapter 3 develops and applies a reduced form of the model in an analysis of the influence of socioeconomic origins on the achievements of the young men in our sample. Chapter 4 examines the role of social psychological factors as variables intervening between socioeconomic origins and socioeconomic achievements. Chapter 5 elaborates and complicates the model still further by interpreting the effects of different types of colleges on occupation and earnings. Chapter 6 departs from the model in an attempt to determine the particular circumstances in which ability seems to matter in the determination of earnings. Chapter 7 briefly summarizes the findings of this research and indicates the directions which our research will take in the future.

2

The Longitudinal Study:
Data Sources and Quality[1]

Sources of Data

The data on which our research is based were collected from a large probability sample of Wisconsin high school seniors who have been followed over a period of years in order to measure their educational and socioeconomic achievements. While men and women both were covered in the 1957 survey of high school seniors and in the 1964 follow-up, earnings were available and analyzed only for males. For this reason, the analyses of response rates and data quality reported in this chapter pertain only to males. Data were collected from several sources which are described in the paragraphs that follow.

In April and May of 1957, a questionnaire survey of all high school seniors in Wisconsin public, private, and parochial schools was carried out by Professor J. Kenneth Little of the School of Education of the University of Wisconsin, with the cooperation of the State Superintendent of Schools, to obtain information that would be useful in the planning of statewide programs of higher educa-

[1] This chapter was prepared by Robert M. Hauser, William H. Sewell, and Vimal P. Shah.

tion. Completed questionnaires were obtained from almost 95% of the high school seniors who graduated in the spring semester of 1957. In this survey, information was obtained on several matters, including the post-high school educational and vocational plans of the seniors; the educational, occupational, and economic backgrounds of their parents; the students' perceptions of the influence of their teachers, parents, and friends on their plans; their interest and activity in applying for admission to college and for scholarships; their opinions about the value of going to college; and a number of related matters. The 1957 questionnaire is reproduced in Appendix A. The seniors' percentile scores on the Henmon–Nelson Test of Mental Ability, which at that time was administered annually to all high school juniors in Wisconsin, were obtained from the State Testing Service of the Student Counseling Center of the University of Wisconsin. The rank of each student in his high school class was obtained from his school. Little (1958, 1959) published reports summarizing the results of this survey, based on a working sample of approximately one-sixth of the total respondents.

The original questionnaires and the punched cards were turned over to William H. Sewell in June 1962. A random sample of approximately one-third of the total respondents to the 1957 survey was selected for further study. After checking the reliability of coding, some of the original survey data were recoded, and several new indexes were constructed both from the original data and from information derived from various public sources. A series of studies of educational and occupational aspirations has been published using these data (Sewell, 1963, 1964; Sewell and Orenstein, 1965; Sewell and Armer, 1966a,b; Haller and Sewell, 1967; Sewell and Shah, 1968a; Portes, Haller, and Sewell, 1968).

In the late spring of 1964, seven years after the students were seniors in high school, a follow-up study was carried out for all students in the one-third sample. Information on the post-high school educational and occupational attainments, marital status, military service, and present residence of these seniors was obtained from their parents by means of a mailed questionnaire (Appendix B) and by telephone interviews. After four waves of mailed questionnaires, followed by telephone interviews to nonrespondents for whom telephone numbers could be obtained, responses were obtained for 87.9% of the males in the sample.

In the fall of 1965, with the cooperation of the Wisconsin Department of Taxation and following their strict arrangements to guarantee the privacy of individual records, information about parents' occupation, reported income, and number of exemptions claimed was obtained from 1957–1960 state income tax returns. Information on occupation, reported income, and number of exemptions claimed by the male students was also obtained from the same source for all available years during the period 1957–1965. Information on the earnings of the male students and their parents in the period 1957–1967 was obtained from the Social Security Administration, Washington, D.C., following an elaborate procedure for protecting individual identity. These procedures are described in Appendix C. In addition, information was collected from several published and unpublished sources regarding the characteristics of the high schools and colleges attended by the seniors in the sample. Several articles using these data have been published (Sewell and Shah, 1967, 1968b; Sewell, Haller, and Portes, 1969; Sewell, Haller, and Ohlendorf, 1970; Wegner and Sewell, 1970; Sewell, 1971; Hauser, 1972; Sewell and Hauser, 1972).

Definition and Measurement of the Variables

The information from all of the various sources discussed in the preceding section was carefully edited, coded, and collated on magnetic tape for computer analysis. Some of this information was then used to develop indexes using appropriate techniques, e.g., socioeconomic status indexes and an index of the students' values in relation to higher education.

Several categories of variables have been used in the research reported in this volume. The major categories are *Socioeconomic Background, Academic Performance, Social Psychological Factors, Type of College Attended,* and *Socioeconomic Attainments and Achievements.* In the sections that follow, the variables in each of these categories will be briefly defined and their sources indicated.

SOCIOECONOMIC BACKGROUND

Father's educational attainment (V) and *mother's educational attainment* (M) were reported by the students in the 1957 questionnaire (Appendix A, item 7) and were coded in years of schooling completed, although they were originally reported as levels of educational certification. From other studies of the validity of reports of parents' education by youth of the same age, we believe these reports to be reasonably accurate (Kerckhoff, Mason, and Poss, 1973; Borus and Nestel, 1973). *Father's occupational status* (X), coded in the metric of Duncan's Socioeconomic Index (SEI) of occupations (Duncan, 1961), was ascertained from the father's report in his 1957 Wisconsin tax return or from his return for the closest available year. In a few instances, where this information was not available from tax returns, reports made by the students on the 1957 questionnaire (Appendix A, item 9a) were used. *Parents' average income* (I) for all available years, 1957–1960 (coded in hundreds of dollars), was ascertained from Wisconsin income tax returns. By averaging parents' income in this way, we expect to have eliminated most temporary fluctuations in income. In some of our analysis we have also used *father's average income* (I_F) and *mother's average income* (I_M), where their sources and definition parallel that of parents' average income. In a few instances in this report and extensively in earlier articles, an *Index of Socioeconomic Status* (SES) has been used. This is a linear combination of parents' average income and educational attainments with father's occupational status.

ACADEMIC PERFORMANCE

Academic performance is indexed by two variables: measured mental ability and rank in high school class. The first reflects ability as indicated by scores on a standardized test of mental ability, the second is based on overall performance in high school courses. *Mental ability* (Q) refers to the students' performance on the Henmon–Nelson Test of Mental Ability (Henmon and Nelson, 1954), ascertained from the State Testing Service of the Student Counseling Center of the University of Wisconsin. The tests were given during the students' junior year in high school. The scores are expressed in the metric of intelligence quotients, with a mean of 100 and a standard deviation of 15 in the standard population of Wisconsin high school juniors on which it was normed. *Rank in high school class* (G) was obtained from high school records, expressed as a percentile, and then transformed to produce an approximately normal distribution.

SOCIAL PSYCHOLOGICAL FACTORS

The information on the educational and occupational aspirations of the students and their perceptions of the influence of significant others are the social psychological variables taken from the 1957 questionnaire. *Educational aspiration* (E) is represented by a dummy variable which indicates whether the student planned to enroll in a degree-granting college or university in the year following high school graduation (Appendix A, items 1 and 2). *Occupational aspiration* (J) is the Duncan SEI score for the occupation category which the respondent said he eventually hoped to enter (Appendix A, item 9b). The three "significant other" variables are all based on the students' self-reported perceptions. *Parents' encouragement* (P) to attend college (Appendix A, item 25) and *teacher encouragement* (T) to attend college (Appendix A, item 24), were both dichotomized to distinguish those who were encouraged to attend college from those who were not. *Friends' plans* (F) is based on whether or not the student reported that most of his friends were planning to attend college, and is treated as a dichotomous dummy variable (Appendix A, item 26).

TYPE OF COLLEGE ATTENDED

From the 1964 survey we learned the names of all colleges and universities attended by the students in our sample, the dates of attendance, and the degree(s) awarded to them. This information and the use of various published documents about colleges and universities enabled us to develop a system for classifying the institutions into 12 categories that reflect the characteristics of the institutions, their faculties, and their students. Alwin (1972) has demonstrated that this classification scheme accurately reflects the selectivity, the quality, and the prestige characteristics of colleges and universities. This classification scheme is applied to the *last college attended* (C) in the analysis of earnings in Chapter 5.

SOCIOECONOMIC ATTAINMENTS AND ACHIEVEMENTS

The three major socioeconomic achievement variables with which this research is concerned are the post-high school educational attainments, the occupational achievements, and the earnings of the young men in our sample. *Educational attainment* (U) is based on information from the 1964 questionnaire (Appendix B) and is a very close approximation to the Census concept of years of schooling completed. The only differences are that we gave up to one year's credit for vocational or technical education, and in some instances we credited students with a last year of regular schooling when we did not know for certain if the year had been completed. In most cases we were able to assign a normative number of school years completed that corresponded to the level of certification achieved, e.g., 16 years for college graduates with no further schooling. *Occupational status* (W) is the occupation in which the person was engaged in 1964 and is based on information from the 1964 survey (Appendix B). It is scaled in Duncan SEI units. Finally, *Earnings* (Y) were ascertained from Social Security records, adjusted for effects of multiple job holding and the ceiling on covered earnings, and expressed in thousands of dollars. Earnings for the specific years 1965, 1966, and 1967 are designated respectively as (Y_1), (Y_2), and (Y_3). We also make use in some of our analysis of a canonically weighted average of the three years of earnings (Y). The derivation of this average is given in Chapter 3, where it is used.

Sampling

THE 1957 SAMPLE

The 1957 class of Wisconsin high school graduates included approximately 36,171 persons.[2] The survey conducted at that time yielded 34,151 questionnaires, a 94.4% response rate. The principal source of nonresponse in the 1957 survey was the failure of 47 of Wisconsin's 501 high schools to administer and return questionnaires. Also, a small but unknown number of students were absent during the period of administration of the questionnaire at the cooperating schools. There is no way of knowing the exact bias attributable to the loss of these students from the 1957 survey. It is reasonable to assume that the small number of students who were

[2] The number of public high school graduates is known to be 31,112, and the estimate for parochial and private schools is placed at 5059. At that time there was no official record of the total enrollment or number of graduates in Wisconsin private and parochial schools.

not included differ little, if at all, from the students in the survey with respect to characteristics relevant to the analysis and that their exclusion does not contribute any important bias to the findings reported in this study. Moreover, the total loss is so small and the noncooperating schools so scattered that even if the nonrespondents were not randomly distributed, their exclusion could not have had any large influence on conclusions drawn for the total cohort of high school seniors.

From this set of 34,151 questionnaires, we wished to select a sample of adequate size to permit rather precise estimates of important population parameters and reliable multivariate statistics. After numerous calculations, it was decided that approximately 10,000 cases with usable information would be optimal. Preliminary examination and past experience with similar surveys made it clear that some questionnaires would be unusable. To be on the safe side, a random sample of 10,750 cases was selected in the hope that it would yield approximately 10,000 usable questionnaires. A computer program for random selection of cases was employed to obtain this sample. The program produced random numbers corresponding to the questionnaire numbers in the file of respondents to the 1957 survey. These cases were then identified, edited, and checked for reliability of coding and for missing data. Cases with missing data on important items or a large number of items had to be eliminated from the sample. Practically all of the losses were due to failure to obtain intelligence test scores, either because those students had not taken the tests or because, for some unknown reason, their scores did not appear on the records of the State Testing Service. A comparison of those omitted with those included, with respect to sex, residence, father's occupation, rank in high school class, and college plans, showed that the omitted cases did not differ significantly in distribution from those in the sample. This sample, consisting of 10,317 cases, has been and will henceforth be referred to as the 1957 sample. It should be kept in mind that the 1957 sample represents a cohort of high school seniors and not a birth cohort. Thus, it would be strictly incorrect to relate our findings to all young men completing their schooling in the late 1950s or at any other time. At the same time, it is worth noting that rates of high school completion in Wisconsin in the late 1950s are similar to those in the total United States in the middle to late 1960s. Of necessity there is some variation in age (birth cohort) within the 1957 sample, and some youths might never appear in a sample of high school seniors. For a number of reasons it is difficult to construct an exact measure of population coverage, but we estimate that 75% to 80% of male Wisconsin youth might have appeared in a survey of high school seniors in the late 1950s. Several estimates of population coverage are described in Appendix D.

THE 1964 FOLLOW-UP SURVEY

In the late spring of 1964, seven full years after graduation from high school, a follow-up study of the students in the 1957 sample was initiated. Because the only addresses available were those of the parents of the students, as given on the 1957 questionnaire, it was necessary to address the follow-up questionnaires to the parents. This posed something of a dilemma, because it meant that for all practical purposes there was no choice but to rely upon the parents to provide either the information on the students or the students' addresses. To follow the latter alternative would not only have been very time consuming and expensive, it would also have greatly increased the nonresponse to the follow-up, since it would have involved obtaining responses from two sets of persons. Relying on the experience of the University of California Center for the Study of Higher Education (Trent and Medsker, 1968) in eliciting reliable responses from parents concerning the post-high school educational experiences of their children, it was decided to construct a questionnaire to be directed to parents.

The California experience had indicated that a high proportion of response could be obtained if only a few questions bearing on important topics were asked and if the questions could be included on one panel of a double postcard, allowing the other three panels for the parent's name and address, a brief explanation of the reasons for requesting the information, and the return address. Following this technique, such a questionnaire was designed with a slightly different format for girls than for boys (see Appendix B). The parents were asked to indicate whether or not their child had attended any school or college, the name(s) of the school(s) or college(s), the dates of each attendance, and whether or not the youth had graduated. They were also asked to indicate their child's present occupation, marital status, military status (in the case of boys), and address.

For present purposes, we will be concerned only with the responses for the males in our sample. The first mailing resulted in a yield of 2382 responses (47.7%) and 2612 nonresponses (52.3%). In the first mailing approximately 20% of the questionnaires were returned by the post office as undeliverable for a variety of reasons including "moved, left no address," and "forwarding period expired." An attempt was made to obtain up-to-date addresses for these persons from State of Wisconsin tax rolls. This resulted in finding usable addresses for all but 424 persons (8.5% of the 1957 sample).

If the parents who received the first questionnaire did not return it within three weeks, they were sent a second double postcard questionnaire stamped "Urgent Second Request." Nonrespondents after the second wave were sent the same questionnaire stamped "Urgent Third Request." Third-wave nonrespondents were sent (1) a letter explaining again the nature of the survey and urging their participation, (2) the returnable portion of the questionnaire stamped "Urgent Fourth Request," and (3) a postage-paid return envelope. An attempt was also made to obtain a telephone interview with those persons who still had not responded after four mailings. This technique was highly successful once the persons were reached; however, telephone numbers could be found for only about half of the fourth-wave nonrespondents.

By means of these techniques, 4571 (91.5%) of the parents of the male seniors in the 1957 sample were finally contacted. Of those who could be contacted through the use of these methods, 4388 (96.0%) responded (92.0% responded to the mailings, and information was obtained by telephone for an additional 4.0%). An indication of the overall effectiveness of the successive mailing waves and telephone interviews can be obtained from the data given in Table 2-1. In this table, the simple and cumulative percentages of the respondents to each wave of response are indicated separately for the total 1957 sample and for those presumed to have been contacted. In addition, the percentages are shown separately for the two sources of addresses used in the follow-up.

Several observations concerning the effectiveness of the follow-up procedures can be made from the information in this table. First, had the follow-up study been concluded after the first mailing to the 1957 addresses, the total yield of responses would have been less than one-half (47.7%) of the cases. By use of new ad-

TABLE 2-1

Male Respondents by Wave of Response in the 1957 Sample and among Those Ever Contacted

Wave of response	1957 sample		1957 sample excluding those never contacted	
	Percent-age	Cumulative percentage	Percent-age	Cumulative percentage
First wave	51.8	51.8	56.6	56.6
1957 address	47.7	47.7	52.1	52.1
Tax return address	4.1	4.1	4.5	4.5
Second wave	20.6	72.4	22.5	79.1
1957 address	18.6	66.3	20.3	72.4
Tax return address	2.0	6.1	2.2	6.7
Third wave	6.8	79.2	7.4	86.5
1957 address	6.3	72.6	6.9	79.3
Tax return address	0.5	6.6	0.5	7.2
Fourth wave	5.0	84.2	5.5	92.0
1957 address	4.3	76.9	4.7	84.0
Tax return address	0.7	7.3	0.8	8.0
Telephone interview	3.6	87.8	4.0	96.0
Refusals	3.7	91.5	4.0	100.0
Never contacted	8.5	100.0	—	—
Total	100.0		100.0	
N	(4994)		(4571)	

dresses for those questionnaires that were not deliverable, the total response rate from those who presumably received a first mailing was built up to 51.8%. The second mailing increased the overall yield by two-fifths, to 72.4%. The two succeeding waves were somewhat less productive but brought the total yield from mailing to 84.2%—a figure seldom achieved in mail inquiries to relatively unselected populations, and one which compares quite favorably with the response rates of the best sample surveys using personal interviewing techniques. Thus, the extra effort expended on the various mailings and in finding up-to-date addresses paid off in an almost unprecedented response rate.

Second, the additional yield from the telephone interview was modest in magnitude, but it increased the total response rate by about 4%, to 87.8%—an unusually high response rate for a follow-up study with a lapse of seven years between data-gathering periods.[3]

Third, no doubt a number of factors contributed to the high response rate. Persistence in the mailing effort, which increased the initial yield by one-half, was obviously important. The effort to find new addresses for those who had moved added another 7.6% to the response rate. The telephone calls were also effective when telephone numbers could be found. However, by this last stage it was very difficult to locate the nonrespondents.

Fourth, the major source of attrition was not refusal to respond but failure to contact potential respondents. If only the responses from those for whom viable addresses were available from the original survey are considered, a very high total response rate (96.0%) was achieved; the nonresponse rate among those presumably contacted was only 4.0%. For the total sample, the refusal rate (failure to respond when presumably reached by the mailings) was 3.7%, whereas 8.5% were inaccessible.

Fifth, there is no way to estimate the influence on the response rate of the various techniques and strategy decisions employed in the follow-up survey. However, the decision to contact the parents rather than the subjects themselves doubtless resulted in dealing with a geographically less mobile group and, therefore,

[3] A wide range of response rates, depending upon the subjects, sample size, interval between the original and the follow-up studies, and several other matters concerning the follow-up procedures, is found among the past longitudinal studies in the area of educational and occupational aspiration and achievement. For example, the response rate in the Project Talent studies ranged from a minimum of 37% in a four-year follow-up of the ninth graders to a maximum of 69% in a one-year follow-up of the twelfth graders (Flanagan and Cooley, 1966:16) and from a low of 28.2% in an eight-year follow-up of ninth graders to a high of 40.1% in a five-year follow-up of twelfth graders (Flanagan, Shaycoft, Richards, and Claudy, 1971:5). Berdie (1954:36) obtained 77% response in a one-year follow-up of 2735 high school seniors in a Southern Minnesota town that was conducted in 1950, but in another one-year follow-up study of 2103 high school seniors conducted in 1961, Berdie and Hood obtained responses from 80% of the total sample or 87% of those contacted. In two nationwide longitudinal studies conducted for the National Science Foundation (1963), a 64% response rate was obtained in a two-year follow-up, but an 83% response rate was obtained in a five-year follow-up (Sharp, 1965). Eckland (1965:735–746) obtained 88.6% response in a ten-year follow-up of 1332 freshman males at the University of Illinois, and Alexander and Eckland (1973) obtained a 50.0% response in a fifteen-year follow-up of a national sample of high school sophomores.

increased the likelihood of contacting the prospective respondents. No doubt, the short length, the nature of the questionnaire, the sponsorship of the research by the university, the interest of the parents in the subject of the inquiry, and the appeal to the parents for cooperation all contributed to our success in obtaining the follow-up information.

Finally, it is tempting to assume that, because of the large sample size and the high response rate, the omission of nonrespondents (actually, persons whose parents were nonrespondents) could not bias the results of the study. Fortunately, it is possible to shed some light on this question by making comparisons of means and percentages for most of the important variables used in this study in the 1957 sample and among persons in the 1964 follow-up study. The sections that follow will investigate this matter.

Before proceeding to the question of bias due to nonresponse in the questionnaire study, brief comment should be made about sampling error. Since the sample is drawn randomly from a list covering 95% of the population (i.e., the 1957 graduating class), it is reasonable to assume that the missing 5% of the population will not cause undue error. Because of the large size of the sample, sampling error is small, and, since the sample is random, sample error estimates can easily be computed for all statistics presented in this report. Our treatment of sampling error may be excessively conservative, since we have not made the correction for sampling from a finite population. It can be asserted with some confidence that almost any difference large enough to be interesting will prove to be statistically significant. In fact, because the sample size is so large, many differences that have no interpretable importance will probably be statistically significant.

NONRESPONSE BIAS

One of the primary defects of questionnaire research is nonresponse or failure to obtain responses for some of the elements selected and designated for the sample (Kish, 1965:532). Nonresponse in mailed questionnaire studies is due either to inaccessibility of the respondents or to their failure to respond to the questionnaire. The amount of nonresponse varies with the availability of correct addresses, the length, difficulty, and format of the questionnaire, the sponsorship of the study, the mailing and follow-up strategies employed, and similar technical considerations.

There is abundant evidence that respondents to questionnaire surveys differ from nonrespondents on many important social, economic, and psychological dimensions; that early respondents differ from late respondents, especially when it has been necessary to prod the more reluctant respondents with repeated appeals to provide information; that those who never respond, either because they refuse to do so or cannot be located, are likely to be quite different on important characteristics from those who respond to various types of appeals during the course of the survey (Reuss, 1943; Baur, 1947; Edgerton, Britt, and Norman, 1947; Pan, 1950; Beilin and Werner, 1957; Larson and Catton, 1959; Donald, 1960; Lehman, 1963; Kivlin, 1965; Mayer and Pratt, 1966; Schwirian and Blaine, 1966; Spaeth and Ellis, 1969; Wells, 1966; Ellis, Endo, and Armer, 1970). Consequently, estimates of population parameters or of sample statistics may be considerably biased if the proportion of nonrespondents is not held to an absolute minimum or if steps are not taken to correct for nonresponse bias (Cochran, 1953:292–304; Deming, 1960:66–67; Kish, 1965:532–571; Moser, 1959:127–144).

As was indicated earlier, great efforts were made to reduce nonresponse to the follow-up questionnaire by finding new addresses for persons to whom the questionnaires could not be delivered, by repeating mailings and appeals to nonrespondents, and by using telephone interviews for nonrespondents to the mailed questionnaires. However, even with the use of these techniques, the nonrespondents constituted 12.2% of the sample; 8.5% were inaccessibles—never contacted—and 3.7% were considered refusals. The possibility of bias due to nonresponse cannot be dismissed without further examination, despite the fact that the nonrespondents would indeed have to be very different from the respondents to have any great effect on statistics based on responses from such a large proportion of the original sample.

It is possible to evaluate the representativeness of the response finally obtained in the 1965 follow-up study by comparing the known characteristics of the original 1957 sample with those of the 1964 respondents. It is also possible to compare total respondents with nonrespondents, to compare the respondents to different waves of mailings in order to learn more about the characteristics of early and late respondents, and to compare inaccessibles (nonrespondents who were never contacted) with refusals (those who were presumably contacted but never responded). For present purposes, we shall focus our attention on the representativeness of the 1957 responses of persons for whom data were obtained in the 1964 follow-up survey. Pavalko and Lutterman (1973) test several hypotheses about characteristics of persons in the Wisconsin sample which vary with nonresponse or wave of response.

NONRESPONSE BIAS IN UNIVARIATE STATISTICS

We ask first whether or not 1964 respondents (persons for whom we have parents' reports) are a sufficiently unselected subset of the 1957 sample to give unbiased estimates of important characteristics of the population from which the sample was drawn. To answer this question we have computed percentages, means, or standard deviations of selected variables in the 1957 sample and among 1964 respondents and nonrespondents. These are reported in the first three columns of Table 2-2. Of course, these comparisons are not possible for the three main dependent variables: educational attainment, occupational status, and earnings, since none of these was measured in 1957. Thus, an inferential step is required in moving from a finding of no biases in respect to variables in Table 2-2 to a conclusion of no biases in respect to any of the important dependent variables in our study.

The first three columns of Table 2-2 present arithmetic means and the standard deviations of nondichotomous variables for all 4994 males in the 1957 sample and for the 4388 respondents and 606 nonrespondents in the 1964 survey; the fourth column (Error) gives differences between measurements in the 1957 sample and among 1964 respondents; and the last column (Bias) gives these differences as percentages of the standard deviation of each variable in the 1957 sample. For example, the mean of father's occupational status was 29.71 points on the Duncan scale in the 1957 sample, and it was 30.12 points among 1964 respondents. Then, the average status of father's occupation was overstated by 0.41 points on the Duncan scale in the 1964 survey, or about 2% of the standard deviation of father's occupational status (22.10) in the 1957 sample.

The case of father's occupational status is instructive, because it represents one of the larger differences between respondents and nonrespondents. The difference between respondents and nonrespondents is almost 3.5 points on the Duncan scale, or about

Table 2-2

Descriptive Statistics for Selected Variables in the 1957 Sample of Males and among 1964 Respondents

Variable	1957 sample	Respond- ents	Nonre- spondents	Error	Bias
Percentage urban	62.6	61.9	67.8	0.7	1.4
Father's education (years):					
Mean	10.03	10.06	9.80	−0.03	−1.0
Std. dev.	3.12	3.12	3.08	0.00	0.0
Mother's education					
Mean	10.37	10.41	10.10	−0.04	−1.3
Std. dev.	2.97	2.97	2.98	0.00	0.0
Father's occupational status (Duncan scale):					
Mean	29.71	30.12	26.75	−0.41	−1.9
Std. dev.	22.10	22.17	21.33	−0.07	−0.3
Parents' income in hundreds of dollars					
Mean	58.37	58.77	53.75	−0.40	−1.2
Std. dev.	32.81	32.81	32.41	0.00	0.00
Mental ability (IQ):					
Mean	100.80	101.01	99.30	−0.21	−1.4
Std. dev.	14.93	15.01	14.26	−0.08	−0.5
High school grades:					
Mean	97.14	97.45	94.96	−0.31	−2.2
Std. dev.	13.93	13.93	13.68	0.0	0.0
Percentage with teach- ers' encouragement	44.6	45.5	38.8	−0.9	−1.8
Percentage with paren- tal encouragement	58.2	58.9	53.1	−0.7	−1.4
Percentage with friends planning on college	34.2	35.0	27.9	−0.8	−1.7
Percentage with college plans	36.9	37.5	32.7	−0.6	−1.2
Occupational aspiration (Duncan SEI):					
Mean	48.21	48.41	46.56	−0.20	−0.7
Std. dev.	27.35	27.47	26.36	−0.12	−0.4
N	4994	4388	606		

Note: See text for definitions of error and bias. There were 4598 cases with data on high school grades, of which 4038 were respondents, and there were 4638 cases with data on occupational aspirations, of which 4129 were respondents.

one-sixth of the standard deviation in either group. It is undoubtedly a statistically significant difference at any of the conventional probability levels, and we would think it noteworthy if comparisons between respondents and nonrespondents were of substantive interest to us. However, our interest lies in the difference between respondents in 1964 and the total 1964 sample, and this difference is affected both by the selectivity of nonresponse and by the share of nonrespondents in the total sample.

In every case but one, respondents are selected favorably relative to nonrespondents in respect to their 1957 characteristics, where we define "favorably" in terms of the effect of each variable on post-high school educational chances. Thus, respondents had higher levels of father's and of mother's educational attainment than did nonrespondents. They had fathers with higher status occupations and families with more income. Respondents had more academic ability and better grades in high school. Respondents were more likely than nonrespondents to have reported that their parents and teachers encouraged them to attend college and that their friends were planning to attend college. Finally, respondents were more likely than nonrespondents to have reported planning to attend college and aspiring to a high status occupation. However, respondents were less likely than nonrespondents to have been living in an urban place in 1957, although men with an urban background are usually at an advantage in the process of achievement.

If the effects of nonresponse are systematic, on the whole they are also quite small, once one has taken into account the rate of nonresponse as well as the difference between respondents and nonrespondents. Fathers of respondents were 3.5 points higher than those of nonrespondents on the Duncan scale of occupational status, and their families had a $500 advantage in average annual income. Respondents had an advantage of 7 to 8 percentage points in respect to teacher and parental encouragement to attend college and the percentage of friends planning on college, and they had an advantage of 5 points in the percentage planning on college. However, the biases just reported are inconsequential in light of the small proportion of nonrespondents. In only one case does the mean of a variable among 1964 respondents differ from the mean of the same variable in the 1957 sample by even as much as 2% of the standard deviation of the variable in the 1957 sample.

We conclude that nonresponse imparts a very small, but systematic bias to characteristics of the population of Wisconsin high school graduates in 1957. It is possible that biases might prove greater in the case of characteristics of respondents in 1964 if the search process were selective directly with respect to post-1964 activities (like further schooling) and only indirectly with respect to achievement and background in 1957. However, we think it unlikely that 1964 characteristics are much more in error than 1957 characteristics because parents, rather than students, were the source of our data, and, again, because nonrespondents were so small a portion of the 1957 sample.

NONRESPONSE BIAS IN BIVARIATE AND MULTIVARIATE STATISTICS

The foregoing analysis has suggested that estimates of univariate statistics based on the 1964 questionnaire responses are likely to be quite representative. However, an equally important question is whether bias due to nonresponse will influence the nature and extent of the bivariate and multivariate relationships among important variables in the study.

Suchman (1962:110–111) has argued that since a great deal of social research is concerned with the testing of hypotheses which require a comparison of relationships rather than just the estimation of univariate parameters, the important question is not only "Are the data biased?" but also "How does the bias that may exist affect the determination of the relationship?"

It has been demonstrated that bias due to nonresponse in univariate statistics is minimal in this study. The question to be examined now is whether bias due to nonresponse affects important bivariate and multivariate relationships. Because rather arbitrary decisions regarding cutting points are required in crosstabular analysis, it is important that the effects of bias on bivariate and multivariate relationships be examined, using both crosstabular and correlational techniques.

The relationships of socioeconomic status and intelligence to educational aspirations are central to this study. Fortunately, complete data on these variables are available from the 1957 survey for the respondents and the nonrespondents in the 1964 questionnaire follow-up. In Tables 2-3 and 2-4, the percentages of men who planned on college are given, separately as well as simultaneously by socioeconomic status and mental ability, for the 1957 sample and for the respondents and the nonrespondents in the 1964 follow-up. The cutting points of socioeconomic status and mental ability used in these tables are the same as those used in other publications from this study.

From Table 2-3 it is clear that the percentages with college plans are very similar for the 1957 sample and the 1964 respondents— all are within one percentage point, whether or not the data are

TABLE 2-3

Percentage Who Planned on College, by Socioeconomic Status and by Mental Ability: Males in the 1957 Sample and 1964 Respondents and Nonrespondents

	1957 sample	1964 follow-up	
		Respondents	Non-respondents
Socioeconomic status			
Low	17.1	17.8	13.1
	(1187)	(1012)	(175)
Lower middle	25.7	26.0	24.1
	(1193)	(1052)	(141)
Upper middle	39.1	39.5	36.0
	(1341)	(1192)	(150)
High	63.2	63.4	62.1
	(1273)	(1133)	(140)
Total	36.9	37.5	32.7
	(4994)	(4388)	(606)
Mental ability			
Low	11.6	12.2	8.5
	(1235)	(1070)	(165)
Lower middle	25.4	25.5	24.3
	(1186)	(1038)	(148)
Upper middle	43.0	43.7	37.6
	(1268)	(1111)	(157)
High	65.1	65.0	65.4
	(1305)	(1169)	(136)
Total	36.9	37.5	32.7
	(4994)	(4388)	(606)

examined separately by socioeconomic status and by mental ability. The percentages of nonrespondents with college plans are lower than those of the 1957 sample or of the 1964 respondents, except in the highest quartile of mental ability. However, the relationships of socioeconomic status and mental ability with college plans are as pronounced among nonrespondents as among 1964 respondents or in the 1957 sample. In other words, when the bivariate

TABLE 2-4

Percentage Who Planned on College, by Socioeconomic Status and by Mental Ability: Males in the 1957 Sample and 1964 Respondents and Nonrespondents

Socioeconomic status	1957 sample	1964 follow-up	
		Respondents	Non-respondents
Low mental ability			
Low	6.5 (447)	7.4 (380)	7.1 (67)
Lower middle	7.9 (343)	8.1 (296)	6.4 (47)
Upper middle	15.4 (286)	16.1 (255)	9.7 (31)
High	27.7 (159)	26.6 (139)	35.0 (20)
Total	11.7 (1235)	12.2 (1070)	8.5 (165)
Lower middle mental ability			
Low	13.1 (306)	13.6 (258)	10.4 (48)
Lower middle	22.7 (322)	22.2 (288)	26.5 (34)
Upper middle	23.3 (301)	22.7 (260)	26.8 (41)
High	45.9 (257)	46.1 (232)	44.0 (25)
Total	25.4 (1186)	25.5 (1038)	24.3 (148)

(*Continued*)

TABLE 2-4 (Continued)

Socioeconomic status	1957 sample	1964 follow-up	
		Respondents	Non-respondents
Upper middle mental ability			
Low	24.3	25.1	20.0
	(259)	(219)	(40)
Lower middle	31.9	32.9	24.2
	(279)	(246)	(33)
Upper middle	44.3	45.8	32.6
	(386)	(343)	(43)
High	64.5	63.7	70.7
	(344)	(303)	(41)
Total	43.0	43.7	37.6
	(1268)	(1111)	(157)
High mental ability			
Low	40.6	40.0	45.0
	(175)	(155)	(20)
Lower middle	47.4	46.9	51.9
	(249)	(222)	(27)
Upper middle	65.0	64.0	74.3
	(368)	(333)	(35)
High	82.1	83.0	74.1
	(513)	(459)	(54)
Total	65.1	65.0	65.4
	(1305)	(1169)	(136)

relationships of socioeconomic status and mental ability with college plans are examined, nonresponse bias does not affect the pattern of the relationships.

The similarity between respondents and nonrespondents in the relationships among socioeconomic status, mental ability, and college plans becomes even more apparent when we look at the percentages with college plans by quartile of socioeconomic status and mental ability by response status in Table 2-4. The percentages with college plans are virtually the same among respondents and in the 1957 sample within each ability–socioeconomic-status combination. With few exceptions, college plans vary monotonically by socioeconomic status within categories of ability and monotonically by ability within categories of socioeconomic status, whether we look at respondents, nonrespondents, or the total 1957 sample. Indeed, in only 9 of the 16 socioeconomic-status–ability combinations do respondents appear more likely than nonrespondents to have college plans. Using methods suggested by Goodman (1968, 1971), we tested the hypothesis that nonresponse in 1964 was statistically independent of the complete cross-classification of college plans by socioeconomic status by mental ability, and we were unable to reject the null hypothesis at any of the conventional probability levels ($\chi^2 = 30.15$ with 30df, $\alpha > 0.50$). In fact we were unable to reject even the simpler hypothesis that the relationships among socioeconomic status, ability, and college plans were strictly additive, while the classification of those three variables was independent of response in 1964 ($\chi^2 = 40.76$ with 40df, $\alpha = 0.44$).

Our results are encouraging with regard to the extent of nonresponse bias in the measurement of post-high school events in our sample. From earlier research we know that college plans are closely correlated with post-high school educational attainments (Sewell and Shah, 1967:16; Sewell, Haller, and Ohlendorf, 1970: 1018), and from the experience of other surveys we would expect nonresponse to be selective with respect to educational attainment (Sewell, 1971:797). However, in the 1957 Wisconsin sample, nonresponse in 1964 is not significantly related to college plans when the latter variable is cross-classified by socioeconomic status and ability ($\chi^2 = 3.81$, $df = 1$, $\alpha > .05$).

Similar results are obtained when we look at correlation and regression analyses of a larger set of variables. Table 2-5 gives zero-order correlations among eight background, academic achievement, and aspiration variables among respondents and nonrespondents and in the full 1957 sample. Differences between respondents and those in the full sample are virtually nil, and the correlations among respondents and among nonrespondents are also quite similar.

Table 2-6 shows estimates of regression coefficients of a six-equation recursive model of the formation of aspirations, where each equation is estimated among respondents and nonrespond-

TABLE 2-5

Correlations among Selected Variables: Males in 1957 Sample, 1964 Respondents, and 1964 Nonrespondents

	SES	Mental ability	High school rank	Teachers' encouragement	Parents' encouragement	Friends' plans	College plans
Total 1957 sample (N = 4994)							
Mental ability	.295						
High school rank	.191	.587					
Teachers' encouragement	.181	.352	.440				
Parents' encouragement	.363	.357	.344	.419			
Friends' plans	.343	.316	.330	.331	.399		
College plans	.383	.436	.468	.448	.533	.499	
Occupational aspirations	.374	.450	.461	.407	.506	.465	.762
1964 respondents (N = 4388)							
Mental ability	.292						
High school rank	.191	.588					
Teachers' encouragement	.185	.352	.442				
Parents' encouragement	.360	.356	.339	.424			
Friends' plans	.351	.319	.325	.333	.408		
College plans	.381	.433	.465	.448	.533	.499	
Occupational aspirations	.372	.451	.465	.415	.505	.469	.764
1964 nonrespondents							
Mental ability	.301						
High school rank	.176	.573					
Teachers' encouragement	.134	.349	.419				
Parents' encouragement	.378	.364	.370	.381			
Friends' plans	.266	.278	.353	.306	.326		
College plans	.390	.454	.481	.442	.527	.500	
Occupational aspirations	.391	.440	.422	.336	.510	.426	.742

ents and in the full 1957 sample. According to the model, socio-economic background and academic ability affect rank in high school class, and each of those three variables affects each of the three perceptions of the expectations of significant others (teachers, parents, and friends). Finally, college plans and occupational aspirations are each taken to depend upon the six preceding variables.

We shall not interpret the estimated coefficients in Table 2-6 at this juncture, except to note the great similarity between those of respondents and the full 1957 sample. As before, there are more differences between nonrespondents and respondents than there are between respondents and the full sample, but again the overall impression is one of substantial similarity.[4]

Thus, the bivariate and multivariate crosstabular as well as correlational analyses indicate not only that there is little bias due to nonresponse in this study but also that this bias must be rather consistent across the various subgroups of the 1964 respondents and nonrespondents. Consequently, there is little chance that findings based on only the respondents' data would lead to any significantly different conclusions than those using the similar data for the 1957 sample.

These results tend to support Suchman's (1962) conclusion, which was based on crosstabular and zero-order correlational analysis, that bias due to nonresponse in questionnaire studies, although it may seriously affect estimates of important univariate parameters, may not necessarily disturb relationships among variables.[5] The fact that the bivariate and multivariate relationships are essentially the same for the 1957 sample, the 1964 respondents, and the nonrespondents is evidence in support of this assertion when a high response rate has been achieved. Whether this generalization may be applied to other questionnaire studies with lower response rates must be determined by further empirical tests.

---

[4] Although the data are not presented here, neither are there any substantial differences in the zero-order or multiple correlation coefficients and regression coefficients when a similar analysis is made for cumulative samples of respondents by wave of response. When the data are separately analyzed for the respondents to each wave and for the two subgroups of nonrespondents (refusals and inaccessibles), the differences in the coefficients are greater than those reported here, but no significant change in the general pattern of relationships between the selected variables is observed.

[5] For some contrary evidence, see Schwirian and Blaine (1966).

TABLE 2-6

Selected Regressions of Achievement and Aspiration: Males in 1957 Sample, 1964 Respondents, and 1964 Nonrespondents

Dependent variable		Predetermined variables						
	Constant	SES	Mental ability	High school rank	Teachers' encouragement	Parents' encouragement	Friends' plans	R^2
Total 1957 sample (N = 4994)								
High school rank	42.1	.0246 (.0151)	.542 (.011)					.345
Teachers' encouragement	−1.24	.00404 (.00053)	.0126 (.0006)	.00349 (.00059)				.212
Parents' encouragement	−.83	.00525 (.00052)	.0070 (.0006)	.01240 (.00058)				.226
Friends' plans	−.91	.00354 (.00051)	.0073 (.0005)	.01160 (.00057)				.198
College plans	−.86	.00287 (.00043)	.0059 (.0005)	.00579 (.00050)	.136 (.012)	.241 (.012)	.229 (.012)	.475
Occupational aspiration	−27.6	.239 (.025)	.334 (.027)	.330 (.029)	5.48 (.69)	12.9 (.71)	11.3 (.71)	.436

(Continued)

TABLE 2-6 (Continued)

Dependent variable		Predetermined variables						
	Constant	SES	Mental ability	High school rank	Teachers' encouragement	Parents' encouragement	Friends' plans	R^2
1964 respondents (N = 4388)								
High school rank	42.5	.0265 (.0161)	.540 (.012)					.346
Teachers' encouragement	−1.24	.00392 (.00056)	.0128 (.0006)	.00370 (.00063)				.215
Parents' encouragement	−.81	.00537 (.00055)	.0067 (.0006)	.01220 (.00062)				.222
Friends' plans	−.91	.00379 (.00054)	.0069 (.0006)	.01190 (.00060)				.201
College plans	−.86	.00277 (.00046)	.0059 (.0005)	.00568 (.00054)	.135 (.013)	.244 (.013)	.226 (.013)	.472
Occupational aspiration	−28.6	.234 (.027)	.349 (.029)	.323 (.031)	5.82 (.74)	12.7 (.76)	11.3 (.75)	.440

(Continued)

39

TABLE 2-6 (Continued)

Dependent variable	Predetermined variables							
	Constant	SES	Mental ability	High school rank	Teachers' encouragement	Parents' encouragement	Friends' plans	R^2
1964 nonrespondents (N = 606)								
High school rank	40.4	.0051 (.0459)	.549 (.034)					.328
Teachers' encouragement	−1.26	.00523 (.00157)	.0116 (.0016)	.00141 (.00177)				.194
Parents' encouragement	−.98	.00485 (.00155)	.0087 (.0016)	.01390 (.00175)				.250
Friends' plans	−.91	.00168 (.00147)	.0094 (.0015)	.00844 (.00165)				.169
College plans	−.88	.00375 (.00121)	.0051 (.0013)	.00684 (.00143)	.148 (.032)	.217 (.033)	.264 (.034)	.500
Occupational aspiration	−20.9	.288 (.074)	.222 (.078)	.409 (.087)	2.71 (1.96)	14.0 (1.98)	11.5 (2.05)	.417

Note: Entries are regression coefficients; numbers in parentheses are standard errors.

These results should not be interpreted to mean that researchers no longer need be concerned with bias due to nonresponse. In many studies, this one for example, accurate estimates of sample statistics and parameters are important goals of the research. Analysis not reported here indicates that such estimates cannot be obtained unless the response rate reaches very high levels (at least 80%). But even if the only concern of the research is with testing hypotheses dealing with relationships between variables, it is still incumbent on the researcher to demonstrate that nonresponse bias is small and occurs in the same direction for the various subpopulations being examined before asserting that nonresponse will not affect the relationships to be tested.

Selection of Subsamples

The samples used in the analysis reported in the various chapters of this volume depend upon the particular population of interest, the problem being investigated, and the availability of data on the variables involved. Thus, in Chapter 3, where the socioeconomic background and earnings of high school graduates are first examined, we decided to limit our analysis to males from nonfarm background, who were not enrolled in school or college, who were employed in the civilian labor force, and who had Social Security earnings in 1965, 1966, and 1967. In Chapter 4, where we introduce several social psychological variables into our model, our sample is essentially the same as in Chapter 3, but its size is reduced by the number of cases in which the essential data on these variables are lacking. In Chapter 5, where we examine the effects of the type of college on socioeconomic achievements, we of course restrict our analysis to the young men in our sample who went to college. In Chapter 6, on the effects of ability on post-high school earnings, a different analytic strategy is employed, and in effect a series of subsamples are selected that are homogeneous on some characteristics, e.g., military service or rural–urban origins, but differ on others, e.g., ability or educational attainment. In Chapter 3, other data sets are also used for comparative purposes. In each of the chapters the specific sample characteristics will be given in greater detail.

We have no way of comparing the quality of these subsamples with some standard of excellence, especially insofar as the samples are specified in terms of post-high school achievements or activities. We can only say that all of the samples are subsamples of the 1964 follow-up sample described in this chapter, and that we think they are representative of the special populations that they are designed to represent. Of course, it should be pointed out that there are well-known limitations to generalizing findings from such samples to larger, less homogeneous populations.

Summary and Conclusions

This chapter has been devoted to a discussion of a number of matters concerning the longitudinal study, from its inception in 1957 to the present. The design of the original survey and of the follow-up study has been presented. The definition and measurement of the variables used in the research have been given. The 1957 sample, consisting of 4994 males, has been discussed, and analysis has been presented which shows that the 4388 respondents to the 1964 follow-up survey closely represent the 1957 sample on major variables pertinent to the analysis contemplated in this study. Bias due to nonresponse has been shown not to affect materially either the univariate or the multivariate statistics of key variables.

With the clear demonstration that the respondents to the 1964 follow-up closely represent the 1957 sample, it is now possible to proceed with the statistical analysis of the relationship between socioeconomic background and post-high school achievements. The next chapter will examine the relationship between the socioeconomic background of the males in our sample and their schooling, occupational status in 1964, and earnings in 1965, 1966, and 1967.

3

Socioeconomic Background, Ability, and Achievement[1]

Introduction

For several years we have been engaged in an analysis of socioeconomic achievement among Wisconsin high school graduates of 1957. In reports of this work to date we have described the effect of socioeconomic background on aspiration, educational attainment, and occupational achievement, and in so doing have constructed social psychological models of processes of status attainment (Sewell and Shah, 1967, 1968a; Sewell, Haller, and Portes, 1969; Sewell, Haller, and Ohlendorf, 1970; Hauser, 1970a, 1972; Sewell, 1971). In this chapter, we extend our analysis to the earnings of males in the Wisconsin sample.

No lengthy justification of our interest in earnings seems necessary. The generation of income by individuals and families affects welfare, life-style, and psychological well-being (Morgan, David, Cohen, and Brazer, 1962; Hodge, 1970; Jencks *et al.*, 1972), and it is a resource for the enhancement of prestige and power. In the

[1] This chapter was prepared by Robert M. Hauser, William H. Sewell, and Kenneth G. Lutterman. An earlier version was presented at the meetings of the American Sociological Association, Denver, Colorado, September 1971.

43

context of research on social stratification—the process by which social status tends to persist across generations—the analysis of earnings or income provides an opportunity to examine "the inheritance of poverty" (Duncan, 1968a,b; Duncan, Featherman, and Duncan, 1972; Featherman, 1969; Blum, 1971, 1972; Coleman, Berry, and Blum, 1972; Treiman and Hauser, 1970). Further, our interest in the social antecedents of earnings complements recent economic research on rates of return to ability and to investment in education (Becker, 1964; Denison, 1964; Jorgenson and Griliches, 1967; Blaug, 1967; Hanoch, 1967; Weisbrod and Karpoff, 1968; Ashenfelter and Mooney, 1968; Bowman, 1969; Cutwright, 1969; Daniere and Mechling, 1970; Reed and Miller, 1970; Griliches, 1970; Griliches and Mason, 1972; Weiss, 1970; Hansen, Weisbrod, and Scanlon, 1970; Rogers, 1969; Hause, 1971, 1972; Bowles, 1972; Taubman and Wales, 1973; Arrow, 1972; Johnson, 1970).

The primary goal of this chapter is to measure the effect of socioeconomic background on earnings 8 to 10 years after graduation from high school. Second, we look at the differential effects on earnings of three socioeconomic background variables—education, occupation, and income. Third, we ask how much of the effect of each background variable on earnings is mediated by ability and how much by post-high school educational attainment and occupational achievement. Fourth, we ask whether our findings are consistent with other studies of the earnings or income of young United States males that have been based on large and representative samples.

There are obvious limits to the generality of our findings. First, the fact that the base population is drawn from a single state means that it is less heterogeneous in most respects than the total United States population. Second, the analysis excludes non-high school graduates, whom we estimate to comprise about 20% of young men growing up in Wisconsin in the late 1950s (Appendix D). Consequently, we are analyzing "poverty" only insofar as it is an aspect of the more general phenomenon of income generation and distribution. (We think that is how poverty ought to be studied.) As indicated below, our analysis also excludes some high achievers who were still in graduate or professional schools in 1964. Third, there is evidence in our data and from other sources that the members of the Wisconsin sample may have been too young (about 24 to 28 years old in 1965–1967) for the effect of their social background or their own achievement on earnings to be fully felt. For example, in the Current Population Survey Supplement of March 1962, "Occupational Changes in a Generation" (OCG), the correlations between son's income and father's education and occupation and son's education and occupation are larger at ages 35 to 44 than at younger ages (Duncan, Featherman, and Duncan, 1972:38). Similar results have been obtained in the Princeton sample of married men in metropolitan areas (Featherman, 1969:105) and in the Johns Hopkins University sample of men aged 30 to 39 in 1968 (Blum and Coleman, 1970). Finally, in no sense should our analysis be interpreted as an exhaustive effort to estimate an earnings function; we have deliberately limited our analysis to the few variables we believe are most relevant in measuring the effect of socioeconomic background on earnings. We shall refer, subsequently, to some important omissions.

At the same time, we do not intend to sell our effort short. We have unique data of high quality on the social background, ability, educational experience, and socioeconomic achievements of a large and representative sample that cover a crucial ten-year span of the socioeconomic life-cycle. Most important for the present analysis, we can combine our data with a set of measurements of the incomes of the parents of the Wisconsin graduates during the years these students were most likely to have been in college (1957–1960).

The Sample

The analysis presented in this chapter pertains to male Wisconsin high school graduates of 1957 with nonfarm background who were not enrolled in school and were employed in the civilian labor force in 1964. This sample was selected from the one-third sample of Wisconsin high school graduates of 1957 (see Chapter 2 for a description of the basic sample). There were 4863 males in the one-third simple random sample of high school graduates whose achievements we have measured over the past decade. Of these, 1070 persons with farm background (whose fathers were farmers or who lived on farms) were excluded, primarily because of the difficulty of measuring the income and earnings of farmers.

TABLE 3-1

Disposition of Sample Cases: Male Wisconsin High School Graduates of 1957 with Nonfarm Background

Source	Frequency	Percentage of total	Percentage of eligible respondents
Males with nonfarm background	3,793	100.0	—
Nonrespondents	452	11.9	—
Deceased	37	1.0	—
In school	466	12.3	—
In military service	352	9.3	—
Unemployed or not in labor force	45	1.2	—
Eligible respondents	2,441	64.4	100.0
With data on parents' income and nonzero earnings, 1965–1967	2,069	—	84.7

Thus, the sample base is 3793 male high school graduates with nonfarm background. The disposition of these cases is described in Table 3-1. All measurements of post-high school achievement other than earnings were obtained in a 1964 mail survey, which it will be recalled had an 87.9% response rate (see Chapter 2).

Persons were also excluded for whom we had a response in 1964 but who had died, were enrolled in school, were on active military duty, or were unemployed or not in the civilian labor force for some other reason. Only a small number of men were in the first or last of these categories. Students and members of the armed forces were excluded because we wanted to define a sample of persons with a permanent commitment to the civilian labor market. Members of the armed forces in 1964 are a heterogeneous group, but persons still enrolled in school at that time were drawn disproportionately from the upper tails of the distributions of background, ability, and schooling. These four restrictions reduced the sample by 900 cases, or 23.7% of the males with nonfarm background. After applying these restrictions the sample included 2441 eligible persons. For all of the eligible men, data are available on all variables of interest here except parents' income and earnings,

1965–1967. The sample on which most of the following analysis is based includes the 2069 eligible men for whom data are available on parents' income and who had nonzero earnings in 1965, 1966, and 1967. This sample constitutes 84.7% of the eligible men.

The Variables

The variables used here have been ascertained from a variety of sources, including a 1957 school-administered questionnaire, school records, the Wisconsin State Testing Service, the Wisconsin State Tax Department, the 1964 mail survey, and federal Social Security earnings records. (See Chapter 2 for sources and definitions of variables.) Father's educational attainment (V) and mother's educational attainment (M) were reported by the student in the 1957 questionnaire and were coded in years of schooling completed. Father's occupational status (X), coded in the metric of Duncan's index of the socioeconomic status of occupations (Reiss, 1961), was ascertained from the Wisconsin tax return in 1957 or the closest available year. Parents' average income (I) for all available years in the period 1957–1960 (coded in thousands of dollars) was ascertained from Wisconsin tax returns. In certain parts of the analysis, we have also used father's average income (I_F) and mother's average income (I_M), whose source and definition parallel that of parents' average income. Son's mental ability (Q) refers to performance on the Henmon–Nelson test, ascertained from the Wisconsin State Testing Service, expressed in the metric of intelligence quotients. Son's educational attainment (U) approximates the number of years of schooling that respondents had completed by 1964. Son's 1964 occupation (W) was ascertained in the 1964 survey and coded into Duncan's SEI. Son's 1965, 1966, and 1967 earnings (Y_1, Y_2, and Y_3, respectively) were ascertained from Social Security records, adjusted for the effects of multiple jobholding and the ceiling on covered earnings, and expressed in thousands of dollars.[2] We have also made extensive use of a canonically weighted average of the three earnings measures (Y), whose derivation is described below.

[2] See Appendix C for a definition of earnings and a description of adjustment procedures.

Effects of Eligibility and Nonresponse

In order to give some impression of the effect of our eligibility criteria and of nonresponse bias on our results, we have displayed in Table 3-2 the characteristics of three subgroups of male Wisconsin high school graduates with nonfarm background. As might be expected from the exclusion of persons enrolled in school in 1964, a comparison of lines 1 and 2 of Table 3-2 discloses that eligible respondents are slightly lower in status and more homogeneous with respect to socioeconomic background and ability than were all respondents with nonfarm background who were alive in 1964. The mean difference in educational attainment and the reduction in its variance among the eligible respondents are quite striking. Of course, these differences do not detract from the

TABLE 3-2

Characteristics of Sample Subgroups on Selected Variables: Male Wisconsin High School Graduates of 1957 with Nonfarm Background

	Variable				
Subgroup	V	M	X	Q	U
(1) Respondents, alive in 1964 (N = 3304)					
Mean	10.42	10.59	34.2	102.0	13.70
Standard deviation	3.17	2.92	23.3	14.8	2.03
(2) Eligible respondents (N = 2441)					
Mean	10.19	10.39	32.4	100.1	13.25
Standard deviation	3.03	2.87	22.4	14.5	1.70
(3) Eligible respondents, with data on parents' income and nonzero earnings, 1965–1967 (N = 2069)					
Mean	10.19	10.41	33.1	99.9	13.22
Standard deviation	3.01	2.84	22.4	14.6	1.68

Note: Item identifications are: V = father's educational attainment; M = mother's educational attainment; X = status of father's occupation (Duncan SEI); Q = son's score on Henmon–Nelson Test of Mental Ability; U = son's educational attainment.

validity of our findings, provided one is cognizant of the population to which they apply.

With respect to validity, the more important comparison is between line 2 and line 3. Fortunately, there are only trivial and uninterpretable differences between all eligible respondents and those with data on parental income and nonzero earnings, 1965–1967. This is mildly surprising, because those with zero earnings include employed persons not covered by Social Security, of whom many are employed in high-status occupations. Perhaps, the failure of this differential to appear is a consequence of the fact that many high achievers were still in colleges and universities in 1964. We shall not be especially cautious in generalizing from the sample of eligible respondents with all data present to the population of all eligible sons.

The Model

The path diagram in Figure 3-1 describes the assumptions and hypotheses guiding our analysis. The reader's familiarity with path analysis is assumed (Duncan, 1966, 1970; Land, 1969; Heise, 1969; Hauser, 1971). We postulate that socioeconomic background affects mental ability, that background and ability affect educational at-

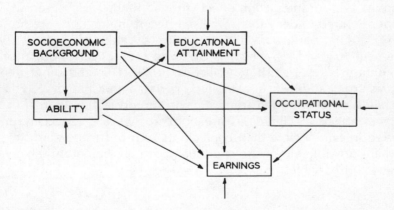

Figure 3-1. Schematic path diagram of the influence of socioeconomic background on earnings.

tainment, that background, ability, and education affect occupational achievement, and that all of the preceding variables affect earnings. With the exception of the link between socioeconomic background and ability, this causal ordering is consistent with the temporal ordering of the variables. The socioeconomic background measurements were all obtained after ability was measured. Thus, while our ordering of ability and background conforms to a common assumption, it is not strictly correct in these data. Moreover, insofar as parental achievement and son's ability are joint consequences of psychological attributes of parents—whether by way of social or genetic mechanisms—our estimate of the effect of socioeconomic background on ability will be too large. Beyond that point, specification of the model presents little difficulty. While both educational attainment and occupational status were measured in 1964, our eligibility criteria insure that most of the men completed their schooling well before that time. Finally, our earliest earnings measure pertains to the year following that in which educational attainment and occupational status were ascertained.

We have estimated coefficients for the four equations represented by the model of Figure 3-1 under the assumption of uncorrelated error using ordinary least squares. In most of our analysis, we have assumed interval measurement in all variables, and linearity and additivity of effects. In some of our analyses the assumption of linearity has been relaxed. For the present purpose we have not looked for interaction effects (nonadditivity). However, we are not prepared to deny that some significant interactions are present in our data, particularly the education by ability interaction with respect to earnings, which is of some theoretical importance to economists (Hause, 1971; Griliches, 1970). This and other departures from additivity are treated in detail in Chapter 6. Finally, while we are willing to admit a priori the possibility that all of the direct effects in Figure 3-1 are nonzero, we are especially interested in cases where path coefficients turn out to be zero, that is, where possible effects are spurious or are mediated entirely by intervening variables.

Data Analysis

In order to exploit the unique aspects of our data while maintaining comparability with other important studies, we have estimated four versions of the model in Figure 3-1. In Model I, son's academic ability is omitted, and socioeconomic background is represented by only two indicators, father's education and father's occupation. In Model II, son's ability is added. In Model III, ability is omitted, but father's income is added as a third indicator of socioeconomic background. Thus, Model III is a two-wave, three-variable panel analysis, with measurements of the education, occupation, and earnings of young men and of their fathers. After trying still other sets of background indicators, we construct Model IV, in which socioeconomic background is represented by father's education, mother's education, father's occupation, and parents' average income, with son's ability included in the model.

MODEL I

In Table 3-3, estimates of Model I based on the Wisconsin data are presented. The first panel displays regression coefficients in

TABLE 3-3

Effects of Father's Education and Occupation on the Education, Occupation and Earnings of Male Wisconsin High School Graduates of 1957 with Nonfarm Background

Dependent variable	Predetermined variables				
	V	X	U	W	
Standardized coefficients					R^2
(1) U	.235	.191	—	—	.130
(2) W	.185	.183	—	—	.096
(3) W	.047	.071	.586	—	.395
(4) Y_1	.026[a]	.029[a]	—	—	.002
(5) Y_1	.002[a]	.010[a]	.102	—	.011
(6) Y_1	−.004[a]	.001[a]	.028[a]	.126	.021
(7) Y_2	.046[a]	.070	—	—	.010
(8) Y_2	.010[a]	.041[a]	.156	—	.031
(9) Y_2	.003[a]	.031[a]	.078	.133	.042

(Continued)

TABLE 3-3 (*Continued*)

Dependent variable	Predetermined variables				
	V	X	U	W	
Standardized coefficients					R²
(10) Y_3	.061	.071	—	—	.012
(11) Y_3	.018a	.036a	.182	—	.041
(12) Y_3	.011a	.026a	.096	.148	.055
(13) Y	.061	.076	—	—	.013
(14) Y	.017a	.040a	.186	—	.043
(15) Y	.010a	.030a	.100	.147	.057
Regression coefficients					Constant
(1) U	.131	.0143	—	—	11.4
(2) W	1.43	.191	—	—	21.2
(3) W	.37	.074	8.16	—	71.9
(4) ·Y_1	.019a	.0028a	—	—	5.93
(5) Y_1	.001a	.0009a	.133	—	4.41
(6) Y_1	—.003a	.0001a	.036a	.0119	5.27
(7) Y_2	.036a	.0074	—	—	6.41
(8) Y_2	.007a	.0042a	.218	—	3.93
(9) Y_2	.002a	.0032a	.109	.0134	4.89
(10) Y_3	.053	.0082	—	—	6.73
(11) Y_3	.016a	.0042a	.282	—	3.52
(12) Y_3	.010a	.0029a	.148	.0164	4.69
(13) Y	.052	.0088	—	—	6.71
(14) Y	.015a	.0047a	.287	—	3.44
(15) Y	.009a	.0035a	.154	.0163	4.61

Note: Item identifications are: V = father's educational attainment; X = status of father's occupation (Duncan SEI); U = son's educational attainment; W = son's 1964 occupation (Duncan SEI); Y_1 = son's 1965 earnings (in thousands of dollars); Y_2 = son's 1966 earnings (in thousands of dollars); Y_3 = son's 1967 earnings (in thousands of dollars); Y = canonically weighted average of son's 1965–1967 earnings (in thousands of dollars). Data pertain to 2069 respondents with nonfarm background, who were employed in the civilian labor force in 1964, were not enrolled in school, had nonzero earnings, 1965–1967, and for whom there were data on parents' income.

a $p > .05$

standard form and the second, unstandardized or metric regression coefficients. The former describe the effect of a change of one standard-deviation in a predetermined variable on a dependent variable in standard-deviation units. Thus, in line 2 of the first panel, one standard-deviation shift in father's education (V) produces a .185 standard-deviation change in occupational status of the son (W), net of the influence of father's occupation (X), which has a similar net effect. In this regression the coefficient of determination (R^2) is .096, so the two background characteristics jointly and separately account for 9.6% of the variance in son's occupational status. Regression coefficients describe effects in the original units of the predetermined and dependent variables. Thus, looking at the corresponding line in the second panel, we see that for each additional year of father's education, a son's occupation averaged 1.43 points higher on the Duncan SEI, and for each additional point on the Duncan scale achieved by fathers, a son's occupational status increased by .191 points.

For each dependent variable, we have estimated each reduced-form equation as well as the most complete equation in the model. Thus, in the case of educational attainment (U), we estimate only the one equation describing its dependence on father's education and occupation (V and X). In the case of son's occupational attainment (W), we estimate its regression on father's education and occupation, and we also estimate the more complete equation which includes son's educational attainment (U) as an additional regressor. Likewise, we regress earnings first on father's education and occupation, then on these two variables and son's educational attainment, and last on these three variables and son's occupational attainment. By comparing coefficients for the variables which appear in these successive equations, we can readily determine the extent to which the effect of any prior variable is mediated by each subsequent predetermined variable. For example, comparing lines 2 and 3 in either the first or second panel (for this type of interpretation is indifferent to standardization), three-fourths of the effect of father's education (V) on son's occupation (W) and three-fifths of the influence of father's occupation (X) on son's occupation (W) are mediated by son's education (U). Thus, in Model I, socioeconomic background influences occupational achievement mainly by way of educational attainment. Correspondingly, son's education (U) has the large net effect on son's occupation (W) of .586 in standard form or 8.16 points on the Duncan SEI per year of post-high school education, net of father's education and occupation.

Turning to the earnings regressions, we present estimates for son's earnings in 1965, 1966, and 1967 (Y_1, Y_2, and Y_3), and also for their canonically weighted average (Y). In most of our discussion, we shall refer only to the equations for son's canonically weighted average earnings (Y), which we believe to be the best representation of earnings performance in our data; but the regressions for its components hold some separate interest. Comparing standardized or metric coefficients of son's earnings in 1965, 1966, and 1967, in almost every case the coefficients in 1966 are larger than those in 1965, and the coefficients in 1967 are larger than those in 1966. We believe this pattern represents a stabilization of earning capacity with labor force experience with respect both to social background and to educational and occupational achievements. Viewing this pattern in conjunction with the extremely low proportions of variance in earnings explained by the model, we thought it would be useful to average the earnings data over the available years and to ask whether the changes in earnings coefficients over time represent a true stabilization of earnings relative to all of their causes or merely a shift in the relative importance of some of their causes.

In order to accomplish both of these objectives, a canonical correlation analysis of the earnings data was carried out. Canonical correlation is a statistical model that chooses weights for the variables in each of two designated groups in order to produce the largest possible correlation between the weighted composites of the variables in the two groups (Cooley and Lohnes, 1963; Hauser and Goldberger, 1971). If the variables in one group are thought of as predetermined and in the other as dependent, the canonical correlation model can be viewed as a generalization of multiple correlation analysis to the case of multiple dependent variables. Because the extraction of a first pair of canonical variates need not account fully for the correlation between variables in the two groups, it may be possible to extract more than one pair of canonical variates. All of the variables in Model IV (X, V, M, I, Q, U, and W), except earnings, were placed in the first group and the three earnings measures (Y_1, Y_2, and Y_3) in the second group. The weights for earnings in the first canonical correlation produce the desired average earnings index. The existence of more than one pair of canonical variates would mean that information about earnings would be lost in constructing a single average of them or, put more concretely, that there are shifts in the effects of variables in the first group on earnings from year to year that represent true changes in the relative importance of those variables over time. We found a statistically significant first canonical correlation (.273), but no second or third canonical correlation. Thus, the data are consistent with a general stabilization of earning capacity relative to its causes over the period in question. The canonical weight of 1967 earnings (.92) is far larger than that of 1966 earnings (.38), while that of 1965 earnings (−.13) is essentially zero. As one might expect from these results, the behavior of the canonically weighted average earnings (Y) in the regression analyses is very similar to that of 1967 earnings (Y_3). The canonical correlation procedure is indifferent to the metric of the constructed variates, and we arbitrarily assigned to the canonically weighted average earnings the same mean and standard deviation as 1967 earnings. Thus, in most instances the metric coefficients of canonically weighted average earnings are larger than those of 1967 earnings, reflecting the slight difference in standardized coefficients of the two variables.

As has already been noted, the coefficients of determination in the earnings regressions are rather small, much smaller than those for educational attainment or occupational achievement. Indeed, as we show later in this chapter, they are smaller than those in regressions of income on the socioeconomic background and educational and occupational achievement of slightly older cohorts of United States males. We believe three facts are responsible for this. First, as has already been demonstrated, earnings more strongly reflect background and later achievements as labor force experience increases. Second, several of the eligibility criteria (Wisconsin residence in 1957, high school graduation, nonfarm background, nonenrollment in 1964) tend to restrict the variance in the sample relative to that, say, in a birth cohort of about the same age, and to reduce the observed correlations correspondingly. Third, the dependent variable, adjusted Social Security earnings, excludes all forms of unearned and, indeed, of noncovered income. Because earnings are a component of income, it is an algebraic necessity that the regression of income on any regressor on which both earnings and other income have coefficients of the same sign be greater in absolute value than the regression coefficient of earnings alone.

If β_1 and β_2 are the regression coefficients of earnings and of all other income on any variable, say, X, then the regression coefficient of income on X will be the sum, $\beta_1 + \beta_2$. Also, we would ordinarily expect the standardized regression coefficient of income on X to be larger than that of earnings on X. In fact, for the subsample of eligible males who were Wisconsin residents in 1964, we have measured Wisconsin income in 1965 as well as 1965 earnings, and in this subgroup the income regressions are about one-third stronger (in standardized or metric form) than the earnings regressions.

Fortunately, none of these factors need affect the interpretation of the system, that is, the degree to which each successive variable mediates the effects of those which come before it. Indeed, we have already produced strong evidence that the interpretations are identical for our three earnings measures. The fact that there is only one canonical earnings variate indicates that the interpretations of 1965, 1966, and 1967 earnings are the same (within the limits of sampling error) even though we can explain 2.1% of the variance in the first, 4.2% of the variance in the second, and 5.5% of the variance in the last.

Looking at line 13 of Table 3-3, father's education (V) and occupation (X) have rather small effects on earnings. Even in the reduced form, the standardized regression coefficients are only .061 and .076, which is to say that a year of father's education is worth $52 per year in son's earnings 10 years after high school graduation, while a point of father's occupational status is worth $8.80. Most of the influence of socioeconomic background in Model I appears to be mediated by the son's educational attainment (U); the effects of father's education and occupation are statistically insignificant when son's educational attainment is taken into account (see line 14). Net of education, a year of father's education is worth only $15, and a one unit change in father's occupational status only $4.70. At the same time the rewards of education are substantial, if not overwhelming. Net of father's education and occupation, a single year of the son's· post-high school education is worth $287 in earnings, which is to say that a college degree is worth almost $1200 more in annual earnings than a high school diploma. When son's occupational status (W) is entered into the equation (see line 15), the coefficients of father's education and occupation are reduced still more, though not by the same amount as when son's education was entered, and the coefficient of son's education is reduced by nearly one-half. That is, the effect of education on earnings is due almost equally to the higher paying jobs of men with more education and to the higher occupation–specific earnings of better educated men.

It is especially instructive to contrast the metric regression coefficients of education and occupation across generations in the equation of line 15. Neither the coefficient of father's education (V) nor that of father's occupation (X) is statistically significant at even the .05 level, while those of son's education (U) and son's occupation (W) are clearly significant. Net of the other variables, a year of father's education is worth $9 in earnings, while a year of son's education is worth $154; in the case of father's occupation a point on the Duncan SEI is worth only $3.50, while in the case of the son's occupation a point is worth $16.30. Of course, the reduced-form coefficients, rather than the net effects of each variable, represent their total effects. Even so, the preponderant influence of a son's own achievements relative to those of his father is evident. The total effect of a year of father's education is $52 in earnings, while the total effect of a year of son's own education is $287; the total effect of a unit of father's occupational status is $8.80 in earnings, while the total effect of a unit of son's own occupational status is $16.30 in earnings. If Model I is to be believed, the effect of socioeconomic background on earnings is quite modest, and it is attributable primarily to the influence of background on son's education and secondarily to its influence on son's occupational status.

We now ask whether these findings are consistent with those in other roughly comparable bodies of data. We have been able to locate published correlation matrices that contain major variables of interest for three broadly representative samples of young United States males. The first of these pertains to the cohort of non-Negro United States males with nonfarm background, aged 25 to 34 in 1962, for whom data were obtained in the Current Population Survey Supplement of March 1962, "Occupational Changes in a Generation," henceforth referred to as OCG. This is the sample on which the important monograph by Blau and Duncan (1967) is based, and also much of the analysis reported by Jencks et al. (1972). The correlation matrix, means, and standard deviations are reported by Duncan, Featherman, and Duncan

(1972:38). Major elements of noncomparability with the Wisconsin data include the more advanced age of the cohort, its national coverage, the fact that the education of the men in the cohort was completed, and the use of total income rather than Social Security earnings as the ultimate dependent variable.

The second study pertains to the cohort of white United States males aged 25 to 34 in 1964, of which a sample was taken in the Current Population Survey Supplement of October 1964, undertaken in cooperation with the National Opinion Research Center; it is henceforth referred to as CPS–NORC. A correlation matrix obtained from this sample is reported by Duncan (1968a:2). These data, too, were used extensively by Jencks et al. (1972). Because there are so few non-Negro nonwhites, the CPS–NORC sample is quite comparable to the OCG sample, except for the exclusion of men with farm background from the former, and the points of noncomparability of the CPS–NORC sample with the Wisconsin sample are much the same as those of the OCG sample, plus the effect of including men with farm background. The similarity of the OCG and CPS–NORC data is so great that both would not have been treated here, except that the latter includes an ability measure, the Armed Forces Qualification Test score (AFQT), while means and standard deviations were reported only in the former. An additional factor affecting the CPS–NORC data is that AFQT scores were ascertained only among veterans, and correlations involving that variable were adjusted to compensate for the homogeneity of that part of the population.

The third sample for which a correlation matrix, means, and standard deviations are reported by Kohen (1971:Tables 4 and 6) represents black and white United States males aged 18 to 24 in 1966 who had completed at least one year of high school but were not currently enrolled in school, and who were employed in the civilian labor force in 1966. This sample represents a subgroup of one panel of the National Longitudinal Surveys of Labor Force Participation and Employment that have been carried out by Herbert Parnes and his associates at Ohio State University in cooperation with the United States Bureau of the Census (Parnes et al., 1969); it is henceforth referred to as NLS. Here, the major elements of noncomparability with the Wisconsin cohort include the slightly younger age of the NLS men, their lower levels of educational attainment, the representation of large numbers of blacks and of men with farm background, and the use of hourly earnings in the 1966 occupation as the ultimate dependent variable. Also, educational attainment in the family of orientation was expressed by the number of persons with some college experience, rather than by father's educational attainment. A major virtue of these data is the inclusion of a standardized ability measure, which was obtained by a follow-back match to the last school attended by each respondent.[3]

In Table 3-4, we present selected comparisons between men in the Wisconsin sample and in the OCG and NLS samples. Fathers of the Wisconsin men are more highly educated but less variable in education than those of OCG men. The occupational status composition of the Wisconsin and OCG fathers is quite similar, while the fathers of NLS men are lower and less variable in occupational status. Men in the NLS sample are lower and less variable in ability than those in the Wisconsin sample. Men in the OCG and NLS samples completed about a year less of schooling than Wisconsin men. Educational attainment was far more variable in the OCG sample than in the Wisconsin sample, as we already have been led to expect, and educational attainment is less variable in the NLS sample than in the Wisconsin sample. Both the mean and the standard deviation of occupational status are similar in the Wisconsin and OCG samples; we suppose that the more extensive labor market experience of the OCG men compensates for their lower levels of educational attainment. Both the mean and the standard deviation of occupational status in the NLS sample are far lower than in the Wisconsin or OCG samples, and, unlike the others, the NLS men have not experienced any improvement over the occupational status of their fathers. In short, we find real and substantial differences among the Wisconsin, OCG, and NLS samples that are large enough to make us wary of generalizing from the Wisconsin sample to the national situation without undertaking a more detailed interpretation of the determination of earnings in the national samples.

[3] There are other studies that we might have tried to compare with our own but that we chose to exclude because of even greater differences in population coverage, variables measured, or availability of published data. For example, see Coleman, Berry, and Blum, 1972; Featherman, 1969; Weiss, 1970; Taubman and Wales, 1973.

TABLE 3-4

Means and Standard Deviations of Selected Variables in Three Studies of Socioeconomic Achievement

Sample	Variable					
	V	X	Q	U	W	Y
(1) Male Wisconsin high school graduates of 1957 with nonfarm background (N = 2069)						
Mean	10.19	33.1	99.9	13.22	42.1	7.54
Standard deviation	3.01	22.4	14.6	1.68	23.3	2.59
(2) OCG: Non-Negro U.S. males with nonfarm background, 25–34 in 1962 (N = 3141)						
Mean	9.17	34.6	—	12.38	43.3	(6.14)
Standard deviation	3.53	22.4	—	3.04	25.0	(4.29)
(3) NLS: Black and white U.S. males with at least one year high school, 18–24 in 1966 (N = 669)						
Mean	(0.4)	31.3	96.9	12.1	30.8	(2.47)
Standard deviation	(0.7)	20.7	13.6	1.5	19.8	(1.30)

Note: Wisconsin data pertain to male high school graduates of 1957 with nonfarm background who were employed in the civilian labor force, were not enrolled in school in 1964, and had nonzero earnings, 1965–1967. Data from the OCG (Occupational Changes in a Generation) pertain to non-Negro U.S. males with nonfarm background who were in the experienced civilian labor force and aged 25–34 in 1962—reported in Duncan, Featherman, and Duncan (1972:38). Data from the NLS (National Longitudinal Survey) pertain to black and white U.S. males who were employed in the civilian labor force in 1966, were not enrolled in school, and had completed at least one year of high school—reported in Kohen (1971:Tables 4 and 6). Item identifications for the Wisconsin sample are: V = father's educational attainment; X = father's occupational status when the son graduated from high school (Duncan SEI); Q = score on Henmon–Nelson Test of Mental Ability; U = son's educational attainment; W = son's occupational status (Duncan SEI); Y = son's 1967 Social Security earnings (in thousands of dollars). In the OCG data, the items are the same as in the Wisconsin data, except that X refers to occupation when the son was 16 years old, and Y is self-reported 1961 income (in thousands of dollars). In the NLS data, the items are the same as in the Wisconsin data, except that V refers to the number of members of the respondent's family who had ever attended college, X refers to father's occupation when the son was 14 years old, Q is a standardized score on any ability test for which a score could be located, and Y is earnings per hour in the 1966 occupation. Figures in parentheses are not measured in the same metric as in the Wisconsin sample.

In Tables 3-5, 3-6, and 3-7, we present estimates for Model I derived from published data for the OCG, CPS–NORC, and NLS samples. Considering the major differences among the samples we have described, the interpretations of education, occupation, and earnings in the four sets of data are remarkably similar, in spite of the numerous differences in individual coefficients, both metric and standardized. In each sample, father's education (V) and father's occupation (X) have large and nearly equal effects on son's educational attainment (U) (see line 1 of the first panel in Tables

TABLE 3-5

Effects of Father's Education and Occupation on the Education, Occupation and Earnings of Non-Negro U.S. Males with Nonfarm Background, 25–34 in 1962

Dependent variable	Predetermined variables				
	V	X	U	W	
Standardized coefficients					R^2
(1) U	.262	.285	—	—	.223
(2) W	.222	.245	—	—	.163
(3) W	.067	.076	.593	—	.436
(4) Y	.072	.167	—	—	.045
(5) Y	.013[a]	.103	.225	—	.084
(6) Y	−.005[a]	.082	.068	.265	.124
Regression coefficients					Constant
(1) U	.226	.0388	—	—	9.0
(2) W	1.58	.274	—	—	19.4
(3) W	.47	.085	4.88	—	−0.0
(4) Y	.087	.0320	—	—	4.23
(5) Y	.016[a]	.0197	.318	—	1.38
(6) Y	−.006[a]	.0158	.096	.0455	2.49

Note: Item identifications are: V = father's educational attainment; X = status of father's occupation when son was 16 (Duncan SEI); U = son's educational attainment; W = son's 1962 occupation (Duncan SEI); Y = son's income, 1962 (in thousands of dollars). Data pertain to 3141 respondents in the experienced civilian labor force in March 1962. Regressions computed from data in March 1962 Current Population Survey supplement, "Occupational Changes in a Generation," reported in Duncan, Featherman, and Duncan (1972:38).

[a] $p > .05$

TABLE 3-6

Effects of Father's Education and Occupation on the Education, Occupation and Earnings of White U.S. Males 25–34 in 1964 (Standardized Regression Coefficients)

Dependent variable	Predetermined variables				
	V	X	U	W	R^2
(1) U	.262	.301	—	—	.237
(2) W	.196	.294	—	—	.181
(3) W	.047	.123	.568	—	.427
(4) Y	.128	.147	—	—	.057
(5) Y	.047	.055	.307	—	.128
(6) Y	.034[a]	.021[a]	.152	.272	.171

Note: Item identifications are: V = father's educational attainment; X = status of father's occupation when respondent was 16 (Duncan SEI); U = son's educational attainment; W = son's 1964 occupation (Duncan SEI); Y = son's 1964 earnings. Data pertain to about 3000 men. Regressions computed from correlations for the October 1964 CPS–NORC study reported in Duncan (1968a:2).

   [a] $p > .05$

3-3, 3-5, 3-6, and 3-7). The possible exception here is the NLS sample, where the effect of father's education appears to be about twice that of father's occupation. In the two nonfarm samples, the effects of father's education and occupation on son's occupation (W) are also large and about equal in size (see line 2 of each table), while father's occupation is relatively more important in the samples that include men with farm origins. Except for the effect of father's occupation on son's occupation in the NLS sample, son's educational attainment mediates two-thirds to three-quarters of the effects of father's education and occupation on son's occupation in each sample (compare lines 2 and 3 of each table). Moreover, in each sample, with son's educational attainment taken into account, father's occupational status is relatively more important in determining son's occupational status than is father's educational attainment. Overall, in each sample, father's occupation also has more influence on son's earnings (Y) than does father's education (see line 4 of each table). In each sample, the effects of father's education and occupation on son's earnings are mediated to a substantial degree by son's educational attainment and occupa-

TABLE 3-7

Effects of Father's Education and Occupation on the Education, Occupation and Wages of Black and White U.S. Males 18–24 in 1966

Dependent variable	Predetermined variables				
	V	X	U	W	
Standardized coefficients					R^2
(1) U	.291	.157	—	—	.132
(2) W	.125	.219	—	—	.077
(3) W	.032[a]	.168	.321	—	.166
(4) Y	.013[a]	.133	—	—	.017
(5) Y	−.051[a]	.113	.131	—	.032
(6) Y	−.055[a]	.096	.099	.099	.040
Regression coefficients					Constant
(1) U	.623	.0114	—	—	11.5
(2) W	3.55	.209	—	—	22.8
(3) W	.91[a]	.161	4.23	—	−0.0
(4) Y	−.025[a]	.0084	—	—	2.22
(5) Y	−.096[a]	.0071	.114	—	.91
(6) Y	−.101[a]	.0060	.086	.0065	1.08

Note: Item identifications are V = number of family members, excluding respondents, who ever attended colleges; X = status of father's occupation when son was 14 (Duncan SEI); U = son's educational attainment; W = son's 1966 occupation (Duncan SEI); Y = son's hourly wage, 1966. Data pertain to 669 respondents who were employed in the civilian labor force, were not enrolled in school, had attended at least the first year of high school, and for whom there were data on all variables. A small number of nonwhite nonblacks were excluded. Regressions computed from data reported in Kohen (1971).

[a] $p > .05$

tional achievement; in all four samples the net intergenerational effect of education on earnings is not statistically significant, while the effect of father's occupational status is nonsignificant in two of the four samples (compare lines 4 and 6 of each table). Finally, a substantial share of the influence of education on earnings is mediated by occupational status in each of the samples: one-half in the Wisconsin sample, two-thirds in the OCG sample, one-half in the CPS–NORC sample, and one-fourth in the NLS sample (compare lines 5 and 6 of each table). In general, we are impressed with the similarity of these interpretations across all four samples, though more in the case of the first three than of the last.

MODEL II

Model II is the same as Model I, except that we add an equation for the effect of socioeconomic background (V and X) on mental ability (Q), and we add ability to the regressors of son's education (U), occupation (W), and earnings (Y). In shifting from Model I to Model II, one set of data is lost (OCG), but it is now possible to interpret the effects of ability and to determine the extent of specification bias in the effect of education on earnings due to the omission of ability from Model I.

Estimates of Model II for the Wisconsin sample are presented in Table 3-8. In describing these estimates, we shall mention only the changes which occur when ability is introduced. As shown in line 1, the effects of father's education and occupation on son's ability are smaller than their effects on son's educational attainment. In view of the upward bias in those coefficients to which we have earlier referred, we find these results to be consistent with other suggestions (Duncan, 1968a; Hauser, 1969) that the dependence of ability on socioeconomic background is often overstated by critics of intelligence testing. However, ability mediates a modest share of the influence of father's occupation and education on son's education, 35% in the former case and 18% in the latter, by virtue of the large net effect of ability on educational attainment. That effect, almost half a year of schooling for each 10-point shift in ability, is, again, largely independent of background. Looking at line 5, son's ability also has a large effect on son's occupational status, 5 points on the Duncan SEI for each 10-point shift in ability net of father's education and occupation, and son's ability mediates 37% of the effect of father's education on son's occupational status in 1964 and 16% of the effect of father's occupational status on son's occupational status in 1964 (compare lines 4 and 5). Comparing lines 5 and 6, it is seen that the effect of ability in mediating the influence of father's education and occupation on son's occupational status is due mainly to the effect of son's ability on his educational attainment. That is, ability helps to explain the influence of background on occupational status because ability influences educational attainment, which in turn has a large effect on occupational status. About two-thirds of the effect of ability on occupational attainment is mediated by education, while the latter continues to have a modest net effect on occupational status. When the mediating role of ability and schooling is taken into account, father's education no longer has a statistically significant direct effect on occupational status, and the direct effect of father's occupation is reduced by 62%.

Looking at the earnings regressions, we see that ability mediates about half the effect of father's education on son's earnings, but

TABLE 3-8

Effects of Ability and Father's Education and Occupation on the Education, Occupation and Earnings of Male Wisconsin High School Graduates of 1957 with Nonfarm Background

Dependent variable	Predetermined variables					
	V	X	Q	U	W	
Standardized coefficients						R^2
(1) Q	.215	.092	—	—	—	.072
(2) U	.235	.190	—	—	—	.130
(3) U	.153	.156	.381	—	—	.264
(4) W	.185	.183	—	—	—	.096
(5) W	.116	.154	.319	—	—	.191
(6) W	.034[a]	.070	.114	.539	—	.405
(7) Y_1	.026[a]	.029[a]	—	—	—	.002
(8) Y_1	.006[a]	.021[a]	.091	—	—	.010
(9) Y_1	−.006[a]	.009[a]	.062	.076	—	.014
(10) Y_1	−.010[a]	.000[a]	.048[a]	.012[a]	.119	.023
(11) Y_2	.046[a]	.070	—	—	—	.010
(12) Y_2	.023[a]	.060	.108	—	—	.021
(13) Y_2	.003[a]	.040[a]	.057	.133	—	.034
(14) Y_2	−.002[a]	.031[a]	.043[a]	.064	.127	.043
(15) Y_3	.061	.071	—	—	—	.012
(16) Y_3	.030[a]	.057	.148	—	—	.033
(17) Y_3	.007[a]	.035[a]	.092	.145	—	.048
(18) Y_3	.003[a]	.025[a]	.077	.071	.136	.059
(19) Y	.061	.076	—	—	—	.013
(20) Y	.030[a]	.063	.143	—	—	.033
(21) Y	.007[a]	.040[a]	.086	.151	—	.049
(22) Y	.002[a]	.030[a]	.070	.077	.137	.060

(Continued)

TABLE 3-8 (*Continued*)

Dependent variable	Predetermined variables					Constant
	V	X	Q	U	W	
Regression coefficients						Constant
(1) Q	1.041	.0601	—	—	—	87.3
(2) U	.131	.0143	—	—	—	11.4
(3) U	.085	.0116	.0438	—	—	7.6
(4) W	1.43	.191	—	—	—	21.2
(5) W	.90	.160	.512	—	—	−23.5
(6) W	.26[a]	.073	.183	7.51	—	−80.5
(7) Y_1	.019[a]	.0029[a]	—	—	—	5.93
(8) Y_1	.005[a]	.0020[a]	.0137	—	—	4.73
(9) Y_1	−.004[a]	.0009[a]	.0093	.100	—	3.97
(10) Y_1	−.007[a]	.0000[a]	.0073[a]	.016[a]	.0112	4.88
(11) Y_2	.036[a]	.0074	—	—	—	6.41
(12) Y_2	.018[a]	.0063	.0173	—	—	4.90
(13) Y_2	.002[a]	.0042[a]	.0092	.185	—	3.50
(14) Y_2	−.001[a]	.0032[a]	.0069[a]	.090	.0127	4.52
(15) Y_3	.053	.0082	—	—	—	6.73
(16) Y_3	.025[a]	.0066	.0262	—	—	4.44
(17) Y_3	.006[a]	.0040[a]	.0164	.224	—	2.75
(18) Y_3	.002[a]	.0029[a]	.0136	.110	.0151	3.96
(19) Y	.052	.0088	—	—	—	6.71
(20) Y	.026[a]	.0073	.0255	—	—	4.49
(21) Y	.006[a]	.0046[a]	.0153	.233	—	2.72
(22) Y	.002[a]	.0035[a]	.0125	.119	.0152	3.94

Note: Item identifications are: V = father's educational attainment; X = status of father's occupation when son graduated from high school (Duncan SEI); Q = mental ability; U = son's educational attainment; W = son's 1964 occupation (Duncan SEI); Y_1 = son's 1965 earnings (in thousands of dollars); Y_2 = son's 1966 earnings (in thousands of dollars); Y_3 = son's 1967 earnings (in thousands of dollars); Y = canonically weighted average of son's 1965–1967 earnings (in thousands of dollars). Data pertain to 2069 respondents with nonfarm background who were employed in the civilian labor force in 1964, not enrolled in school, had nonzero earnings, 1965–1967, and for whom there were data on parents' income.

[a] $p > .05$

only one-sixth of the influence of father's occupation on son's earnings. The total effect of ability on earnings is substantial, amounting to $255 per year per 10-point shift in ability, net of father's education and occupation (see lines 19 and 20). Educational attainment mediates 40% of the influence of ability on earnings, and an additional 11% is mediated by occupational status, but about half the effect of ability on earnings is unmediated (compare lines 20, 21, and 22). As in Model I, we find that socioeconomic background, represented by father's education and occupation, has no direct effect on earnings when the intervening variables have been taken into account.

With regard to bias in the education coefficient of the earnings regression when ability is omitted, the total effect of educational attainment (U) on earnings (Y) is reduced by 19% when ability (Q) is entered in the earnings regression (compare line 14 of Table 3-3 with line 21 of Table 3-8). If we regard the zero-order effect of educational attainment as its total effect ($r_{UY} = .203$ in Table 3-11), we see that the regression of earnings on education is reduced by 25% when we take into account the mutual influence of father's education, father's occupation, and son's ability on son's education and earnings. With regard to specification bias in the education coefficient, we think these findings lend greater support to the position taken by Denison (1964) and Bowman (1969) than that of Griliches (1970). Our findings are also in general agreement with the argument of Gintis (1971) that educational attainment has a substantial effect on earnings, net of ability, but we see nothing persuasive about his interpretation of that effect.

Estimates of Model II for the CPS–NORC and NLS samples are displayed in Tables 3-9 and 3-10. Again, in spite of substantial differences in the populations represented and in the metric and standardized coefficients, the interpretation is rather similar across samples. In each, we find modest effects of father's education (V) and occupation (X) on son's ability (Q) (compare line 1 of Tables 3-8, 3-9, and 3-10). In each sample there is a large net effect of ability on educational attainment. Ability mediates a larger share of the effect of father's occupation (X) on son's education (U), one-third in both the CPS–NORC and NLS samples and a smaller share (10%) of the effect of father's education on son's education in the NLS sample (compare lines 2 and 3 of Tables 3-8, 3-9, and 3-10).

TABLE 3-9

Effects of Ability and Father's Education and Occupation on the Education, Occupation and Earnings of White U.S. Males 25–34 in 1964 (Standardized Regression Coefficients)

Dependent variable	Predetermined variables					
	V	X	Q	U	W	R²
(1) Q	.181	.201	—	—	—	.109
(2) U	.262	.301	—	—	—	.237
(3) U	.175	.205	.482	—	—	.444
(4) W	.196	.294	—	—	—	.181
(5) W	.133	.224	.348	—	—	.289
(6) W	.043	.120	.102	.511	—	.434
(7) Y	.128	.147	—	—	—	.057
(8) Y	.081	.095	.260	—	—	.117
(9) Y	.042	.050	.154	.221	—	.144
(10) Y	.031	.019[a]	.127	.089	.258	.181

Note: Item identifications are: V = father's educational attainment; X = status of father's occupation when son was 16 (Duncan SEI); Q = Armed Forces Qualification Test (AFQT) score; U = son's educational attainment; W = son's 1964 occupation (Duncan SEI); Y = son's 1964 earnings (in thousands of dollars). Data pertain to about 3000 men. Regressions computed from correlations for the October 1964 CPS–NORC study reported in Duncan (1968a:2).

[a] $p > .05$

We can offer no explanation for the latter result beyond the possibility that the measure of parents' college experience behaves differently from that of father's educational attainment, while it is possible that the former difference follows from the inclusion of men with farm background in the CPS–NORC and NLS samples.

The findings are more consistent across samples with regard to the role of ability in mediating background effects on occupational status. In the CPS–NORC sample, ability mediates 32% of the influence of father's education (V) on son's occupation (W) and 24% of the influence of father's occupation on son's occupation, while in the NLS sample, the corresponding figures are 19% and 20%, respectively (see lines 4 and 5 of Tables 3-9 and 3-10). In the OCG sample, as in the Wisconsin sample, educational attainment mediates about two-thirds of the influence of ability on occupational

TABLE 3-10

Effects of Ability and Father's Education and Occupation on the Education, Occupation and Earnings of Black and White U.S. Males 18–24 in 1966

Dependent variable	Predetermined variables					
	V	X	Q	U	W	
Standardized coefficients						R^2
(1) Q	.125	.219	—	—	—	.077
(2) U	.291	.157	—	—	—	.132
(3) U	.260	.103	.247	—	—	.189
(4) W	.125	.219	—	—	—	.077
(5) W	.101	.175	.198	—	—	.113
(6) W	.026[a]	.146	.127	.287	—	.058
(7) Y	−.013[a]	.133	—	—	—	.017
(8) Y	−.032[a]	.100	.151	—	—	.038
(9) Y	−.058[a]	.090	.127	.098	—	.046
(10) Y	−.060[a]	.078[a]	.116	.074[a]	.084	.052
Regression coefficients						Constant
(1) Q	2.44	.144	—	—	—	91.4
(2) U	.623	.0114	—	—	—	11.5
(3) U	.556	.0075	.0273	—	—	9.0
(4) W	3.55	.209	—	—	—	22.8
(5) W	2.84	.168	.288	—	—	−3.5
(6) W	.73[a]	.139	.185	3.79	—	−37.7
(7) Y	−.025[a]	.0084	—	—	—	2.22
(8) Y	−.060[a]	.0063	.0144	—	—	.90
(9) Y	−.107[a]	.0057	.0121	.085	—	.14
(10) Y	−.111[a]	.0049[a]	.0111	.064[a]	.0055	.35

Note: Item identifications are: V = number of family members, excluding respondents, who ever attended college; X = status of father's occupation when son was 14 (Duncan SEI); U = son's educational attainment; W = son's 1966 occupation (Duncan SEI); Y = son's 1966 hourly wage; Q = mental ability. Data pertain to 669 respondents who were employed in the civilian labor force, not enrolled in school, had attended at least the first year of high school, and for whom there were data on all variables. A small number of nonwhite nonblacks were excluded. Regressions computed from data reported in Kohen (1971).

[a] $p > .05$

status, while taken together ability and educational attainment mediate about three-quarters of the influence of father's education on son's occupational status and three-fifths of the influence of father's occupational status on son's occupational status (compare lines 4, 5, and 6 of Tables 3-8 and 3-9). In the NLS sample, educational attainment mediates only one-third of the effect of ability on occupation, and ability and educational attainment together account for a smaller share (one-third) of the effect of father's occupation on son's occupational attainment (see lines 4, 5, and 6 of Table 3-10).

We also detect substantial similarity across samples in our interpretation of the earnings regressions. In the CPS–NORC sample, the coefficients of father's education (V) and occupation (X) are reduced by 37% and 35%, respectively, when ability is entered in the earnings equation. In the NLS sample, the effect of father's education is nonsignificant with or without the introduction of son's ability (Q), while 25% of the influence of father's occupation on son's earnings (Y) is mediated by son's ability (compare lines 19 and 20 of Table 3-8 with lines 7 and 8 of Tables 3-9 and 3-10). In the CPS–NORC sample, as in the Wisconsin sample, educational attainment mediates about two-fifths of the effect of ability on earnings, while, again, the reduction of the ability coefficient is less similar (one-sixth) in the NLS sample (compare lines 20 and 21 of Table 3-8 with lines 8 and 9 of Tables 3-9 and 3-10). Together, son's education and occupation account for about 50% of the effect of ability on earnings in both the CPS–NORC sample and the Wisconsin sample, while their mediating effect is lower (about 25%) in the NLS sample.

In all three samples, the effects on earnings of socioeconomic background, represented by father's education and occupation, are almost entirely mediated by son's ability and by intervening educational and occupational achievements of the sons. Indeed only one of the six net intergenerational effects on earnings is statistically significant (see lines 21 and 22 of Table 3-7 and lines 9 and 10 of Tables 3-9 and 3-10). With regard to the issue of specification bias in the education coefficient, we find a reduction in the effect of education on earnings, net of father's education and occupation, of 28% in the CPS–NORC sample (compare line 5 of Table 3-6 with line 9 of Table 3-9) and of 25% in the NLS sample (compare line 5 of Table 3-7 with line 9 of Table 3-10), each of which is consistent with our finding in the Wisconsin sample.

In summary, we are impressed with the similarity across samples in the interpretation of the determination of educational attainment, occupational achievement, and earnings. The likeness is especially strong in the case of comparisons between the Wisconsin and CPS–NORC samples, and we think this important because we wish to generalize from our own sample to the national situation of representative birth cohorts (Hauser, 1970a). The tedious comparisons described above have been undertaken in the hope of establishing some basis for generalization of our findings with regard to aspects of the Wisconsin data for which there exist no parallel national measurements. With this in mind, we begin a more intensive analysis of the Wisconsin data. Table 3-11 presents a correlation matrix, means, and standard deviations of background, ability, and achievement measures for the Wisconsin sample.

MODEL III

In Model III we again omit ability, but we add father's average income (I_F) as a third measure of socioeconomic background. Table 3-12 presents estimates for this model in the Wisconsin sample. Our findings with regard to the determination of earnings are strikingly changed from those reported above. Here, we direct our attention to the equations for 1967 earnings (Y_3) in lines 10–12 of Table 3-12; we omitted canonically weighted average earnings (Y) from Model III, because father's income was not entered explicitly in the canonical correlation analysis. As soon as father's income is entered as a variable, even in the reduced-form equation (line 10), the regression coefficients of father's education (V) and occupation (X) are reduced to statistical and substantive nonsignificance. A father's educational attainment and occupational status are correlated with his son's earnings only by virtue of their correlation with the father's income, which has a substantial direct effect on the son's earnings.[4] The total effect of father's income is to increase son's annual earnings by $116 for each $1000 increase in father's

---

[4] This is the specification on which Treiman and Hauser (1970) have based their effort to estimate the inheritance of earning propensity in the OCG sample.

TABLE 3-11

Correlations among Social Background and Achievement Variables: Male Wisconsin High School Graduates of 1957 with Nonfarm Background

	V	M	X	I	Q	U	W	Y₁	Y₂	Y₃	Y
V	1.000										
M	.524	1.000									
X	.425	.288	1.000								
I	.320	.238	.457	1.000							
Q	.254	.211	.184	.184	1.000						
U	.316	.260	.291	.279	.448	1.000					
W	.263	.211	.262	.237	.377	.621	1.000				
Y₁	.038	.039	.040	.128	.096	.105	.143	1.000			
Y₂	.076	.065	.090	.175	.125	.171	.191	.738	1.000		
Y₃	.091	.083	.097	.177	.166	.199	.217	.648	.795	1.000	
Y	.093	.083	.102	.184	.162	.203	.220	.645	.878	.985	1.000
Mean	10.20	10.41	33.11	6.443	99.86	13.22	42.11	6.218	7.022	7.538	7.538ᵃ
St. dev.	3.008	2.848	22.41	3.141	14.57	1.676	23.34	2.202	2.337	2.589	2.589ᵃ

Note: Item identifications are: V = father's educational attainment; M = mother's educational attainment; X = status of father's occupation when son graduated from high school (Duncan SEI); 1 = parents' average income, 1957–1960 (in thousands of dollars): Q = son's score on Henmon–Nelson Test of Mental Ability; U = son's educational attainment; W = son's 1964 occupation (Duncan SEI); Y₁ = son's 1965 earnings (in thousands of dollars); Y₂ = son's 1966 earnings (in thousands of dollars); Y₃ = son's 1967 earnings (in thousands of dollars); Y = canonically weighted average of son's 1965–67 earnings (in thousands of dollars). Data pertain to 2069 respondents with nonfarm background who were employed in the civilian labor force in 1964, were not enrolled in school, had nonzero earnings, 1965–67, and for whom there were data on parents' income.

ᵃ Arbitrarily assigned values for Y₃.

income. Moreover, relatively little—only 16%—of the influence of father's income is mediated by the son's educational attainment or occupational status. Net of those two achievement variables, father's income is still worth $98 per $1000 per year in earnings in this cohort of young Wisconsin men. We would find this outcome less striking if our dependent variable included sources of income other than earnings, but our finding of inherited earning propensity refers strictly to earned income. Of course, we do not wish to overstate the size of the income effect. We account overall for less

TABLE 3-12

Effects of Father's Education, Occupation, and Income on the Education, Occupation, and Earnings of Male Wisconsin High School Graduates of 1957 with Nonfarm Background

Dependent variable	Predetermined variables					
	V	X	I_F	U	W	
Standardized coefficients						R^2
(1) U	.221	.143	.118	—	—	.141
(2) W	.175	.158	.086	—	—	.102
(3) W	.046	.065	.017[a]	.584	—	.395
(4) Y_1	.009[a]	−.030[a]	.146	—	—	.019
(5) Y_1	−.011[a]	−.043[a]	.136	.087	—	.025
(6) Y_1	−.016[a]	−.051[a]	.134	.015	.123	.035
(7) Y_2	.029[a]	.010[a]	.150	—	—	.027
(8) Y_2	−.003[a]	.011[a]	.133	.142	—	.045
(9) Y_2	−.009[a]	−.019[a]	.131	.066	.130	.055
(10) Y_3	.044[a]	.012[a]	.145	—	—	.029
(11) Y_3	.007[a]	−.012[a]	.125	.169	—	.053
(12) Y_3	.000[a]	−.022[a]	.122	.084	.145	.066
Regression coefficients						Constant
(1) U	.123	.0107	.0614	—	—	11.3
(2) W	1.36	.154	.62	—	—	19.8
(3) W	.35	.067	.12[a]	8.13	—	−71.9
(4) Y_1	.006[a]	−.0030[a]	.100	—	—	5.71
(5) Y_1	−.008[a]	−.0042[a]	.093	.114	—	4.42
(6) Y_1	−.012[a]	−.0050[a]	.091	.020	.0116	5.25
(7) Y_2	.022[a]	.0010[a]	.108	—	—	6.17
(8) Y_2	−.002[a]	−.0011[a]	.096	.198	—	3.94
(9) Y_2	−.007[a]	−.0020[a]	.095	.092	.0131	4.88
(10) Y_3	.038[a]	.0014[a]	.116	—	—	6.47
(11) Y_3	.006[a]	−.0014[a]	.100	.261	—	3.53
(12) Y_3	.000[a]	−.0025[a]	.098	.130	.0161	4.68

Note: Item identifications are: V = father's educational attainment; X = status of father's occupation when son graduated from high school (Duncan SEI); I_F = father's average income, 1957–1960 (in thousands of dollars); U = son's educational attainment; W = son's 1964 occupation (Duncan SEI); Y_1 = son's 1965 earnings (in thousands of dollars); Y_2 = son's 1966 earnings (in thousands of dollars); Y_3 = son's 1967 earnings (in thousands of dollars). Data pertain to 2069 respondents with nonfarm background who were employed in the civilian labor force in 1964, were not enrolled in school, had nonzero earnings, 1965–1967, and for whom there were data on parents' income.

[a] $p > .05$

than 7% of the variance in earnings, so a young man's earnings are not completely or even mainly determined by his socioeconomic background, schooling, or occupational status. Even when the possibility of explaining more variance in total income or earnings measured at a later age is taken into account, it is likely that the predictability of remuneration will not be dramatically increased.

Our finding of an intergenerational income effect is augmented by the fact that a father's income is not an especially powerful cause of his son's educational attainment or occupational achievement. This aspect of our results may be emphasized by contrasting them with interpretations offered by Schiller (1970). By comparing the educational and occupational achievement of a collection of sons whose mothers had received Aid to Dependent Children (ADC) payments with the educational attainment and first job status of young men in the OCG sample, Schiller draws the conclusion that "opportunity stratification" is best represented by income in the family of orientation, and that, so measured, it would account for most of the sizable difference in achievement between the ADC and OCG sons.[5] We find in Table 3-8 that, in the determination of educational attainment and of occupational status (lines 1–3), the effects of father's education, occupation, and income (V, X, and I_F, respectively) are of the same order of magnitude and that, if anything, the coefficients of father's income are smaller than those of father's education and occupation in both regressions. Indeed, net of father's education and occupation and son's education (U), the effect of father's income on son's occupation (W) is not statistically significant. Our findings also conflict with Schiller where he allocates to income of the family of orientation a share of the effects of father's occupation (75%) and son's education (65%) on son's occupational status. Comparing line 3

---

[5] Schiller's ADC data are of questionable external validity, for the sampling design of the study from which his data were obtained (Burgess and Price, 1963) guaranteed that the less successful sons of welfare mothers would be represented in disproportionately large numbers among all adult sons in his sample. Moreover, in assigning educational and occupational differentials to the effects of income, Schiller nowhere takes account of the handicap imposed by greater than average fertility and by the nonintactness of virtually all welfare families. Further, his argument concerning the supposed lack of an ability effect on the differential is invalid.

of Table 3-3 with line 3 of Table 3-12, it is seen that introducing father's income into the regression for son's occupational status reduces the effect of father's occupational status by less than 9%, and it reduces the effect of son's education by less than 1%.

The objection may be raised that our sample of high school graduates does not represent all of the population in poverty, and this is surely the case. However, the Wisconsin sample does represent a broad range of income distribution; some 18% of the young men in the Wisconsin cohort came from families with average incomes below $3000 in the years 1957–1960. With regard to the influence of family income on educational attainment, we believe that its effects are probably larger in the case of higher education than in the case of secondary education because of larger direct costs and opportunity costs (foregone earnings) at that level. Moreover, we have been able to locate no evidence which conflicts with our modest estimates of the effect of family income on higher education (see Jencks, 1968). In summary, we conclude that paternal income plays a unique role in the process of stratification, but it is certainly not the one suggested by Schiller.

MODEL IV

In constructing Model IV, we again enter mental ability (Q) into the model, and choose a "best set" of measures of socioeconomic background. Table 3-13 presents a set of results that bear on the choice of measures of socioeconomic background. The first three columns contain coefficients of determination from the reduced-form regressions of each dependent variable on three sets of background variables. The first set, father's education, occupation, and income (V, X, and I_F, respectively), are those used in Model III. The second set includes these as well as two measures on our respondents' mothers, their educational attainment (M) and their average annual income, 1957–1960 (I_M). As shown by the F-ratios in the fourth column, the second set of background variables explains significantly more variance in all but one of the dependent variables than do those in the first set. Clearly, the explanation is improved by including socioeconomic characteristics of mothers. With as many as five background variables, it would be cumbersome to display all of the results, and we questioned whether it was necessary to include separate measurements of mother's and

TABLE 3-13

Coefficients of Determination in Regressions of the Education, Occupation, and Earnings of Male Wisconsin High School Graduates with Nonfarm Background on Three Combinations of Socioeconomic Background Variables

Dependent variable	Background variables			F-ratios	
	(a)V,X,I_F	(b)V,M,X,I_F,I_M	(c)V,M,X,I	(b)vs.(a)	(b)vs.(c)
Q	.0772	.0851	.0848	8.91	0.68[a]
U	.1406	.1552	.1552	17.83	0.00[a]
W	.1022	.1126	.1123	12.09	0.70[a]
Y_1	.0189	.0198	.0170	0.95[a]	5.89
Y_2	.0274	.0318	.0312	4.69	1.28[a]
Y_3	.0288	.0339	.0334	5.45	1.07[a]

Note: Item identifications are: V = father's educational attainment; M = mother's educational attainment; X = status of father's occupation when son graduated from high school (Duncan SEI); I_F = father's average income, 1957–1960 (in thousands of dollars); I_M = mother's average income, 1957–1960 (in thousands of dollars); I = parents' average income, 1957–1960 (in thousands of dollars); Q = son's score on Henmon–Nelson Test of Mental Ability; U = son's educational attainment; W = son's 1964 occupation (Duncan SEI); Y_1 = son's 1965 earnings (in thousands of dollars); Y_2 = son's 1966 earnings (in thousands of dollars); Y_3 = son's 1967 earnings (in thousands of dollars). Data pertain to 2069 respondents with nonfarm background who were employed in the civilian labor force in 1964, were not enrolled in school, had nonzero earnings, 1965–1967, and for whom there were data on parents' income.
  [a] $p > .05$

father's income. Here, the appropriate statistical test compares coefficients of determination in the second column with those in the third column, which pertain to the set including father's education, mother's education, father's occupation and parents' average income (V, M, X, and I). The effect of using parents' average income as a regressor is to force our estimated regression coefficients to be the same for father's income and mother's income. The F-ratios for these tests, displayed in the last column of Table 3-13, are not statistically significant at even the .05 level; we conclude, therefore, that it is unnecessary to use both father's income and mother's income in the regression analyses. Taking into account the desirability of both completeness and parsimony, we have chosen father's education, mother's education, father's occupation and parents' average income as our final measures of socioeconomic background.

Brief consideration has been given to the possible nonlinearity of the equations in Model IV. Each interval regressor was represented by a series of dummy (binary) variables and each reduced-form and structural equation in Model IV was estimated using the dummy-variable regressors. By contrasting coefficients of determination in these regressions with those in the corresponding interval regressions shown in Table 3-14, we can determine whether our assumption of linearity seriously distorts the true regressions. The nonlinear dummy-variable regressions must explain more variance than does linear regression, but if it is not too much more, we will have confidence in the validity of our linear estimates. On the whole, we are impressed with the fit obtained in linear regression. The effect of background on ability is clearly linear. Nonlinearity adds a statistically significant 3 percentage points to the explained variance in educational attainment (U), whether or not ability (Q) is entered in the regression; from other analyses not yet reported, we know this to be a consequence of heterogeneity in the data with regard to other (social psychological) variables. There is statistically significant nonlinearity in two of the occupational-status regressions, but we regard it as substantively trivial. Finally, while the assumption of nonlinearity adds increments to explained variance in earnings that are not small in relation to the proportion of variance explained by linear regression, not one of these increments is statistically significant at even the .05 level. Consequently, we believe that it is safe to interpret the major relationships in our data using linear regression.[6]

Our estimates of the statistically significant effects in the linear version of Model IV are displayed on the path diagram in Figure 3.2.[7] Each of the previously mentioned socioeconomic background variables, father's education (V), mother's education (M), father's occupation (X), and parents' average income (I), has a modest direct effect on son's mental ability (Q), while a son's ability has a large effect on his educational attainment (U). The direct effects of each

[6] These results do not rule out the possibility of statistically significant and substantively interpretable nonlinear effects of one or two criteria of classification.

[7] The following findings are in marked conflict with the polemical interpretation of similar materials by Bowles and Gintis (1972).

TABLE 3-14

Coefficients of Determination in Linear and Nonlinear (Dummy Variable) Regressions of Education, Occupation, and Earnings on Socioeconomic Background, Ability, and Achievement: Male Wisconsin High School Graduates of 1957 with Nonfarm Background

Predetermined variables	Dependent variable					
	Q	U	W	Y_1	Y_2	Y_3
(1) V,M,X,I						
Linear	.0848	.1552	.1123	.0170	.0312	.0334
Nonlinear	.0986[a]	.1827	.1281	.0284[a]	.0445[a]	.0438[a]
(2) V,M,X,I,Q						
Linear	—	.2782	.1995	.0229	.0395	.0499
Nonlinear	—	.3072	.2120[a]	.0376[a]	.0556[a]	.0656[a]
(3) V,M,X,I,Q,U						
Linear	—	—	.4059	.0256	.0491	.0617
Nonlinear	—	—	.4226	.0471[a]	.0699[a]	.0806[a]
(4) V,M,X,I,Q,U,W						
Linear	—	—	—	.0334	.0579	.0720
Nonlinear	—	—	—	.0587[a]	.0803[a]	.0976[a]

Note: Item identifications are: V = father's educational attainment; M = mother's educational attainment; X = status of father's occupation when son graduated from high school (Duncan SEI); I = parents' average income, 1957–1960 (in thousands of dollars); Q = son's score on Henmon–Nelson Test of Mental Ability; U = son's educational attainment; W = son's 1964 occupation (Duncan SEI); Y_1 = son's 1965 earnings (in thousands of dollars); Y_2 = son's 1966 earnings (in thousands of dollars); Y_3 = son's 1967 earnings (in thousands of dollars). Data pertain to 2069 respondents with nonfarm background who were employed in the civilian labor force in 1964, were not enrolled in school, had nonzero earnings in 1965–1967 and for whom there were data on parents' income.

[a] Indicates *failure* to reject null hypothesis of linearity at the .05 level of significance. The error sums of squares have 2040, 2031, 2026, and 2019 degrees of freedom in models (1), (2), (3), and (4), respectively, while the corresponding degrees of freedom for the increments to explained sums of squares are 24, 32, 36, and 42, respectively.

background variable on educational attainment are essentially equal in size and about as large as their effects on ability. Educational attainment has a very large direct effect on occupational status, which is also directly influenced by father's occupational

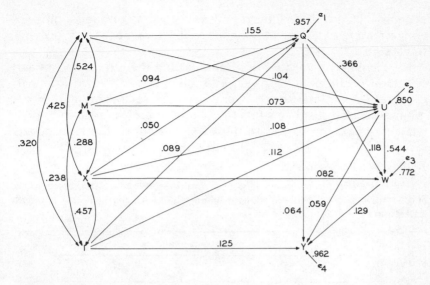

Figure 3-2. A path model of the influence of socioeconomic background on earnings: male Wisconsin high school graduates of 1957 with nonfarm background. Item identifications are: V = father's educational attainment; M = mother's educational attainment; X = status of father's occupation when son graduated from high school (Duncan SEI); I = parents' average income, 1957–1960 (in thousands of dollars); Q = son's score on Henmon–Nelson Test of Mental Ability; U = son's educational attainment; W = son's 1964 occupation (Duncan SEI); Y = son's canonically weighted average of 1965–1967 earnings (in thousands of dollars). Data pertain to 2069 respondents with nonfarm background, employed in the civilian labor force in 1964 and not enrolled in school, who had nonzero earnings in 1965–1967 and for whom there were data on parents' income. Numerical entries are regression coefficients in standard form. All path coefficients shown are statistically significant at the .05 level.

status and by ability. That is, students with equal educational credentials are slightly better off in the job market if they are unusually bright or if their fathers had unusually high-status jobs. However, mother's and father's educational attainments and incomes have no influence on son's occupational achievement, beyond their influence on ability and educational attainment. Finally, in the determination of earnings, ability and educational attainment have modest and roughly equal effects, while the effects of occupational status and parental income, also roughly equal in size, are about twice as large as those of ability and educational attainment. We want to emphasize this last point; at this early stage in the socioeconomic life cycle the effect of parents' income on the earnings of young men is as large as the effect of their own achieved occupational status.

We can interpret Model IV in detail using the reduced-form and structural coefficients displayed in Table 3-15. As shown in line 1, even this complete and powerful set of socioeconomic background measures explains less than 10% of the variance in ability; we are again impressed with the extent to which the later effects

TABLE 3-15

Effects of Socioeconomic Background and Ability on the Education, Occupation, and Earnings of Male Wisconsin High School Graduates of 1957 with Nonfarm Background

Dependent variable	Predetermined variables							
	V	M	X	I	Q	U	W	
Standardized coefficients								R^2
(1) Q	.155	.094	.050	.089	—	—	—	.085
(2) U	.161	.104	.125	.146	—	—	—	.155
(3) U	.104	.070	.107	.113	.367	—	—	.278
(4) W	.129	.078	.131	.118	—	—	—	.112
(5) W	.081	.049	.115	.090	.308	—	—	.200
(6) W	.025[a]	.011[a]	.058	.030[a]	.112	.535	—	.406
(7) Y_1	−.003[a]	.016[a]	−.026[a]	.137	—	—	—	.017
(8) Y_1	−.015[a]	.008[a]	−.030[a]	.130	.080	—	—	.023
(9) Y_1	−.022[a]	.004[a]	−.037[a]	.123	.058	.061	—	.026
(10) Y_1	−.025[a]	.003[a]	−.043[a]	.120	.045[a]	.000[a]	.114	.033
(11) Y_2	.012[a]	.019[a]	.004[a]	.164	—	—	—	.031
(12) Y_2	−.003[a]	.010[a]	−.000[a]	.156	.095	—	—	.040
(13) Y_2	−.015[a]	.002[a]	−.013[a]	.143	.053	.116	—	.049
(14) Y_2	−.018[a]	.000[a]	−.020[a]	.139	.039[a]	.050[a]	.122	.058
(15) Y_3	.021[a]	.032[a]	.006[a]	.160	—	—	—	.033
(16) Y_3	.000[a]	.020[a]	−.001[a]	.148	.134	—	—	.050
(17) Y_3	−.013[a]	.010[a]	−.015[a]	.134	.088	.128	—	.062
(18) Y_3	−.016[a]	.009[a]	−.022[a]	.130	.073	.058	.131	.072
(19) Y	.020[a]	.030[a]	.009[a]	.166	—	—	—	.036
(20) Y	.000[a]	.018[a]	.002[a]	.155	.130	—	—	.051
(21) Y	−.014[a]	.009[a]	−.012[a]	.140	.081	.133	—	.064
(22) Y	−.017[a]	.007[a]	−.020[a]	.136	.066	.063	.131	.074

(Continued)

TABLE 3-15 (*Continued*)

Dependent variable	Predetermined variables							
	V	M	X	I	Q	U	W	
Regression coefficients								Constant
(1) Q	.751	.481	.0326	.412	—	—	—	83.4
(2) U	.090	.061	.0094	.0776	—	—	—	10.8
(3) U	.058	.041	.0080	.0602	.0422	—	—	7.3
(4) W	1.00	.64	.136	.87	—	—	—	15.1
(5) W	.63	.40	.120	.67	.494	—	—	−26.1
(6) W	.19[a]	.09[a]	.060	.22[a]	.180	7.45	—	−80.7
(7) Y_1	−.002[a]	.012[a]	−.0026[a]	.096	—	—	—	5.58
(8) Y_1	−.011[a]	.006	−.0030[a]	.091	.0121	—	—	4.57
(9) Y_1	−.016[a]	.003[a]	−.0036[a]	.086	.0087	.080	—	3.98
(10) Y_1	−.018[a]	.002[a]	−.0042[a]	.084	.0068[a]	.000[a]	.0108	4.85
(11) Y_2	.009[a]	.015[a]	.0005[a]	.122	—	—	—	5.96
(12) Y_2	−.002[a]	.008[a]	−.0000[a]	.116	.0152	—	—	4.69
(13) Y_2	−.011[a]	.001[a]	−.0013[a]	.106	.0084	.161	—	3.51
(14) Y_2	−.014[a]	.000[a]	−.0020[a]	.104	.0063[a]	.070[a]	.0122	4.50
(15) Y_3	.018[a]	.029[a]	.0006[a]	.132	—	—	—	6.18
(16) Y_3	.000[a]	.018[a]	−.0001[a]	.122	.0239	—	—	4.19
(17) Y_3	−.011[a]	.010[a]	−.0017[a]	.110	.0155	.197	—	2.74
(18) Y_3	−.014[a]	.008[a]	−.0026[a]	.107	.0129	.089	.0146	3.92
(19) Y	.018[a]	.028[a]	.0010[a]	.137	—	—	—	6.16
(20) Y	.000[a]	.016[a]	.0003[a]	.127	.0230	—	—	4.23
(21) Y	−.012[a]	.008[a]	−.0014[a]	.115	.0144	.206	—	2.72
(22) Y	−.014[a]	.007[a]	−.0023[a]	.112	.0118	.097	.0146	3.90

Note: Item identifications are: V = father's educational attainment; M = mother's educational attainment; X = status of father's occupation when son graduated from high school (Duncan SEI); I = parents' average income, 1957–1960 (in thousands of dollars); Q = son's score on Henmon–Nelson Test of Mental Ability; U = son's educational attainment; W = son's 1964 occupation (Duncan SEI); Y_1 = son's 1965 earnings (in thousands of dollars); Y_2 = son's 1966 earnings (in thousands of dollars); Y_3 = son's 1967 earnings (in thousands of dollars); Y = son's canonically weighted average of 1965–1967 earnings (in thousands of dollars). Data pertain to 2069 respondents with nonfarm background who were employed in the civilian labor force in 1964, not enrolled in school, had nonzero earnings, 1965–1967, and for whom there were data on parents' income.

[a] $p > .05$

of mental ability on achievement are independent of socioeconomic background. Comparing lines 2 and 3 we see that ability (Q) has a large direct effect on educational attainment (U) net of socioeconomic background, more than two-fifths of a year of school for each 10-point shift in ability, which accounts for 15% to 35% of the influence of each of the background variables on educational attainment. At the same time, relatively little (18%) of the association between ability and educational attainment needs to be attributed to their mutual dependence on socioeconomic background.[8] The remaining effects of background are still appreciable. For example, net of ability, each year of father's education (V) and each $1000 increment in family income (I) are worth .06 years of post-high school educational attainment.

In the occupational status (W) regressions (lines 4, 5, and 6), ability has a powerful total effect—5 points on the Duncan SEI scale for each 10-point shift in ability. Again, this represents only a moderate reduction (18%) of the zero-order association of ability with occupational status. Nearly two-thirds (64%) of the effect of ability on occupational status is mediated by educational attainment; thus, academic ability is valuable in the job market mainly insofar as it is translated into salable skills and credentials through institutions of post-secondary education. Still, ability has a moderate direct effect on occupational status, 1.8 points on the Duncan SEI for each 10-point shift in ability. Educational attainment has a very large direct effect on occupational status net of background and ability, nearly 7.5 points on the Duncan index for each additional year of education. Only 14% of the association of educational attainment and occupational achievement may be attributed to their mutual dependence on background and ability; the rest is due to the direct and pertinent effect of education on occupation.

Each of the background variables affects occupational status. The combined influence of father's (V) and mother's (M) education is the largest, followed by father's occupation (X) and parents' income (I). Each one-year shift in father's education produces a one-point change in occupational status on the Duncan SEI, and each one-year shift in mother's education, a change of two-thirds of a point. A one-point change in father's occupational status yields a

---

[8] These findings conflict with Schiller's (1970) contention that ability plays a minor role in mediating the effect of family income on educational attainment.

shift of one-seventh of a point in son's occupational status. Interestingly, this total effect is almost identical to the regression of son's earnings on parents' income (compare lines 4 and 19 of Table 3-15). A $1000 shift in parents' income produces a .87-point change in occupational status on the Duncan SEI scale, so, as in the case of educational attainment, $1000 in parents' average annual income is worth slightly less than a year of father's education. Ability mediates almost 40% of the effects of mother's and father's education on occupational status, and about 25% of the effect of parents' income,[9] but it accounts for only 12% of the influence of father's occupation on son's occupation. Educational attainment mediates an additional 40% of the effects of father's education and of father's occupation and an additional 50% of the influence of mother's education and of parents' income on occupational status. In all, son's mental ability and educational attainment account for about 75% of the effects of father's and mother's education and income. Their direct effects on son's occupational status in the last equation (line 6) are not even statistically significant, but the model mediates only 50% of the influence of father's occupation on son's occupation. After taking into account the influence of other background variables and of ability and educational attainment, a 10-point shift in father's occupational status is still worth three-fifths of a point of son's occupational status.

Among the background variables, only parents' income (I) influences son's earnings (Y). A thousand dollars of parents' income in 1957–1960 is worth about $137 per year in son's earnings ten years after his high school graduation (see line 19 of Table 3-15). Neither mental ability (Q) nor educational attainment (U) and occupational achievement (W) account for the influence of parents' income on son's earnings. Taken as a group, they mediate only 18% of the effect of parents' income (compare lines 19 and 22). In view of the moderate intercorrelations among the background variables, we wanted to be sure that the apparent intergenerational income effect was not a consequence of large sampling errors due to multicollinearity. In a statistical test comparing the assumption that each background variable has an equal effect on son's earnings

[9] This finding conflicts with Schiller's (1970) contention that ability plays a minor role in mediating the effect of parental income on occupational achievement.

with the model in line 19 of Table 3-15, we were able to reject the null hypothesis of equal effects with a less than 1% chance of error. We also tested the hypothesis that father's education (X), mother's education (M), and father's occupation (V) jointly added nothing to the effect of parents' income (I) and were unable to reject the null hypothesis at even the .05 level of significance. There is little doubt that the association of socioeconomic background variables with son's earnings is due solely to the intergenerational effect of parents' income, while the latter cannot to any large extent be explained by the differing abilities, educational attainments, or occupational achievements of the sons of rich and poor families.

Mental ability has an important effect on earnings net of socioeconomic background; a 10-point shift in ability is worth $230 in annual earnings (see line 20). Further, only 20% of the zero-order association between ability (Q) and earnings (Y) need be attributed to their mutual dependence on socioeconomic background, the remainder being attributable to the direct and indirect effects of ability (compare line 20, Table 3-15, with $r_{QY} = .162$ in Table 3-11). A large component (38%) of the total effect of ability on earnings is mediated by educational attainment (U), and an additional 11% is mediated by occupational status (W). This leaves half of the total effect of ability on annual earnings, $118 for each 10-point shift in ability, as an unmediated differential among men of equal socioeconomic background, educational attainment, and occupational status.

When the effects of background and ability are taken into account, a year of educational attainment is worth just over $200 in annual earnings. Of this effect, just over half is explained by the higher status jobs open to better educated men; even for men with jobs of equal status, an additional year of schooling is worth $97 in annual earnings about 10 years after high school graduation (see lines 21 and 22 of Table 3-15). We find the coefficient of education on earnings would be biased upward if ability were omitted from the model. The apparent influence of son's educational attainment is reduced by 18% when ability (Q) is added to an equation for earnings (Y) that also contains the socioeconomic background variables (V, M, X, and I). The education coefficient falls by 35% when both background and ability (V, M, X, I, and Q) are added to an equation in educational attainment alone (compare $r_{UY} = .203$

from Table 3-11 with line 21 of Table 3-15). Consequently, while educational attainment has an important effect on earnings, its influence would be overestimated by about 50% if the effects of background and ability were not taken into account.

Finally, a 10-unit shift in occupational status (W) yields $146 in annual earnings. This direct effect is about equal to the total (direct and indirect) effects on earnings (Y) of ability (Q) and education (U) and slightly less than that of parents' income (I) (compare lines 19–22 of Table 3-15). This is only 60% as large as the zero-order association between occupational status and earnings; the remaining 40% of the association is explained by the mutual dependence of occupational status and earnings on socioeconomic background, mental ability, and educational attainment (compare $r_{WY} = .220$ in Table 3-11 with line 22 of Table 3-15).

Summary and Conclusions

In this chapter, we have analyzed the effects of socioeconomic origins on the earnings of a sample of Wisconsin men approximately 10 years after their graduation from high school. The sample is made up of 1957 high school graduates with nonfarm background who were not enrolled in postsecondary education and who were employed in the civilian labor force in 1964. Some of our findings may be specific to this early period of the socioeconomic life cycle and to the experiences of the three-fourths of the graduation cohort who had entered the civilian labor market by 1964. In this analysis, we have presented a basic model for explaining and interpreting the direct and indirect influences of socioeconomic background on earnings, as mediated by ability, post-high school educational attainment, and occupational achievement. We have demonstrated that socioeconomic background affects ability, that socioeconomic background and ability affect educational attainment, that socioeconomic background, ability, and educational attainment affect occupational achievement, and that all of the preceding variables affect earnings.

More specifically, we have estimated four versions of our basic model. In Model I, son's academic ability is omitted and socioeconomic background is represented only by father's education and occupation. Using this model, we compared our results with those obtained with similar data from three national samples. We are impressed by the extent to which the effects of father's education and occupation are mediated by son's education and occupational achievements, and by the fact that a substantial share of the effect of education on earnings is mediated by occupational status in each of our samples.

Model II is the same as Model I, except for the addition of son's ability. With this model we can compare the Wisconsin results with only two national samples. Again, the results are quite similar across samples. Father's education and occupation have modest effects on son's ability, and son's ability has a large net effect on son's educational attainment. Ability mediates a large share of the effects of the background variables on education, and education mediates most of the effect of ability on occupational achievement. In all these samples, the effects on earnings of father's education and occupation are almost entirely mediated by son's ability and by the intervening educational and occupational achievements of the sons. Again, we are impressed by the comparable interpretations of the determinants of educational attainment, occupational achievement, and earnings, across samples.

In Model III, we again omit son's ability but add father's income and focus only on the Wisconsin sample. Our findings regarding the determination of earnings are now strikingly changed. When father's income is entered as a variable, the regression coefficients for father's education and occupation are reduced to nonsignificance; they are associated with son's earnings only by virtue of their correlations with father's income, which has a direct effect on son's earnings. Relatively little of the influence of father's income is mediated by son's educational or occupational attainments.

In Model IV, we again enter son's ability into the model and add two measures of socioeconomic background: mother's education and parents' income. This more complex model can only be applied to the Wisconsin sample, because of lack of data on comparable variables elsewhere. The results again show the critical importance of ability in the determination of educational attainment. Relatively little of the association between ability and education is attributable to their mutual dependence on socioeconomic background. Ability also has a powerful total effect on occupational attainment, mainly mediated by educational attainment. Father's occupation has a notable effect on son's occupation, independent of the other socioeconomic background variables, son's ability and educational attainment. Ability also has an important effect on earnings net of socioeconomic background and educational attainment. Educational attainment in turn has a large effect on earnings, about half of which is due to the better jobs that higher educated men obtain. Occupational status, of course, has a marked direct effect on earnings, but almost 40% of the association between occupation and earnings is due to the dependence of these variables on socioeconomic background, ability, and education.

Finally, none of the socioeconomic background variables has any effect on earnings that is not due to its association with other variables in the model—with the exception of parents' income. But this is a very significant exception; $1000 in parents' average income is worth $137 in son's earnings 10 years after graduation from high school. This effect is independent of the influence of the other socioeconomic variables, son's ability and son's educational and occupational status.

Having documented a new effect—the direct social inheritance of earnings performance—we hope in the future to explain it, but our limited effort to date has not met with much success. One possibility is that the social psychological mechanisms that mediate the effects of background on son's educational and occupational status also mediate the effect of parents' income on earnings (Sewell, Haller, and Portes, 1969; Sewell, Haller, and Ohlendorf, 1970). This possibility is considered along with other matters in Chapter 4, but, to anticipate the results, we find that when social psychological variables are added to regression of earnings on socioeconomic background, ability, and educational and occupational achievement, they do not mediate the influence of parents' income on son's earnings—although they add substantially to the effects of background and ability on educational and occupational achievement.

A second possibility that we have briefly examined is the mediating effects of other social variables—place of origin, place of residence, length of labor force experience, military experience, and marital status. This analysis is not presented here, but our preliminary conclusion is that none of these variables accounts for much of the intergenerational income effect. After gathering new data, we expect to examine these possibilities in greater detail and to explore others. Meanwhile we have examined one of the social variables most frequently emphasized in the literature, the effect of college quality on earnings. The detailed analysis of this effect is reported in Chapter 5.

Again, we do not wish to exaggerate the size of the effect of parents' income on son's earnings that we have estimated. While the predictability of our earnings measure may be low relative to that of later earnings or income, we know that, in general, income is less predictable than educational attainment or occupational achievement. By no means are we attempting to suggest that sons are bound in lock-step to the pecuniary achievements of their fathers. At the same time, our analysis leaves no room for doubt that families confer a modest economic advantage or disadvantage on their sons which is independent of the son's ability, educational attainment, or occupational achievement.

4

Social Psychological Factors in Achievement[1]

Introduction

In the previous chapter, we measured the influence of parents' socioeconomic characteristics on son's socioeconomic achievements, with particular reference to the earnings of the young men in our sample 10 years after their graduation from high school. Using a linear causal model, we demonstrated that several socioeconomic characteristics of parents' influence their son's earnings, principally through their effects on his academic ability and his post-high school educational and occupational achievements. We also found that one background variable, parents' income, has an impressive direct effect on son's earnings which is independent of ability, schooling, and occupational status.

In the present chapter, we further examine the relationship be-

[1] This chapter was prepared by William H. Sewell and Robert M. Hauser. Much of the analysis reported in this chapter was included in an invited paper presented at the General Session of the American Agricultural Economics Association, held in Gainesville, Florida, on 22 August 1972. This paper was subsequently published in the Association's journal under the title "Causes and Consequences of Higher Education: Models of the Status Attainment Process" (Sewell and Hauser, 1972).

tween socioeconomic origins and later achievements. We proceed by elaborating our model of the achievement process with a set of social psychological variables which we believe intervene between socioeconomic background and achievement. We expect that these social psychological variables mediate the influence of the background variables on achievement and also have independent effects on the achievement outcomes.

The Variables and the Sample

Before discussing our model and the results of our analysis, we should point out that the measures of socioeconomic background and ability used in this chapter are the same as those used in Chapter 3 and defined in detail in Chapter 2. They include *father's education* (V); *mother's education* (M); *father's occupation* (X); *parents' income* (I); and *mental ability* (Q). The socioeconomic achievement variables have also been used extensively in Chapter 3 and are defined in Chapter 2. They are *son's educational attainment* (U); *son's occupational attainment* (W); and *son's earnings in 1967* (Y_3).[2] The intervening social psychological variables have not been used up to this point but are defined in Chapter 2. They are son's academic performance as indicated by his *rank in high school class* (G); his perception of *teachers' encouragement* (T) to attend college; his perception of *parents' encouragement* (P) to attend college; his perception that most of his *friends plan* (F) to attend college; his *educational aspirations* (E), as indicated by his plans to attend college; and his *occupational aspirations* (J), as indicated by the socioeconomic status of the occupation he hopes to enter. All of these variables come from the 1957 survey and, of course, are based on high school experiences. Each of these variables has been shown to be related to social origins and to educational and occupational attainment (Sewell, 1971; Hauser, 1972), and each is among the social psychological variables most commonly discussed in the status attainment literature (Haller and Portes, 1973).

The analysis reported in this chapter is based on the 1789 men

---

[2] Our analyses of 1967 earnings are so much like those for the two preceding years that we have not presented those analyses here.

who in 1964 were employed in the civilian labor force but were not in school and for whom information on 1965–1967 Social Security earnings and on all of the other variables in the model was available. The main sources of loss from the original sample were the exclusion of men with farm background, men in the military, and men who were still in college in 1964 (many of whom were pursuing professional and graduate education). The principal effect of these limitations is to lower the means and variances of the variables in our models, because the excluded men tend to rank high on background measures, social psychological factors, and educational and socioeconomic achievements (see Table 3-2). While the extension of our analyses to earnings has required us to restrict our sample, it should be noted that the present analyses of educational attainment do closely parallel those reported earlier for a larger portion of the total sample (Sewell, 1971; Hauser, 1972).

A Social Psychological Model of Achievement

The extended model used in our analysis is described by a path diagram in Figure 4-1. As has become conventional, the curved, two-headed arrows represent correlations for which no causal interpretation is offered, while the straight, unidirectional arrows represent direct paths of causal influence. Initially, the model included every unidirectional effect implied by the ordering of the variables from left to right in the diagram, but in the final model of Figure 4-1, the statistically insignificant paths were eliminated. The correlations, means, and standard deviations of the variables are shown in Table 4-1, while Table 4-2 gives the final equation for each intervening or dependent variable in the model.

The model begins by positing the dependence of mental ability (Q) on socioeconomic background (V, X, and I). High school grades (G) depend both on socioeconomic background and on ability, but only ability turns out to affect grades directly (see Table 4-2, line 2). Thus, the higher academic ability of men from socioeconomically advantaged homes fully accounts for the modest effect of the background variables on grades. At the same time ability has a very large effect on grades, most of which is independent of background.

Socioeconomic background, ability, and grades are next assumed

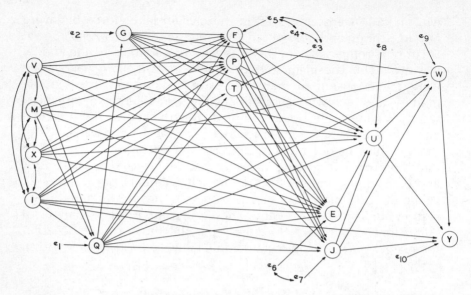

Figure 4-1. A social psychological model of post-high school achievement. Variables are: V = father's education, M = mother's education, X = father's occupational status, I = parents' average income (in tens of dollars), Q = mental ability, G = high school grades, T = teachers' encouragement, P = parents' encouragement, F = friends' plans, E = college plans, J = occupational aspiration, U = educational attainment, W = occupational status in 1964, Y = earnings, 1967.

to affect three perceptions of social support from significant others: teachers' encouragement to attend college (T); parents' encouragement to attend college (P); and the perception that most of the youth's friends plan to attend college (F). As indicated by the curved arrows connecting the unmeasured disturbances (e_3, e_4, and e_5) affecting T, P, and F, we do not postulate any causal nexus among these three types of social support beyond their mutual determination by prior measured variables. Perceived support from teachers is more heavily influenced by ability and, especially, grades, than are parents' encouragement or friends' plans, while the latter are more affected by socioeconomic background than is teachers' encouragement (compare lines 3, 4, and 5 of Table 4-2). In this respect, teachers may be more meritocratic than parents or peers. Only about half the effect of ability on each perception of social support is mediated by high school grades, so there are

TABLE 4-1

Correlations among Variables in a Social Psychological Model of Post-High School Achievement: Male Wisconsin High School Graduates of 1957 with Nonfarm Background

	V	M	X	I	Q	G	T	P	F	E	J	U	W	Y₃
V	—													
M	.520	—												
X	.439	.287	—											
I	.321	.247	.448	—										
Q	.246	.205	.181	.178	—									
G	.154	.140	.131	.121	.557	—								
T	.150	.140	.154	.173	.347	.415	—							
P	.248	.231	.261	.241	.345	.315	.437	—						
F	.237	.210	.219	.233	.288	.307	.339	.398	—					
E	.270	.257	.266	.275	.426	.450	.447	.522	.493	—				
J	.227	.227	.242	.238	.428	.460	.399	.477	.455	.755	—			
U	.306	.273	.290	.273	.446	.512	.406	.472	.474	.656	.580	—		
W	.252	.215	.268	.231	.376	.414	.331	.358	.360	.473	.476	.623	—	
Y₃	.082	.064	.083	.173	.163	.159	.113	.121	.091	.178	.190	.204	.211	—
Mean	10.310	10.514	33.627	650.00	100.67	96.010	.4444	.6082	.3611	.3868	49.380	13.298	43.299	757.36
Std. dev.	3.0242	2.8787	22.543	315.85	14.539	13.642	.4970	.4883	.4804	.4872	26.506	1.7156	23.409	260.71

Note: Variables are: V = father's education; M = mother's education; X = father's occupational status; I = parents' average income (in tens of dollars); Q = mental ability; G = high school grades; T = teachers' encouragement; P = parents' encouragement; F = friends' plans; E = college plans; J = occupational aspiration; U = educational attainment; W = occupational status in 1964; Y₃ = son's 1967 earnings (in tens of dollars). Data pertain to 1789 respondents with nonfarm background who were employed in the civilian labor force in 1964, were not enrolled in school, had nonzero earnings, 1965–1967, and for whom all data were present.

TABLE 4-2

Structural Coefficients of a Social Psychological Model of Post-High School Achievement: Male Wisconsin High School Graduates of 1957 with Nonfarm Background

						Predetermined variables								
	V	M	X	I	Q	G	T	P	F	E	J	U	W	Constant
A. Regression coefficients														
(1) Q	.787	.475	—	.00472										84.49
(2) G	—	—	—	—	.523									43.37
(3) T	—	—	—	—	—									−1.298
(4) P	.0081	.0147	.00249	.000169	.00514	.0116								−1.005
(5) F	.0118	.0121	.00143	.000153	.00619	.0059								−1.097
(6) E	.0030	.0088	.00085	.000179	.00364	.0071	.127	.242	.235					−1.043
(7) J	—	—	—	.000100	.00346	.0060	4.42	12.29	12.12					−30.51
(8) U	.030	.022	.0046	.0058	.239	.398		.313	.453	1.190	.0043			8.355
(9) W	—	—	.0868	—	.0069	.0263		—	—		.1155	6.250		−70.41
(10) Y₃	—	—	—	.0934	.0928	.1309		—	—		.7397	9.123	1.246	484.9

(Continued)

TABLE 4-2 (Continued)

						Predetermined variables							
	V	M	X	I	Q	G	T	P	F	E	J	U	W	R²

B. Regression coefficients in standard form

	V	M	X	I	Q	G	T	P	F	E	J	U	W	R²
(1) Q	.164	.094	—	.102										.078
(2) G	—	—	—	—	.557									.311
(3) T	—	—	—	.108	.150	.318								.203
(4) P	.050	.087	.115	.099	.184	.166								.202
(5) F	.074	.072	.067	.118	.110	.201								.168
(6) E	.019	.052	.040	.065	.103	.168	.130	.242	.232					.465
(7) J	—	—	.069		.131	.205	.083	.226	.220					.408
(8) U	.054	.037	.060	—	.058	.209	—	.089	.127	.338	.067			.540
(9) W	—	—	.084	—	.058	.076	—	—	—	—	.131	.458		.423
(10) Y₃	—	—	—	.113	—	—	—	—	—	—	.075	.060	.112	.070

Note: Variables are V = father's income (in tens of dollars); M = mother's education; X = father's education; Q = mental ability; G = high school grades; T = teachers' encouragement; P = parents' encouragement; F = friends' plans; E = college plans; J = occupational aspiration; U = educational attainment; W = occupational status in 1964; Y₃ = son's 1967 earnings (in tens of dollars). Data pertain to 1789 respondents with nonfarm background who were employed in the civilian labor force in 1964, were not enrolled in school, had nonzero earnings, 1965–1967, and for whom all data were present.

apparently alternative means by which an individual's academic potential may be demonstrated to significant others (see Table 4-3, lines 5, 6, 8, 9, 11, and 12).

Educational aspirations (E) and occupational aspirations (J) are assumed to depend on all of the preceding variables: background, ability, grades, and perceived encouragment. Each of the prior variables affects educational aspiration directly, but the effects of parents' education and father's occupational status on occupational aspiration are fully mediated by intervening variables (see Table 4-2, lines 6 and 7). Ability has a large effect on each aspiration measure when socioeconomic background is controlled (Table 4-3, lines 14 and 18). Almost half the effect of ability is attributable to the higher grades of more able men and the large effect of grades on aspirations (compare lines 14 with 15, and lines 18 with 19, in Table 4-3). While ability does mediate a significant share of the effect of socioeconomic background on aspirations, high school grades do not add to this because they are not affected by background when ability is controlled. Finally, the measures of support from significant others jointly make a large independent contribution to the variability in aspirations. The effects of parents' encouragement and friends' plans are each about twice that of teachers' encouragment. Thus, while the latter is more meritocratically determined than are the former measures, teachers' encouragement has weaker effects on aspirations as well as on other variables yet to be discussed.

Following aspirations, educational attainment (U), occupational status in 1964 (W), and earnings in 1967 (Y_3) are entered into the recursive model in that order. Educational attainment is affected directly by all of the preceding variables except parents' income and teachers' encouragement. Occupational status is influenced directly by ability, grades, and occupational aspiration as well as by father's occupational status and son's educational attainment. Earnings in 1967 are directly affected only by parents' income and by son's occupational aspiration and his educational and occupational attainment (see Table 4-2, lines 8, 9, and 10). Thus, to anticipate our more detailed analysis of post-high school achievements, the social psychological variables are less important in explaining the influence of background on earnings than they are in explaining its influence on educational attainment or occupational status.

TABLE 4-3

Coefficients of Structural and Reduced-form Equations in a Social Psychological Model of Achievement

Dependent variables	Predetermined variables													
	V	M	X	I	Q	G	T	P	F	E	J	U	W	Constant
Regression coefficients														
(1) Q	.710	.464	.0336[a]	.00391										84.80
(2) G	.340	.343	.0314[a]	.00241										86.28
(3) G	−.026[a]	.104[a]	.0141[a]	.00040[a]	.514									42.65
(4) T	.0086[a]	.0116	.00136	.000176										.0737
(5) T	.0009[a]	.0066[a]	.00099[a]	.000134	.01075									−.8381
(6) T	.0012[a]	.0054[a]	.00083[a]	.000130	.00482									−1.3296
(7) P	.0145	.0196	.00288	.000192										.0308
(8) P	.0079[a]	.0153	.00257	.000155	.00924									−.7526
(9) P	.0081[a]	.0147	.00249	.000153	.00619	.00592								−1.0052
(10) F	.0168	.0162	.00177	.000210										−.1783
(11) F	.0116	.0128	.00153	.000182	.00728									−.7956
(12) F	.0118	.0121	.00143	.000179	.00364	.00708								−1.0973
(13) E	.0161	.0225	.00244	.000246										−.2573
(14) E	.0076[a]	.0170	.00204	.000200	.01185									−1.2626
(15) E	.0079	.0159	.00189	.000196	.00643	.01055								−1.7127
(16) E	.0030[a]	.0088	.00085[a]	.000100	.00346	.00600	.127	.242	.235					−1.0433
(17) J	.991	.977	.122	.0108	.667									17.76
(18) J	.517	.668	.100	.0082	.356	.603								−38.78
(19) J	.532	.605	.092	.0079	.220	.400	4.50	11.66	11.64					−64.51
(20) J	.295[a]	.269[a]	.042[a]	.0035										−34.03

(Continued)

TABLE 4-3 (Continued)

Dependent variables					Predetermined variables									
	V	M	X	I	Q	G	T	P	F	E	J	U	W	Constant
(21) U	.0778	.0774	.00991	.000751	.0433									10.86
(22) U	.0470	.0573	.00846	.000582	.0194									7.19
(23) U	.0482	.0525	.00780	.000563	.0116	.0465								5.21
(24) U	.0338	.0328	.00496	.000300	.0066	.0345	.248	.621	.763	1.166				7.00
(25) U	.0291	.0214[a]	.00379	.000168[a]		.0258	.080[a]	.290	.439		.0043			8.36
(26) W	.820	.735	.153	.0080										16.66
(27) W	.467	.504	.136	.0061	.499									−25.62
(28) W	.479	.453	.129	.0059	.247	.490								−46.52
(29) W	.350[a]	.274[a]	.103	.0034	.172	.370	3.44	5.12	7.10					−29.01
(30) W	.291[a]	.189[a]	.093	.0024[a]	.123	.281	2.13[a]	2.18[a]	4.20	5.17	.145			−18.69
(31) W	.113[a]	.058[a]	.070	.0014[a]	.082	.123	1.64[a]	.41[a]	1.51[a]	−1.97[a]	.119	6.123		−69.88
(32) Y_3	2.2[a]	1.0[a]	−.1[a]	.136										637.8
(33) Y_3	.5[a]	−.1[a]	−.1[a]	.126	2.45									429.9
(34) Y_3	.5[a]	−.3[a]	−.2[a]	.126	1.52	1.81								352.9
(35) Y_3	.4[a]	−.6[a]	−.2[a]	.122	1.39	1.63	8.0[a]	17.0[a]	−3.0[a]					378.3
(36) Y_3	.0[a]	−1.0[a]	−.3[a]	.117	1.11	1.13	2.0[a]	1.0[a]	−19.0[a]	19.0[a]	.950			430.5
(37) Y_3	−.4[a]	−1.4[a]	−.3[a]	.114	1.00[a]	.69[a]	0.0[a]	−3.0[a]	−26.0[a]	−0.0[a]	.878	16.91		289.1
(38) Y_3	−.6[a]	−1.4[a]	−.4[a]	.112	.90[a]	.54[a]	−1.0[a]	−4.0[a]	−28.0[a]	2.0[a]	.731	9.37	1.231	375.2

(Continued)

TABLE 4-3 (Continued)

Dependent variables	Predetermined variables													R²
	V	M	X	I	Q	G	T	P	F	E	J	U	W	
Regression coefficients in standard form														
(1) Q	.148	.092	.052ᵃ	.085										.080
(2) G	.075	.072	.052ᵃ	.056										.035
(3) G	—.006ᵃ	.022ᵃ	.023ᵃ	.009ᵃ	.548									.312
(4) T	.052ᵃ	.067	.062	.112										.046
(5) T	.006ᵃ	.038ᵃ	.045ᵃ	.085	.314									.137
(6) T	.008ᵃ	.032ᵃ	.038ᵃ	.082	.141	.316								.206
(7) P	.090	.116	.133	.124										.114
(8) P	.049ᵃ	.090	.119	.100	.275									.183
(9) P	.050ᵃ	.087	.115	.099	.184	.166								.202
(10) F	.106	.097	.083	.138										.096
(11) F	.073	.077	.072	.119	.220									.140
(12) F	.074	.072	.067	.118	.110	.201								.168
(13) E	.100	.133	.113	.160										.135
(14) E	.048ᵃ	.100	.095	.130	.354									.250
(15) E	.049	.094	.088	.127	.192	.296								.310
(16) E	.019ᵃ	.052	.040ᵃ	.065	.103	.168	.130	.242	.232					.465
(17) J	.113	.106	.104	.129										.109
(18) J	.059	.072	.085	.098	.366									.232
(19) J	.061	.066	.078	.095	.196	.310								.298
(20) J	.034ᵃ	.029ᵃ	.036ᵃ	.042	.121	.206	.084	.215	.211					.409

(Continued)

TABLE 4-3 (Continued)

Dependent variables	V	M	X	I	Q	G	T	P	F	E	J	U	W	R^2
(21) U	.137	.130	.130	.138										.153
(22) U	.083	.096	.111	.107	.367									.277
(23) U	.085	.088	.102	.104	.164	.369								.371
(24) U	.060	.055	.065	.055	.098	.274	.072	.177	.214					.465
(25) U	.051	.036[a]	.050	.031[a]	.056	.205	.023[a]	.082	.123	.331	.066			.541
(26) W	.106	.090	.147	.109										.111
(27) W	.060	.062	.131	.082	.310									.199
(28) W	.062	.056	.124	.080	.153	.286								.255
(29) W	.045[a]	.034[a]	.100	.046	.107	.216	.073	.107	.146					.300
(30) W	.038[a]	.023[a]	.090	.032[a]	.076	.164	.045[a]	.046[a]	.086	.108	.164			.334
(31) W	.015[a]	.007[a]	.067	.018[a]	.051	.072	.035[a]	.008[a]	.031[a]	−.041[a]	.134	.449		.426
(32) Y_3	.026[a]	.011[a]	−.005[a]	.164										.031
(33) Y_3	.005[a]	−.001[a]	−.012[a]	.153	.137									.048
(34) Y_3	.006[a]	−.004[a]	−.014[a]	.152	.085	.094								.054
(35) Y_3	.004[a]	−.006[a]	−.018[a]	.148	.077	.085	.017[a]	.032[a]	−.006[a]					.055
(36) Y_3	.001[a]	−.011[a]	−.023[a]	.142	.062	.060	.004[a]	.003[a]	−.034[a]	.036[a]	.097			.064
(37) Y_3	−.005[a]	−.015[a]	−.028[a]	.138	.056[a]	.036[a]	.001[a]	−.006[a]	−.048[a]	−.001[a]	.089	.111		.070
(38) Y_3	−.007[a]	−.016[a]	−.036[a]	.136	.050	.028[a]	−.003[a]	−.008[a]	−.052[a]	.003[a]	.074	.062	.111	.076

Note: Variables are: V = father's education; M = mother's education; X = father's occupational status; I = parents' average income (in tens of dollars); Q = mental ability; G = high school grades; T = teachers' encouragement; P = parents' encouragement; F = friends' plans; E = college plans; J = occupational aspiration; U = educational attainment; W = occupational status in 1964; Y_3 = son's 1967 earnings (in tens of dollars). Data pertain to 1789 respondents with nonfarm background who were employed in the civilian labor force in 1964, were not enrolled in school, had nonzero earnings, 1965–1967 and for whom all data were present.

[a] not significant at .05 level, two tailed

Data Analysis

In the following sections our analytic strategy is to concentrate serially on each of our attainment variables. We first examine the influence of socioeconomic origins on educational attainment. We then introduce the social psychological variables in their presumed causal sequence in order to assess their role as mediators of the effects of prior variables in the model and, also, their independent contribution to educational attainment. Next, we repeat the above analysis, with occupational status as the final dependent variable and educational attainment as an additional intervening variable. Last, with earnings in 1967 as the ultimate dependent variable, we analyze the direct and indirect effects of the socioeconomic origin variables, the social psychological variables, and the two causally prior achievement variables.

This interpretative analysis is based on Table 4-3, which presents standardized and metric regression coefficients for each structural and reduced-form equation in our model. The coefficients in the most complete equation for each variable differ from those reported in Table 4-2, where we eliminated the statistically insignificant coefficients and reestimated each equation without them.

EDUCATIONAL ATTAINMENT

We begin our analysis with an equation that includes only the four socioeconomic background variables and educational attainment. We find that mother's education (M), father's education (V), father's occupation (X), and parents' income (I) taken together account for 15% of the total variance in years of son's post-high school educational attainment (see Table 4-3, line 21). Whether we examine linear or nonlinear effects, each of the four socioeconomic variables has an approximately equal effect on son's educational attainment and on all of the intervening variables in the model (Sewell, 1971; Hauser, 1972). This approximate equality of effects of the four stratification variables suggests that there may be little merit in the efforts of some social scientists to interpret all social inequalities in terms of income differences or any other single status characteristic.

The extent to which socioeconomic origins reduce the average educational achievement of those from the lower socioeconomic strata is impressive. For example, each year of father's or mother's education was worth .08 years of higher education for their son— after controlling for the effects of father's occupation and family income. Consequently, the sons of parents with only grade school education obtained on the average one and one-fourth fewer years of higher education than the sons of parents who were college graduates—even when their fathers had similar jobs and their families had similar incomes.

A \$1000 increase in the annual income of the family on the average also yielded .08 years of educational attainment. Thus, a shift from the poverty level of \$3000 (below which almost one-fifth of the families in the sample fell) to \$6000, the median income at that time, increased the average years of education by one-fourth of a year when the effects of parents' education and father's occupation were taken into account. A shift in family income from \$3000 to \$10,000 led to an increase of more than half an additional year in postsecondary schooling.

When son's academic ability (Q) is added to the model, the explained variance in educational attainment (U) almost doubles—rising from 15% to 28%. The additional 13% represents a large component in the variance in the educational attainment of sons that is completely independent of socioeconomic status. An important component, varying between 15% and 40%, of the effect of each socioeconomic variable is mediated by academic ability (compare lines 21 and 22 of Table 4-3). At the same time, less than one-fifth of the association of ability with educational attainment may be attributed to its association with socioeconomic origins (compare $r_{UQ} = .446$ from Table 4-1 with $p_{UQ} = .367$ in line 22 of Table 4-3). Clearly, the effect of measured ability on schooling is not merely a reflection of an individual's socioeconomic status, the assumptions of some social scientists to the contrary notwithstanding.

In order to explain more fully the ways in which socioeconomic origins affect post-high school educational attainment, we further complicate our model by adding three sets of social psychological intervening variables: (1) high school performance, (2) significant others' influence, and (3) educational and occupational aspirations. On the basis of evidence from our previous research, we believe that these sets of variables intervene in the order indicated and help to mediate the effects of socioeconomic origins and academic ability on higher educational attainment. Taken as a group, these intervening variables account for a very large portion of the effects of each socioeconomic status variable on post-high school educational attainment. With regard to son's educational attainment, about 60% of the effect of father's education, 70% of the effect of mother's education, 60% of the effect of father's occupation, and 80% of the effect of parents' income is mediated by the other variables in the model (compare lines 21 and 25 of Table 4-3). Their remaining effects represent the direct influence of socioeconomic resources and discrimination (or perhaps a critic might attribute them to our failure to include some relevant intervening variable). Even with this model, which explains 54% of the variance in higher educational attainment, socioeconomic origins continue to influence directly an individual's chances for higher education.

The extent to which our model explains the effects of socioeconomic origins on eventual educational attainment is remarkable because all of our intervening variables pertain to the secondary school experiences of the men in our sample. Even for young men who succeed in finishing high school, the effects of social background on later educational attainment are largely explained by social psychological experiences during the high school years.

Again, with this complex model, the interpretations for the total associations are generally similar for each of the socioeconomic status variables. Between 32% and 60% of the mediated effect of each background variable is due to the higher ability and grades of the socioeconomically advantaged, 30% to 45% is due to the higher expectations of their significant others, and the remaining 10% to 20% is due to their higher levels of aspiration (compare lines 21, 23, 24, and 25 of Table 4-3).[3]

Of course, the model not only interprets the several ways in which the socioeconomic variables influence higher education, but

[3] In describing how the effects of each variable are mediated, we have consistently referred to the earliest intervening variable in the chain as the mediating variable. Thus, when we say school performance mediates a percentage of the effect of background, this does not exclude the further mediation of those effects by subsequent intervening variables.

also the effect of academic ability on higher educational attainment. Recall that of the total association between academic ability and higher educational attainment, only 18% is due to the mutual dependence of ability and schooling on socioeconomic background. The total effect of academic ability on post-high school educational attainment is large; for each 10-point increase in measured intelligence the average student obtains nearly one-half of a year of post-secondary schooling (Table 4-3, line 22). Of this total effect, 85% is mediated by the other intervening variables in our model (55% by high school performance, 18% by perceived expectations of others, and 11% by educational and occupational aspirations). Less than one-sixth of the influence of ability is unmediated by the variables in our model (compare lines 22–25 of Table 4-3). This means that the influence of academic ability can only in a minor way be attributed to socioeconomic status considerations, but that it rests quite solidly on its direct and pertinent influence on academic performance and on its direct and indirect effects on significant others and on educational and occupational aspirations. In this connection it should also be stressed that socioeconomic status has no effect on academic performance in high school independent of academic ability.

Next in the interpretation of this causal model, we examine the effects of parents' encouragement (P), teachers' encouragement (T), and friends' educational plans (F) on post-high school educational attainment (V). Recall that parents' encouragement and friends' plans depend heavily on son's socioeconomic origins, while teachers' encouragement is more heavily dependent on the student's academic ability (Q) and performance (G). Indeed, teachers are not perceived to engage in direct socioeconomic discrimination, as parents and peers apparently do, but rather depend mainly on judgments of the student's academic ability as it is validated by school performance.

The influence of parents and peers on educational attainment (U) is about equal and is two to three times that of teachers. Holding constant all other factors included in the model up to this point (the four socioeconomic origin variables, academic ability, school performance, parental encouragement, and friends' plans), we find that strong teachers' encouragement (T) is worth an additional one-quarter of a year of higher education—whereas the net effects of strong parents' encouragement (P) and of having friends who plan on college (F) are six-tenths and three-fourths of a year, respectively (line 24 of Table 4-3). Shifts in educational plans and occupational aspirations account for about one-half of the effects of parents' encouragement and friends' plans and for about two-thirds of the effect of teachers' encouragement (compare lines 24 and 25 of Table 4-3). Although all three significant others variables have important effects on son's educational attainment, we are led to conclude that teachers' expectations for students do not account for much of the effect of socioeconomic background on higher educational attainment. Far from reflecting overt or covert discrimination, teachers' expectations appear to be based on ability and performance and, as such, make a fundamental though modest contribution to the equalization of educational opportunities.

OCCUPATIONAL ATTAINMENT

When we extend our model to include occupational status (W) seven years after high school graduation, as measured by Duncan's SEI, we observe the central role that post-high school education plays in occupational attainment. Educational attainment (U) alone adds 9% to the variance in occupational attainment explained by all of the other variables in the model (compare lines 30 and 31 of Table 4-3). Almost three-fourths of the association between educational and occupational attainment is attributable to the direct influence of educational attainment; the remaining one-fourth is due to the mutual dependence of schooling and jobs on causally prior variables (compare $r_{UW} = .623$ from Table 4-1 with $p_{WU} = .449$ in line 31 of Table 4-3).[4] Each year of education after high school is worth about 6 points of occupational status on the Duncan index.

Except in the case of father's occupational status, all of the effects

---

[4] Bowles (1972) suggests that Duncan and others have underestimated the spurious component in the association of schooling with later social and economic achievements because of a failure to measure socioeconomic background reliably. In our research, we have found that no reasonable adjustment for unreliability in our socioeconomic background measures affects our results to an appreciable degree. Moreover, our estimates of spurious components of association between schooling and occupation or earnings are increased by our inclusion of social psychological variables that are mainly unrelated to socioeconomic background.

of the socioeconomic background variables on son's occupational attainment are mediated by intervening variables. About 40% of the effects of parents' education and income are mediated by academic ability and performance (compare lines 26 and 28 of Table 4-3). Most of the remaining effects are mediated by significant others' influences and by aspirations. Since significant others' expectations and the students' educational aspirations ultimately affect occupational achievement by way of educational attainment, so also do the effects of socioeconomic background—father's occupation excepted. However, 46% of the effect of father's occupational status represents direct status inheritance, which is unmediated by any of the intervening achievements in our model (compare lines 26 and 31 of Table 4-3).

Just as in the case of educational attainment, more than 80% of the association of ability with occupational status represents its direct and indirect effects (compare $r_{QW} = .376$ from Table 4-1 with $p_{WQ} = .310$ in line 27 of Table 4-3). A 10-point increase in measured ability (Q) leads to an average increase of 5 points in status on the Duncan SEI. Of this total effect, 50% is attributable to the higher grades of more able students, 15% to higher perceived expectations of significant others, 10% to higher aspirations, and 8% to longer schooling; the remaining 17% is a direct effect of ability on the occupational achievement of men with similar levels of academic performance, significant others' expectations, aspirations, and educational attainment (compare lines 27–31 of Table 4-3). The effect of academic performance (G) on occupational status is nearly as great as that of ability, and only 30% of the association between grades and occupational status is spurious (compare $r_{GW} = .414$ in Table 4-1 with $p_{WG} = .286$ in line 28 of Table 4-3). With regard to the effect of academic performance on occupational status, one-fourth is mediated by significant others' influence, about one-sixth by educational and occupational aspirations, and one-third by educational attainment; the remaining one-fourth represents a direct effect (compare lines 28–31 of Table 4-3).

Net of prior variables, strong teachers' encouragement (T) is worth 3.4 points on the Duncan SEI (W), while high values on the parents' encouragement (P) and the peer plans (F) variables are worth 5.1 and 7.1 points, respectively (see line 29 of Table 4-3). One-third to one-half of the effect of these three variables is mediated by educational and occupational aspirations and the remainder by educational attainment, so none of them has a significant direct effect on occupational status (see lines 29–31 of Table 4-3).

The effect of planning on college (E) on occupational status (W) is 6.7 points on the Duncan SEI, all of which is attributable to the greater schooling obtained by those with college plans. An increase of 10 points of occupational aspiration (J) on the Duncan index is worth 1.5 points in occupational status (W), net of prior variables in the model (see lines 30 and 31 of Table 4-3). It is interesting that this total effect is virtually identical to the regression of son's occupational status on father's occupational status (line 26 of Table 4-3). Less than one-fifth of the effect of occupational aspiration on occupational status is mediated by educational attainment. The remainder represents an effect of aspiration on achievement over a seven-year period which is completely independent of socioeconomic background, ability, high school performance, and educational attainment.

It is apparent from our analysis that the path to high occupational status is through higher education. Higher status families appear to make greatest use of this route, in part by providing the genes and the stimulating environment that result in superior cognitive abilities and school performance. Further, their encouragement of high educational and occupational aspirations leads to higher educational attainment and, ultimately, to higher levels of occupational achievement. In addition, but to a lesser degree, higher status families also manage to help their sons through direct occupational inheritance, but the evidence from our analysis is that the social psychological influences that result in higher educational attainment are much more important than are direct economic influences.

EARNINGS IN 1967

When our model is finally extended to include Social Security earnings in 1967 (Y_3), 10 years after high school graduation, some expected and some surprising findings result. As expected, educational attainment (U) and occupational attainment (W) each play an important role in earnings. About one-half of the effect of educational attainment on earnings is due to the higher paying jobs held by men with more education, and one-half represents higher earnings within occupations (compare lines 37 and 38 of Table 4-3). In the case of both educational and occupational attainment, their effects on earnings represent just one-half of their correlation with earnings; the remaining half is attributable to the mutual dependence of earnings and of educational attainment or occupational status on prior variables (compare $r_{UY_3} = .204$ and $r_{WY_3} = .211$ from Table 4-1 with $p_{Y_3U} = .111 = p_{Y_3W}$ in lines 37 and 38 of Table 4-3). Net of all prior variables, one year of post-high school education is worth $169 in 1967 earnings, and 10 points on the Duncan SEI is worth $123.

The most surprising finding is that parents' average income (I) during the four years following the son's graduation from high school has the largest effect on earnings (Y_3) of all of the variables in the model ($p_{Y_3I} = .164$ in line 32 of Table 4-3). One thousand dollars in parents' income is worth about $136 in son's earnings (note: earnings, not income) 10 years after graduation from high school. Neither the social psychological variables nor educational or occupational achievements explains this effect of parents' income on son's earnings; these variables together mediate only one-fifth of the effect of parents' income. Thus, after all intervening achievements are taken into account, $1000 in parents' income is still worth $112 in son's earnings (compare lines 32 and 38 of Table 4-3). Moreover, none of the other socioeconomic background variables affects earnings significantly, once the influence of parents' income has been taken into account. Statistical tests indicate that this income effect is not a consequence of large sampling errors due to multicollinearity among the socioeconomic background variables in the model (see Chapter 3, p. 83–84). Thus, to return to the question raised in the conclusion of Chapter 3, there appears to be little doubt that the intergenerational effect of parents' income cannot in any large measure be explained by the set of social psychological variables that we have introduced in this chapter. Neither can it be accounted for by the differing abilities, educational attainments, or occupational achievements of the sons of wealthy or poor families.

Academic ability has an important effect on earnings which is almost entirely mediated by later variables in the model. Of the correlation between ability (Q) and earnings (Y_3), only 16% is attributable to the mutual dependence of ability and earnings on socioeconomic background; the remaining 84% represents an increase in earnings of $245 for each 10-point increase in measured ability (compare $r_{QY_3} = .163$ from Table 4-1 with $p_{Y_3Q} = .137$ in line 33 of Table 4-3). Of this effect, 38% is attributable to the influence of ability (Q) on high school performance (G); 17% to its effect on significant others' influence (T, P, and F) and aspirations (E and J); and most of the remaining 45% is due to a nonsignificant direct effect of ability on earnings (see lines 33–38 of Table 4-3). The effects of high school performance are slightly less than those of ability, and they are mediated in much the same fashion.

Neither significant others' influence (T, P, and F) nor educational plans (E) has a significant effect on 1967 earnings, but son's occupational aspiration does have a rather important effect on earnings 10 years after high school graduation. A 10-point increase in occupational aspiration (J) on the Duncan SEI is worth $95 in 1967 earnings, net of all prior variables in the model (line 36 of Table 4-3). Of this effect, 8% is attributable to the greater educational attainment of those with higher occupational aspirations, and an additional 15% is due to their higher status occupations. The remaining 76% represents a direct effect of aspiration on earnings; net of intervening educational and occupational achievements, each 10 points in occupational aspiration (on the Duncan index) is worth $73 in 1967 earnings (see lines 36–38 of Table 4-3).

Again, the other social psychological variables—significant others' influence and educational aspirations—have no significant direct or indirect effects on earnings. The limited capacity of our social psychological model to explain earnings contrasts markedly with its contributions to the explanation of post-high school education and of occupational attainment. We are in no position to dispute the possibility that the propensity to earn has a social psychological basis or that it may be manifest before the completion of secondary schooling. Thus, our results might have come out differently had we directly ascertained encouragement and aspirations for pecuniary success in the 1957 survey. At the same time, our analysis leads us to believe that the social psychological roots of strictly economic success are different from those of educational or occupational achievement. Recalling the differential effects of father's education, occupation, and income on son's achievements, the present findings suggest the importance of avoiding a singular interpretation of the causes or effects of socioeconomic achievement.

Conclusions

Our model has proved to be a rather powerful predictor of status attainment. It is especially effective in explaining educational achievement, accounting for 54% of the variance. It is a bit less efficient in accounting for occupational attainment, but still explains over 43% of its variance. It is much less effective in predicting earnings, where it accounts for only 7% of the variance in 1967 earnings.[5] Its better showing for educational and occupational attainment may be largely due to the fact that these attainments were probably more fixed by the time they were measured than were earnings. Other evidence seems to indicate that earnings patterns had not stabilized by 1967, when the last data were available for this sample. The most likely explanation for this is the greater investment in on-the-job training among the more highly educated individuals with less labor force experience. We will be following the earnings careers of our sample in the future and will be able to test this explanation at a later date.

It is also true that the earlier variables in our model were all selected for their pertinence to educational and occupational attainment rather than to earnings. Important as these variables are, it must be recognized that there are probably more pertinent and proximate influences on earnings that need to be considered in future models. For example, our occupational information is for 1964. We need information on more current jobs. Moreover, job-relevant information, such as years of experience on the job, on-the-job training, and additional formal schooling, would probably increase the efficacy of a model that sought to predict current earnings. Our interest has been primarily to interpret the effects of socioeconomic background on educational and socioeconomic achievements, and we have not yet fully exploited some of the

---

[5] It should be noted that Solmon's (1972a) semilog earnings equation explains about the same amount of variance in early income in the NBER–Thorndike sample as ours does when expressed in that functional form.

data we currently hold which might improve our ability to specify an earnings function. For example, we can also consider such factors as the extent and timing of military service, family formation, size of family, geographic mobility, and characteristics of the labor market, and similar contingencies that doubtless have some effect on earnings experiences. We plan to restudy our sample during the next 18 months, and will gather additional information on these and related matters.

But, to return to our model, we feel that the inclusion of the social psychological variables has resulted in a more complete explication of the attainment process in the educational, occupational, and economic spheres—and this is what we as sociologists are concerned with. Our disaggregated model, discussed in Chapter 3, had clearly demonstrated the importance of socioeconomic origins for educational, occupational, and earnings attainments. The expanded model we have discussed in the present chapter has illuminated the rather complex process by which the effects of socioeconomic background on educational, occupational, and economic attainments are mediated by various social psychological experiences. In addition to the various and sometimes quite indirect paths to status attainment, our model has also revealed that there is a modest amount of status inheritance that is completely independent of these social psychological processes and not explained by other variables in the model. Most noteworthy of these elements are the rather sizable net effects of father's occupation in 1957 on son's occupation in 1964 and of average family income in 1957–1960 on son's earnings in 1967. This finding regarding the inheritance of the pertinent status characteristics of the father by the son is indeed remarkable when we consider that the measurements of the son's status characteristics are from different sources and occur from 7 to 10 years later than the measurements on the father. It is even more remarkable that they persist when other socioeconomic, social psychological, and attainment variables in the model are controlled.

We expect that better models of the status-attainment process will be developed in the future, and we hope to contribute to that movement with the data from our longitudinal research program. We also are cognizant of the interest of social scientists in dependent variables other than years of schooling, occupational status, and earnings, such as critical thinking, tolerance, humanitarianism, citizenship, responsibility, and other valued traits.[6] Perhaps we can develop models to explain these outcomes, but at present we do not have the necessary data to study them. Meanwhile, we do have as yet unexploited information on the colleges attended by the young men in our sample. In the next chapter, we will add this information to our model to enable us to estimate the effect of college characteristics on the early socioeconomic achievements of these young men, especially on their earnings.

[6] The literature on the benefits of education has been reviewed in many places. The most comprehensive recent review is by Withey (1972). Withey's book is particularly useful because it stresses the consequences of higher education for economic behavior, political behavior, personality, and life styles.

5

Colleges and Achievement[1]

In the preceding analyses, our discussions of the causes and consequences of education in the stratification process have concentrated on the quantity of education, expressed as years of schooling completed. Some scholars have argued that the quality of schooling must be considered as a separate factor in the stratification process. Although educational quality is hard to define, it is often believed to be an important factor in the later lives of those who attend college, especially in their socioeconomic careers (Jencks, 1968). Further, the quality of schooling is sometimes said to be represented by the college attended by a student, so interinstitutional differentials in the outcomes of schooling reflect differences in the quality of schooling.

Support for the hypothesis that colleges affect economic outcomes is often based on the early *Time* studies, which examined the relationship between the type of college attended and later monetary income (Babcock, 1941; Havemann and West, 1952). For the most part, these studies are inadequate because they fail to control other theoretically relevant variables. Recently, a modest

[1] This chapter was prepared by Duane F. Alwin, Robert M. Hauser, and William H. Sewell. It is based in part on analyses reported in Alwin (1972).

research literature on such effects has developed (Hunt, 1963; Weisbrod and Karpoff, 1968; Reed and Miller, 1970; Sharp, 1970; Daniere and Mechling, 1970; Solmon and Wachtel, 1971; Solmon, 1972b; Wales, 1973; Kinloch and Perrucci, 1969; Laumann and Rapoport, 1968), and there is some support in this literature for the hypothesis of a unique effect of college quality on economic attainments.

In this chapter, we examine the effects of colleges on the early earnings of men in the Wisconsin sample who attended college. The null hypothesis that guides the analysis is that the relationship between type of college attended and earnings is largely spurious, and when the selection and recruitment into different types of colleges have been considered (Wegner and Sewell, 1970), the initial relationship will be considerably reduced. Alternatively, the choice of a college and its subsequent effect on earnings may reflect the influence of socioeconomic background or other prior variables on earnings, or colleges may introduce a component of variation in earnings that is unrelated to socioeconomic background and experiences in secondary school. In the following section, we discuss the process of selection and recruitment in some detail, pointing to factors that should be controlled in the analysis of college effects on earnings. Then, we review our research strategy and methods for assessing the presence of unique college effects in the Wisconsin data. Finally, we present our analysis of college effects on earnings and compare them with college effects on educational attainment and occupational status.

Selection and Recruitment Factors in College Choice

It is now widely recognized that college differences in economic outcomes may be due to the nonrandom allocation of students among colleges. For example, it is generally recognized that certain colleges actively seek out more able students or students with particular interests. The socioeconomic composition of student bodies obviously varies as well, and such selection and recruitment factors may be responsible for the relationship between college differences and socioeconomic achievements.

There are at least four major factors on the basis of which high school graduates are selected for higher learning and allocated differentially into various types of colleges: mental ability, past academic performance, aspirations, and socioeconomic background. If these factors are not measured and controlled, their effects on achievement may wrongly be attributed to such college characteristics as intellectual environment, quality, or prestige.

MENTAL ABILITY

Higher learning has always been viewed in American society as an intellectual challenge requiring above average capacity. This general view is born out by the fact that colleges almost universally have adopted ability as a standard for admission when the demand for higher education has exceeded the supply (Jencks and Riesman, 1968; Wing and Wallach, 1971). The differences between college attenders and nonattenders on measured ability reflect both the requirements of the college educational experience and the academic standards that most colleges maintain for entrance. Such differences have been reported for a variety of time periods, populations, and ability measures (Wolfle, 1954; Sewell and Shah, 1967; Folger, Astin, and Bayer, 1970).

Furthermore, differences in average measured ability have been observed among the student bodies of various colleges and of colleges of different types (Wolfle, 1954; Cooley and Becker, 1966; Wegner and Sewell, 1970). Indeed, colleges are typically defined as being of higher quality if they enroll only students of high ability. Using data on colleges from the College Entrance Examination Board for the period 1965–1967, Wing and Wallach (1971) illustrate a positive relationship between the selectivity of an institution, as defined by Astin (1965), and the percentage of applicants it admits with higher verbal Scholastic Aptitude Test (SAT-V) scores. The high correlation between Astin's Selectivity Index and the measured intelligence of students has been demonstrated by several investigators (Astin and Panos, 1969; Spaeth and Greeley, 1970; Folger *et al.*, 1970).

HIGH SCHOOL ACADEMIC PERFORMANCE

High school students who receive good grades are not only more likely to attend college, they are also more likely to graduate (Wolfle, 1954). High school grades have been one of the traditional standards for admission to college (Wing and Wallach, 1971). As with measured intelligence, high school grades figure importantly in the differential selection and recruitment of students (Wegner and Sewell, 1970).

ASPIRATIONS

Regardless of a student's ability and academic performance, whether he wants to attend is a key factor in the ultimate decision to go to college (Wolfle, 1954). Sewell and Shah (1967) report a strong relationship between plans to attend college during the senior year in high school and actual college attendance during the next seven years. In addition to specific aspirations or plans regarding college attendance, there are other motivational sources of variation in college attendance. A number of studies have found that students' educational or occupational aspirations vary with the quality of the college they attend (Wegner and Sewell, 1970; Spaeth, 1968b; Spaeth and Greeley, 1970).

SOCIOECONOMIC BACKGROUND

Prior to the relatively recent emphasis on admission standards, when colleges were not pressed by large numbers of applicants, admission to a college, particularly a public institution, was a rather simple process. If a student had graduated from high school, could afford the expense of college, and had the desire to attend, it was relatively easy to obtain admission into most institutions of higher learning. The net result of these circumstances was that college attendance depended greatly on socioeconomic background. Apparently this situation still persists (Sewell and Shah, 1967; Folger et al., 1970). Colleges also differ in the investments they demand from their students in the form of tuition and other fees, and to a large extent the ability to meet these costs depends on the financial well-being of the student's family (Jencks and Riesman, 1968:118). In addition to family income, other aspects of the family's socioeconomic standing are associated with the likelihood of attending college, e.g., father's occupation and parents' education (Wolfle, 1954; Sewell and Shah, 1968b; also, see Chapter 3). The influence of socioeconomic background on the distribution of students into different types of colleges has also been documented (Wegner and Sewell, 1970), and a number of studies report variations among colleges in the socioeconomic composition of their student bodies (Astin and Panos, 1969; Spaeth, 1968a, 1968b; Spaeth and Greeley, 1970; Karabel and Astin, 1972).

Religion and ethnicity are known to be important in the allocation of students among colleges (Astin and Lee, 1972), and have also been shown to affect adult socioeconomic achievements (Duncan and Duncan, 1968; Featherman, 1971; Duncan and Featherman, 1972). These variables were not included in our analysis because we have no information on them, and for that reason our analysis may overstate the effects of some types of colleges.

The Research Problem

The literature on school effects suggests a theoretical model that draws attention to the fact that students are not randomly allocated to colleges. This model also underlies what sociologists refer to as contextual analysis (Hauser, 1970a) and certain studies of socialization, particularly adult socialization (Brim and Wheeler, 1966). Werts (1968) calls this the Input–Output model. The basic idea is that persons select themselves or are recruited differentially into groups, contexts, or social institutions, and are influenced, changed, or marked in some way by differential association or by other unique organizational characteristics. In the case of colleges, this effect may be due to differential socialization or certification, or both (Jencks, 1968).

It is convenient to refer to the selection and recruitment factors discussed in the above section as inputs. The inputs partly determine both specific college attendance and later achievements, and in order to speak about a college effect it is essential that inputs be held constant. These causal specifications are described in Figure 5-1. The figure depicts a recursive model with the set of input variables as a major predetermined source of variation in later variables. The causal ordering in Figure 5-1 is consistent with the temporal ordering of the variables. The inputs occur prior to college attendance; the inputs and college experience both occur prior to the social achievements; educational attainment precedes both occupation and earnings; and occupation precedes earnings. The model permits us to ascertain the total (nonspurious) effects of colleges on earnings and, also, to measure the extent to which those effects are produced by way of educational and occupational achievement.

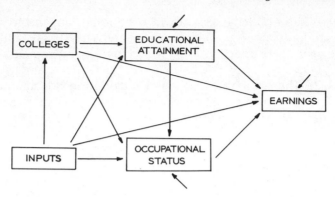

Figure 5-1.   A schematic causal model for the assessment of college effects.

The Sample and Data

The analysis reported in this section assesses college effects on earnings 8 to 10 years after graduation from high school. These effects are estimated for the males in our sample of 1957 Wisconsin high school seniors who had some college experience between 1957 and 1964 and who in 1964 were alive, not enrolled in any school, and not on active duty with the armed forces. A total of 1198 men with college information available meets the eligibility criteria just set forth. The several sources of data for this sample are discussed at length in previous chapters and will not be reviewed at this point.

While most of the variables used here are discussed in Chapter 2 and have been used previously in Chapters 3 or 4, for the convenience of the reader we again list the variables employed in our analysis. Four socioeconomic variables are included: mother's education (M), father's education (V), father's occupational status (X) and father's average income (I_F).[2] Other input variables are mental

---

[2] In preliminary analyses we have found that father's average income has a larger effect on son's earnings among college attenders than does the average combined income of mothers and fathers, and we have used father's income rather than parents' income in our analysis of college effects. It may be recalled from Chapter 3 that combined parents' income was the more powerful variable among male high school graduates of nonfarm origin.

ability (Q), rank in high school class (G), teachers' encouragement to attend college (T), parents' encouragement to attend college (P), friends' college plans (F), educational aspirations (E), occupational aspirations (J), and several measures of commitment to college attendance. Variables treated as intervening between the inputs and the economic outcomes are educational attainment (U) and occupational status (W) in 1964. Finally, annual earnings in 1965, 1966, and 1967 (Y_1, Y_2, and Y_3) are used as the major dependent variables in the analysis.

Our analysis uses 12 categories of colleges attended by the males in our sample. The first 6 of these categories represent single colleges or homogeneous sets of colleges in the state of Wisconsin: *University of Wisconsin—Madison; University of Wisconsin—Milwaukee;* the *University of Wisconsin Center System;* the *Wisconsin State Universities;* the *Wisconsin County Teachers Colleges;* and *Marquette University.* The next 4 categories were created on the basis of a similarities analysis of 134 colleges and universities: *Prestigious Colleges and Universities; Liberal Arts Colleges—General; Liberal Arts Colleges—Catholic;* and *Universities* not in the other categories. For a complete discussion of the procedures used to classify these 134 colleges and universities see Alwin (1972:96–136). In brief, a matrix of similarity coefficients among the 134 schools was subjected to a Q-type factor analysis, and the classification was based on the resulting clusters of schools. The similarity coefficients were constructed from profiles on 31 college characteristics. The last 2 categories—*Technological Colleges and Institutes* and *Other Colleges*—were created primarily on the basis of a priori considerations. The Technological category contains engineering colleges, art schools, and military institutes. The final category is a residual group containing junior colleges, theological seminaries, business colleges, and foreign colleges. In order to give the reader some feeling for the content of the college categories, Table 5-1 gives a partial listing of the schools in the larger groups. In the analysis of the effects of colleges on earnings, we assigned each man to the category of the last college he attended.[3]

[3] College attended is defined as the college from which the son graduated, or, if the son did not graduate, as the first college attended. Among those who attended college this definition gives a very close approximation to the last college attended.

TABLE 5-1

Examples of the Classification of Schools and Colleges

Prestigious Colleges and Universities	Yale University, University of Chicago, Northwestern University, Carleton College, Dartmouth College, Duke University, Beloit College, Lawrence College
Liberal Arts Colleges, General	Spring Hill College, Colorado State College, Lake Forest College, Carthage College, Valparaiso University, McNeese State College, Hope College, Macalester College, Abilene Christian College, Milton College
Liberal Arts Colleges, Catholic	Regis College, Loras College, St. John's University, Xavier University, Christian Brothers College, St. Norbert College
Universities	University of Alabama, University of Arizona, University of Colorado, Georgetown University, University of Illinois, Indiana University, University of Maryland, University of Michigan, Syracuse University, University of Oklahoma, Baylor University
Technological Colleges and Institutes	Georgia Institute of Technology, Rose Polytechnic Institute, Massachusetts Institute of Technology, Michigan College of Mining and Technology, Webb Institute of Naval Architecture, American Academy of Art, U.S. Naval Academy, U.S. Military Academy
Other Colleges	Moody Bible Institute, Sacred Heart Seminary, North Central Bible College, Baltimore College of Commerce, Fort Smith Junior College, Cisco Junior College, Guadalajara University, Conservatoire of Music–Paris

Note: For complete listing, see Alwin (1972: Appendix A).

Analytic Strategy

Following the model of Figure 5-1, we have used multiple regression analysis to estimate and interpret college effects on earnings in 1965, 1966, and 1967. We treated earnings in the three years separately, in order to detect possible changes over time in the determinants of earnings and in the quality of the earnings data.[4]

The first equations estimated for the earnings variables are straightforward dummy-variable regressions in which 11 of the 12 college categories are entered as regressors. Based on these equations, we present the gross college differences in the form of deviations from the grand mean of earnings in each year. The coefficients of determination (R^2) for these regression models provide an upper bound on the potential magnitude of the combined effects of all college characteristics on early earnings.

A second set of regression models was used to examine the functional form of possible college effects. Specifically, we asked whether colleges modify the way in which input or intervening variables affect earnings, or whether the effects of other variables are much the same in any college category. In the latter case, colleges can still affect earnings by means of an additive increment or decrement. This question can be answered with a test for non-additivity or statistical interaction. Following Gujarati (1970) the interaction terms entering the regression equations are created by multiplying a dummy variable for each of the college categories (less one) by each input or intervening variable in the equation, so that there can be a unique slope in each college category. Thus, it takes 11 interaction terms to represent all possible interactions among the 12 college categories and each other variable in the equation. In a typical test for interaction, we estimate two equations, one in which earnings are regressed on the college dummy variables and the input and intervening variables (covariates) and one in which earnings are regressed on the college dummies and covariates as well as on the interaction variables for all covariates in the equation. We then compare the explained sums of squares in the two regression equations to determine whether there are statistically significant differences in slopes among the college categories.

A third set of regression equations is used to interpret the net

[4] For persons at or above the ceiling on covered Social Security earnings, an appropriate algorithm was used to estimate actual earnings (see Chapter 2 and Appendix C). The quality of the earnings data may vary with the proportion of cases for which it was necessary to estimate earnings in each year.

(additive) effects of colleges on earnings. We estimate several regression models in sequential fashion, starting with socioeconomic
background and academic ability as predetermined variables and
systematically adding other input variables, college categories, and
intervening variables in subsequent models. By comparing the coefficients of input and intervening variables in these equations, we
determine the extent to which colleges affect the influence of input
variables on earnings. The interpretive scheme follows that used
in Chapters 3 and 4. Then, we use these same equations to derive
the net effects of the college categories. A comparison of net effects
with gross college differences tells us the extent to which the
latter may be attributed to the input variables.

GROSS COLLEGE DIFFERENCES IN EARNINGS

College differences as reflected in earnings in 1965, 1966, and
1967 are displayed in Table 5-2 as deviations from the annual mean
earnings in dollars and in standard deviations of the earnings
distributions. There are substantial differences in earnings among
the college categories, and these differentials appear to be consistent from one year to the next. Men who attended Technological
Colleges and Institutes or Marquette University earned from $1000
to $1700 more than the average in each year, an advantage that
placed them .38 to .55 standard deviations above the mean. Men
who attended Prestigious Colleges and Universities, Other Universities, or the University of Wisconsin—Madison enjoyed lesser advantages, ranging from $450 to $870 per year, which placed them
about one-fifth of a standard deviation above the grand mean.
The University of Wisconsin—Milwaukee was very close to the
average in all three years. Those who attended the University of
Wisconsin—Center System, the Wisconsin State Universities, or
either type of Liberal Arts College had modest disadvantages
ranging from about $300 to $600 per year, or 0.1 to 0.25 standard
deviations less than the average. Finally, those who attended Wisconsin County Teachers Colleges or Other Colleges experienced
deficits in earnings of from $750 to $1800 per year, which placed
them from one-fourth to one-half of a standard deviation below
the average annual earnings.

In interpreting the differences in mean earnings, it should be
kept in mind that some of the college categories—especially
County Teachers Colleges and Other Colleges—have very few

TABLE 5-2

Earnings by Type of College Attended: Male Wisconsin High School Graduates of 1957 with College Experience

College category	Sample size	Deviations from grand mean					
		1965		1966		1967	
		Dollars	St. dev.	Dollars	St. dev.	Dollars	St. dev.
University of Wisconsin, Madison	205	558	.206	574	.178	868	.239
University of Wisconsin, Milwaukee	108	−11	−.004	278	.086	−7	−.002
University of Wisconsin, Center System	43	−273	−.101	−332	−.103	−352	−.097
Wisconsin State Universities	359	−436	−.161	−488	−.152	−638	−.176
Wisconsin County Teachers Colleges	15	−753	−.277	−1438	−.447	−1828	−.504
Marquette University	72	1041	.383	1249	.388	1711	.472
Prestigious Colleges and Universities	28	456	.168	644	.200	330	.091
Liberal Arts Colleges, General	101	−663	−.244	−753	−.234	−603	−.166
Liberal Arts Colleges, Catholic	38	−441	−.162	−598	−.186	−476	−.131
Universities	54	866	.319	690	.214	591	.163
Technological Colleges and Institutes	39	1486	.547	1352	.420	1274	.351
Other Colleges	19	−1387	−.511	−863	−.268	−1343	−.370
Total sample size	1081	1121		1123		1119	
Grand mean		6199		7246		7916	
Standard deviation		2716		3218		3626	
Coefficient of determination (R²)		.055		.044		.051	

Note: Data pertain to male Wisconsin high school graduates of 1957 with college experience between 1957 and 1964 who were alive and not in school or in the military in 1964. Sample size reported for each college category is the number of cases for which nonzero earnings were reported in all three years, 1965–1967.

sample cases. Further, despite the large differences in earnings we have just described, most of the variability in earnings occurs among men who attended the same college. Only 4.5% to 5.5% of the variance in earnings at this early stage of the socioeconomic career can be attributed to attending different types of colleges. Still, we think these interinstitutional differences in earnings are large enough to warrant further analysis.

INTERACTION EFFECTS

Table 5-3 summarizes a large number of statistical tests of differences among college categories in the effects of input and intervening variables on earnings for the years 1965, 1966, and 1967. The results of these tests are entirely consistent; they give no evidence that input or intervening variables have different effects in different college categories. For example, panel 1 gives the explained proportions of the sums of squares of earnings—both in the sample (R^2) and corrected for loss of degrees of freedom (R^2)—from regressions of 1965, 1966, and 1967 earnings on socioeconomic background, ability, and the college categories. Panel 2 contrasts these results with more complicated regression equations that permit socioeconomic background and ability to interact with the college categories. The model of panel 1 accounts for 9.5% of the variance in 1967 earnings, while the corresponding interaction model accounts for an apparently much larger 15.2% of the variance. However, it takes 55 degrees of freedom to produce this increment of 5.8 percentage points in the explained variance, and the very low F-ratio (1.0138) for the contrast between additive and interaction models indicates that an increment this large could easily have occurred by chance. Indeed, when the percentages of variance explained in the additive and interactive models are adjusted for loss of degrees of freedom, they are virtually the same: 7.8% and 7.9%, respectively.

In panels 3–8 of Table 5-3, this analysis is extended to interaction effects of type of college with academic performance and aspirations, educational attainment, and occupational status. In no case do the effects of these variables on earnings in any year differ significantly among the college categories. Thus, our analysis suggests that the effects of socioeconomic background, ability, and high school experiences on post-high school earnings are not significantly modified by the type of college that a young man

TABLE 5-3

Tests for Interaction Effects of College Categories and Inputs on 1965–1967 Earnings

Independent variables	Year	R^2	$\bar{R}^2$	Increment in R^2	F-ratio	Degrees of freedom
1. Socioeconomic background, ability, and colleges	1965	.064	.047			
	1966	.067	.050			
	1967	.095	.078			
2. (1) plus interactions involving background and ability	1965	.136	.061	.071	1.2266	55,818
	1966	.124	.048	.057	.9696	55,818
	1967	.152	.079	.058	1.0138	55,818
3. (1) plus academic performance and aspirations	1965	.074	.054			
	1966	.077	.057			
	1967	.114	.095			
4. (3) plus interactions involving academic performance and aspirations	1965	.106	.051	.032	.9083	33,837
	1966	.108	.053	.032	.8949	33,837
	1967	.147	.094	.033	.9735	33,837
5. (3) plus education	1965	.077	.056			
	1966	.079	.057			
	1967	.118	.098			
6. (5) plus interactions involving education	1965	.084	.050	.007	.5489	11,858
	1966	.088	.055	.009	.7939	11,858
	1967	.130	.099	.013	1.1171	11,858
7. (5) plus occupation	1965	.101	.080			
	1966	.094	.072			
	1967	.132	.111			
8. (7) plus interactions involving occupation	1965	.112	.079	.011	.9226	11,857
	1966	.106	.073	.012	1.0581	11,857
	1967	.150	.119	.018	1.6784	11,857

Note: Data pertain to male Wisconsin high school graduates of 1957 with college experience between 1957 and 1964, who were alive and not in school or in the military in 1964, with all data present (N = 890).

attends. Rather, this aspect of socioeconomic achievement exhibits a remarkable homogeneity across diverse types of schools, colleges, and universities.

COLLEGE TYPE AS AN INTERVENING VARIABLE

Since we found no evidence that type of college interacts with the other causes of earnings, we now look at several additive models of earnings. The findings in 1965, 1966, and 1967 are so similar that we have chosen to present only the results for 1967.[5] Table 5-4 gives standardized and unstandardized regression coefficients of earnings on input and intervening variables. Each odd-numbered column gives coefficients of a regression equation for the variables indicated, and the following even-numbered column gives the coefficients of the same variables in an equation where the college categories have been added as regressors. (We shall compare gross and net effects of the college categories in a later section.)

In column 1, we see that parents' education (V and M) and father's occupation (X) have no effect on son's 1967 earnings. As in the more inclusive sample treated in Chapter 4, income is the only socioeconomic characteristic of the family of orientation that affects son's earnings a decade after high school graduation. In this case, a $1000 shift in father's income (I_F) leads to a $125 shift in son's earnings, net of ability and other socioeconomic background variables. Even in this college-going sample, mental ability (Q) appears to have a modest effect on earnings, $207 for each 10-point shift in ability, but this effect is not quite large enough to be statistically significant.

By comparing the entries in column 2 with those in column 1, we can contrast the total effects of socioeconomic background and ability on earnings, with their effects net of college type. When the college categories are added to the regression of earnings on socioeconomic background and ability, the percentage of variance explained increases from 4.4% to 7.8%, an increment that is two-thirds as large as the total percentage of variance between types of colleges. Thus, differences among college categories in the mental ability and socioeconomic background of their graduates account for about one-third of the variance in earnings among college

---

[5] Results for all three years are given in Alwin (1972:211–238).

types. There is only a minor (8%) reduction in the coefficient of father's income between columns 1 and 2, so greater financial resources do not increase a son's earning power by facilitating a propitious choice among colleges. Net of college type, $1000 of father's income is still worth $116 in son's 1967 earnings. At the same time, the type of college attended does account for much of the effect of ability on earnings. Of the $200 shift in income effected by a 10-point shift in ability, about $100 is explained by the selection of brighter students into types of colleges whose matriculants later enjoy higher earnings.

Column 3 of Table 5-4 shows the regression of 1967 earnings on socioeconomic background, ability, and high school grades (G). The addition of academic performance to the equation accounts for almost all of the effect of mental ability on earnings (compare columns 1 and 3), but for none of the effect of father's income. In fact, father's income has a marginally greater effect on son's earnings after high school grades have been entered into the equation, presumably because the selection of a college-going subsample sets up a modest negative association between socioeconomic background and high school academic performance (Campbell, 1973). Still, none of the other socioeconomic background measures has a significant effect on earnings.

The reader will recall that we did not ascertain high school grades as such, but rather obtained percentile ranks in class. These were transformed into the same metric as IQ scores, so they had a mean of 100 and a standard deviation of 15 in the total population of high school seniors. Thus, the effects of academic performance are in a metric that is strictly comparable to that of ability.

Each 10-point increase in grades (G) on our scale gives rise to a $335 increase in son's 1967 earnings, after the effects of ability and socioeconomic background have been taken into account. When the college categories are again added to the earnings equation (column 4), the coefficient of father's average income is barely affected, but that of grades is reduced from $335 to $243 per 10-point shift in performance. Thus, about one-fourth of the higher earnings of college-going men with superior high school grades can be attributed to their attending types of colleges that enhance earning capacity at the outset of the socioeconomic career. The college categories add 2.0 percentage points to the explained

TABLE 5-4

Regression Models for 1967 Earnings: Male Wisconsin High School Graduates of 1957 with College Experience

Predetermined variables	Model											
	1	2	3	4	5	6	7	8	9	10	11	12
Regression coefficients in standard form												
V	-.0105	-.0024	-.0062	.0001	-.0092	-.0030	-.0132	-.0065	-.0166	-.0098	-.0215	-.0155
M	.0237	.0290	.0218	.0302	.0149	.0251	.0185	.0268	.0141	.0237	.0172	.0246
X	.0318	.0136	.0401	.0196	.0317	.0119	.0285	.0109	.0247	.0066	.0210	.0042
I_F	.1657a	.1532a	.1684a	.1582a	.1639a	.1546a	.1611a	.1531a	.1602a	.1537a	.1567a	.1485a
Q	.0749	.0365	.0109	-.0052	.0030	-.0124	-.0126	-.0240	-.0184	-.0303	-.0243	-.0361
G			.1193a	.0865a	.1060a	.0737	.0919a	.0641	.0656	.0379	.0583	.0320
T					.0189	.0251	.0131	.0196	.0121	.0186	.0004	.0079
P					.0594	.0531	.0476	.0441	.0468	.0426	.0411	.0376
F					.0371	.0364	.0236	.0255	.0135	.0157	.0070	.0089
E							-.0624	-.0559	-.0692	-.0615	-.0641	-.0572
J							.1551a	.1312a	.1502a	.1249a	.1333a	.1115a
U									.0819a	.0875a	.0055	.0177
W											.1710a	.1552a
R^2	.0437	.0780	.0539	.0828	.0601	.0885	.0746	.0985	.0796	.1040	.0998	.1202

(Continued)

128

TABLE 5-4 (Continued)

Predetermined variables	Model											
	1	2	3	4	5	6	7	8	9	10	11	12
Regression coefficients												
Constant	445.23	442.73	276.63	326.41	62.03	127.31	88.76	140.79	−59.54	−27.14	152.08	180.28
V	−1.18	−.27	−.70	.02	−1.04	−.34	−1.48	−.73	−1.86	−1.10	−2.42	−1.74
M	2.76	3.37	2.54	3.51	1.73	2.92	2.16	3.11	1.64	2.75	2.00	2.86
X	.49	.21	.61	.30	.49	.18	.44	.17	.38	.10	.32	.06
I_F	.1258[a]	.1163[a]	.1278[a]	.1200[a]	.1244[a]	.1173[a]	.1222[a]	.1162[n]	.1216[a]	.1167[n]	.1189[a]	.1127[a]
Q	2.07	1.01	.30	−.14	.08	−.34	−.35	−.66	−.51	−.84	−.67	−1.00
G			3.35[a]	2.43[a]	2.98[a]	2.07	2.58[a]	1.80	1.84	1.07	1.64	.09
T					14.15	18.72	9.78	14.65	9.04	13.90	.33	5.89
P					62.66	56.03	50.17	46.47	49.32	44.94	43.35	39.63
F					27.36	26.82	17.40	18.75	9.92	11.53	5.13	6.53
E							−52.94	−47.42	−58.71	−52.14	−54.43	−48.54
J							2.56[a]	2.16[a]	2.48[a]	2.06[a]	2.20[a]	1.84[a]
U									18.24[a]	19.48[a]	1.22	3.94
W											2.73[a]	2.48[a]

Note: Variables are V = father's education; M = mother's education; X = father's occupational status; I_F = father's income; Q = mental ability; G = rank in high school class; T = teachers' encouragement; P = parents' encouragement; F = friends' college plans; E = college plans; J = occupational status aspirations; U = educational attainment; W = occupational status attainment. Data pertain to male Wisconsin high school graduates of 1957 with college experience between 1957 and 1964 who were alive and not in school or in the military in 1964. Estimates were made from a correlation matrix based on pairwise-present data. In no case were correlations based on fewer than 964 cases. All even-numbered models differ from the preceding odd-numbered models by the inclusion of the college categories, but regression coefficients of the college categories are not shown here.

[a] $p \leq .05$

variance in 1967 earnings, net of socioeconomic background, ability, and academic performance in high school. Thus, an additional one-tenth of the variance in 1967 earnings among college types, which is not accounted for by background and ability differences, can be explained by variability among colleges in the high school grades of their students.

In column 5, our measures of teachers' (T) and parents' (P) encouragement to attend college and friends' college plans (F) are added to the model excluding the college categories. While the effects of these three variables are substantial in terms of dollars, especially in the case of parents' encouragement, none of them is statistically significant at even the .05 level, nor do the three measures collectively add a statistically significant increment to the explained sum of squares.[6] Consequently, adding these variables to the model does not alter the coefficients of father's average income or of son's academic performance. Likewise, adding the college categories to the model (column 6) does not materially affect the coefficients of the three measures of significant others' influence, and the contribution of the college categories to the explained variance is essentially the same here (2.8 percentage points) as in the model of column 4. That is, college differences in perceived levels of social support for college attendance do not contribute anything to the explanation of college differences in earnings. In interpreting these null findings, it should be kept in mind that our measures of perceived social support refer specifically to college-going and not to other facets of social or economic success.

In columns 7 and 8, educational aspirations (E) and occupational aspirations (J) are added to the model. Educational aspiration has a nonsignificant negative coefficient in this sample of college-going youth, but occupational aspiration does have a substantial positive impact on earnings. Net of prior variables, each 10-point shift in occupational aspiration on the Duncan SEI effects a shift of more than $250 in 1967 earnings. Thus, the effect of occupational aspiration among these college-going men is about two and one-half times larger than its effect in the sample of all high school graduates of nonfarm origin (see Table 4-3). While occupational aspiration influences earnings to an important degree, it does not

---

[6] Because of coding differences, the effects of T, P, and F are not strictly comparable to those reported in earlier chapters.

serve to mediate the effects of father's income or of high school academic performance (compare columns 5 and 7). In this sample of college-going men, the relationship between occupational aspiration and earnings is largely independent of father's income and of son's ability and performance in high school. When the college categories are added to the equation for 1967 earnings, the effect of occupational aspiration on earnings is reduced by one-sixth, to $216 per ten-point shift on the Duncan scale, so the allocation of men among types of colleges is not strongly implicated in the effect of occupational aspiration on earnings. Again, we are impressed by the size of the total effect of occupational aspiration on earnings, because the survey item was not narrowly directed to aspirations for pecuniary success.

The college categories add 2.4 percentage points to the explained variance in 1967 earnings net of background, ability, grades, significant others' influence, and aspirations, so those input variables collectively account for just one-half of the variance in earnings among college types. Obversely, one-half of the observed variance in earnings among college types might be attributed to the true effects of institutional types, and the remainder is a spurious consequence of the differential allocation of students among colleges. Since we have great confidence in the accuracy of our data on college attended, while our specification of effects of input variables is more subject to error because of omitted variables and random measurement error, we think that we are more likely to have overestimated than to have underestimated the net effects of the college categories.

This completes our analysis of the ways in which college categories mediate the effects on earnings of socioeconomic background, ability, and high school experiences. To summarize, of the several variables in our linear model of socioeconomic achievement, only three have substantial and statistically significant effects on 1967 earnings in this sample of men with collegiate experience. These are father's average income during the period 1957–1960 (I_F), academic performance in high school (G), and occupational aspiration during the senior year of high school (J). To a modest degree, the effects of these variables on earnings are brought about by the differential selection and recruitment of students among colleges whose graduates later experience earning differentials. Less than one-tenth of the effect of father's income, about one-fourth of the effect of academic performance, and one-sixth of the effect of occupational aspiration are mediated by the type of college attended. At the same time, these and the other input variables do account for more than half of the variance among college categories in 1967 earnings. While 5.1% of the variance in 1967 earnings occurs among college types, only 2.4 percentage points are explained once the effects of the input variables have been taken into account. Thus, we might think of the net effects of colleges on earnings as small relative to the total variability in the earnings of college-going men, but large relative to our ability to specify the factors affecting earnings early in the socioeconomic career.

From the last four columns of Table 5-4, we can determine the extent to which college effects on earnings are brought about by differentials in years of schooling and in occupational achievement. In column 9 of Tables 5-4, we add educational attainment (U) to the regressors of 1967 earnings. In this sample of men with college experience, each year of post-high school education leads to an increase of $182 in 1967 earnings. At the mean of the earnings distribution, this is an increase of just over 2% in earnings for each additional year in school. While this is a low return relative to rates commonly reported by economists of education, we do not think it is surprising, given the restrictions on our sample, their limited labor force experience, and our thorough specification of factors affecting both schooling and earnings. Years of schooling accounts for about one-third of the net influence of academic performance on earnings (compare columns 7 and 9) but does not account for the effects of father's income or of occupational aspiration.

When the college categories are added to the earnings equation (column 10), the coefficient of earnings increases slightly, to $195 per year of schooling. That is, there is a modest tendency for men with more schooling to have attended colleges with depressing effects on earnings. Likewise, the college categories add slightly more to the explained sum of squares in the model of column 10 than they do to those of column 8. Some colleges are more likely than others to hold their matriculants until graduation (Wegner and Sewell, 1970; Alwin, 1974), but the greater or lesser holding power of colleges clearly does not account for their effects on earnings.

When we add occupational status (W) to the regression of 1967 earnings on the input variables and educational attainment (column 11 of Table 5-4), we find that each 10 points on the Duncan SEI is worth $273 in earnings. This is more than twice the payoff of occupation in the sample of nonfarm men with or without college experience (see Table 4-3, line 38). At the same time, the returns to occupational status in 1964 are scarcely larger than the total effect of the occupational aspiration reported in 1957 (compare columns 7 and 11 of Table 5-4). The higher status occupations of men with more education account for almost all of the effect of educational attainment on earnings, but occupational status accounts for few of the effects of the other input variables on earnings (compare columns 9 and 11). Finally, when the college categories are added to the earnings equation, the coefficient of occupational status falls by less than 10% (compare columns 11 and 12). Thus, the modest effects of colleges on earnings are not explained either by differences in their capacity to hold students until graduation or by the higher or lower status jobs of their graduates. Other mechanisms must be invoked to explain the effects of colleges on earnings. As a prelude to further explorations of this issue, we now turn to a detailed examination of the effects of the college categories on earnings.

COLLEGE TYPES AND EARNINGS

Gross and net differences among the college categories in 1967 earnings are displayed in Table 5-5. Again, the results in 1965 and 1966 are so similar to those of 1967 that we have chosen not to present them here. The entries in the table are deviations of the average earnings in each college category from the grand mean of the 1967 earnings distribution. The deviations from the grand mean are expressed both in dollars and in units of the standard deviation of earnings.

The first pair of columns gives the gross, or unadjusted, deviations that were reported earlier in Table 5-2. In the second pair of columns, the deviations have been adjusted to take account of the variation among college categories in the socioeconomic background and ability of their students. That is, the entries in the second pair of columns are coefficients of the college categories in the regression equation of Table 5-4, column 2. In the last pair of columns, the deviations have been adjusted for all of the input variables, so the entries are coefficients of college categories in the regression equation of Table 5-4, column 8.

TABLE 5-5

Gross and Net College Differences in 1967 Earnings: Male Wisconsin High School Graduates of 1957 with College Experience

College category	Deviations from grand mean					
	Unadjusted		Adjusted on V,M,X,I_F,Q		Adjusted on $V,M,X,I_F,$ Q,G,T,P,F,E,J	
	Dollars	St. dev.	Dollars	St. dev.	Dollars	St. dev.
University of Wisconsin, Madison	868	.239	746	.206	533	.147
University of Wisconsin, Milwaukee	−7	−.002	64	.018	58	.016
University of Wisconsin, Center System	−352	−.097	−114	−.031	−146	−.040
Wisconsin State Universities	−638	−.176	−370	−.102	−360	−.099
Wisconsin County Teachers Colleges	−1828	−.504	−1139	−.314	−900	−.248
Marquette University	1711	.472	1571	.433	1330	.367
Prestigious Colleges and Universities	330	.091	−498	−.137	−751	−.207
Liberal Arts Colleges, General	−603	−.166	−642	−.177	−665	−.183
Liberal Arts Colleges, Catholic	−476	−.131	−524	−.145	−372	−.103
Universities	591	.163	536	.148	543	.150
Technological Colleges and Institutes	1274	.351	1358	.375	1057	.292
Other Colleges	−1343	−.370	−1109	−.306	−812	−.224
Grand mean	7916					
Standard deviation	3626					

Note: Variables are F = father's education; M = mother's education; X = father's income; Q = mental ability; G = rank in high school class; T = teachers' encouragement; I_F = father's income; F = friends' college plans; E = college plans; J = occupational status aspirations. Data pertain to male Wisconsin high school graduates of 1957 with college experience between 1957 and 1964 who were alive and not in school or in the military in 1964. Estimates were made from a correlation matrix based on pairwise-present data. In no case were correlations based on fewer than 964 cases. All even-numbered models differ from the preceding odd-numbered models by the inclusion of the college categories, but regression coefficients of the college categories are not shown here.

Recall that the adjustments for input variables do account for a large share of the variance in 1967 earnings among the college categories. Unadjusted college differences accounted for 5.1% of the variance in 1967 earnings, but the college categories explained 3.4% of the variance in earnings net of socioeconomic background and ability and only 2.4% of the variance in earnings net of all of the input variables.

As one would expect from these earlier findings, the adjusted deviations among the college categories are generally smaller than the gross deviations. At the same time they show the same pattern of sign and magnitude as the gross deviations. For example, on a gross basis, men who attended the University of Wisconsin—Madison had an advantage of $868 in 1967 earnings over the average student of other colleges. Of this advantage, $335 could be explained by the favorable distributions of Madison students on the input variables, but the average Madison student still earned $533 more than the average of all college students. The $1711 advantage of men who attended Marquette University fell to $1330 after adjustment for the input variables, but men from Marquette remained the most advantaged earners in both the gross and the adjusted distributions. Similarly, about $200 of the advantage of men from Technological Colleges and Institutes was explained by the input variables, but they still earned $1000 more than average.

At the other extreme, about half of the $1828 earnings disadvantage of men who attended Wisconsin County Teachers Colleges was explained by their unfavorable distribution on the input variables. Similarly, $500 of the $1343 disadvantage of men who attended Other Colleges was explained by their distribution on the input variables. Still, these two categories had the lowest average earnings after adjustment, just as they did before adjustment.

There was one major discrepancy between the gross and adjusted earnings. Before adjustment, men who attended Prestigious Colleges and Universities earned $330 more than average, but after adjustment for the input variables, they earned $750 less than average. This is less than the adjusted earnings in any college category except the Wisconsin County Teachers Colleges and the Other Colleges.

The pattern of adjusted deviations in Table 5-5 only partly confirms the notion that college effects on earnings follow the prestige rankings of institutions. Such a pattern is plainly evident in both the gross and the adjusted deviations of public institutions in Wisconsin, where the University of Wisconsin—Madison ranks first, followed by the University of Wisconsin—Milwaukee, the University of Wisconsin Center System, the Wisconsin State Universities, and the Wisconsin County Teachers Colleges, in that order. At the same time, institutional prestige cannot explain the very high earnings of men from Marquette University and from Technological Colleges and Institutes, nor can it explain the low earnings of men from the Prestigious Colleges and Universities. Indeed, it is difficult to think of any unidimensional classification of the college types that could yield a nontautological explanation of the net differences in earnings among the college categories.

COLLEGE EFFECTS ON EDUCATION, OCCUPATION, AND EARNINGS

By comparing college effects on earnings with those on educational attainment and occupational status, we can obtain further insights about the magnitude of college differences in earnings and, also, about the meaning of college quality as an explanatory construct.[7] In the sample of men with college experience, there is more variability among colleges in the educational attainments of their matriculants than in their earnings, and less variability in their occupational statuses; 7.8% of the variance in years of schooling and 4.6% of the variance in occupational status occurs among the college categories, compared with 5.1% of the variance in 1967 earnings.

The several input variables account for 70% of the between-category variance in educational attainment, 46% of the between-category variance in occupational status, and 53% of the between-category variance in 1967 earnings. Thus, one-half or more of the observed variance among college types in each of the socio-economic outcomes may be attributed to the joint dependence of the type of college attended and the outcome variable on the causally prior input variables. The college categories account for between 2.25% and 2.5% of the variance in each outcome variable, above and beyond the effects of the input variables. Since the

---

[7] College effects on educational attainment and occupational status are analyzed in greater detail in Alwin (1974).

input variables alone explain 27.0% of the variance in educational attainment and 16.6% of the variance in occupational status among the college-going men, but only 7.5% of the variance in 1967 earnings, the net effects of the colleges on earnings represent a much larger share of the explained variance than in the case of the two prior outcomes of schooling.

Table 5-6 gives gross and adjusted differences among the college categories in educational attainment and in occupational status. Differences in educational attainment are expressed as deviations from the grand mean, both in raw units of years of schooling and in standard deviation units. Differences in occupational attainment are expressed both as points on the Duncan SEI and in standard deviation units. The adjusted deviations in years of schooling and in occupational status are comparable to the adjusted deviations in 1967 earnings reported in the last two columns of Table 5-5.

The gross differences in years of schooling among the college categories range from a high of 1.4 years more than average for men from Prestigious Colleges and Universities to a low of about 0.7 years below average in the University of Wisconsin—Center System and Wisconsin County Teachers Colleges. The lower attainments of men in the last two categories are not strictly determined by their two-year programs, since men were classified by the first college they attended in the analyses of educational attainment. Men who first attended the University of Wisconsin—Madison, Marquette University, or one of the Technological Colleges obtained about 0.4 to 0.5 more years of schooling than the average, and men attending the Liberal Arts Colleges obtained about 0.25 more years of schooling than the average. Men from the Wisconsin State Universities and from the Other Colleges spent about one-fourth of a year less in school than the average, while those attending the University of Wisconsin—Milwaukee, spent about half a year less than the average.

Adjustment for the input variables markedly affected the deviations of some college categories from the grand mean of educational attainment. Men who first attended the University of Wisconsin—Madison obtained slightly less schooling than predicted from their distribution on the input variables. The educational advantage of men who attended Prestigious Schools and Universities remained after adjustment, but it was a full year less than the unadjusted deviation. On the other hand, while men who attended

TABLE 5-6

Gross and Net College Differences in Educational Attainment and Occupational Status: Male Wisconsin High School Graduates of 1957 with College Experience

College category	Educational attainment				Occupational status			
	Gross		Adjusted		Gross		Adjusted	
	Years	St. dev.	Years	St. dev.	SEI	St. dev.	SEI	St. dev.
University of Wisconsin, Madison	.40	.24	−.09	−.06	6.7	.30	1.8	.08
University of Wisconsin, Milwaukee	−.57	−.35	−.54	−.33	−4.0	−.18	−2.7	−.12
University of Wisconsin, Center System	−.73	−.45	−.55	−.34	−13.0	−.57	−9.6	−.42
Wisconsin State Universities	−.23	−.14	−.08	−.05	−2.3	−.10	0.6	.03
Wisconsin County Teachers Colleges	−.70	−.43	.22	.13	−6.2	−.27	5.1	.23
Marquette University	.54	.33	.02	.01	8.4	.37	4.3	.19
Prestigious Colleges and Universities	1.41	.86	.40	.25	−0.4	−.01	−11.3	−.50
Liberal Arts Colleges, General	.27	.17	.11	.07	−0.5	−.02	−0.8	−.03
Liberal Arts Colleges, Catholic	.28	.17	.39	.24	−3.6	−.16	−0.6	−.03
Universities	−.15	−.09	−.14	−.09	−2.1	−.09	1.6	.07
Technological Colleges and Institutes	.42	.26	.12	.07	6.9	.30	6.8	.30
Other Colleges	−.26	−.16	.33	.20	−10.2	−.45	−3.9	−.17
Grand mean	15.08				56.54			
Standard deviation	1.63				22.68			

Note: Adjusted deviations from the grand mean are effects of the college categories net of socioeconomic background, mental ability, high school grades, significant others' influence, educational and occupational aspirations, and commitment to college. In the analysis of educational attainment, men were assigned to the category of the first college they attended. Data pertain to male Wisconsin high school graduates of 1957 with college experience between 1957 and 1964 who were alive and not in school or in the military in 1964.

Wisconsin County Teachers Colleges and Other Colleges obtained less schooling than the average, they obtained more schooling than expected, given their distribution on the input variables.

Men who last attended the University of Wisconsin—Madison, Marquette University, or the Technological Colleges and Institutes enjoyed an advantage of from 7 to 8 points in occupational status relative to the grand mean. Men from the University of Wisconsin Center System, the Wisconsin County Teachers Colleges, or the Other Colleges held occupations 6 to 13 points below the average in status. The remaining college categories were scattered between these extremes.

In the case of occupational status, the pattern of adjusted deviations from the grand mean was generally similar to that of the gross deviations. After adjustment for the effects of input variables, the major shifts were the elimination of the apparent disadvantage of students attending the Wisconsin County Teachers Colleges and the elimination of much of the apparent advantage of men from the University of Wisconsin—Madison and Marquette University. Further, while men from Prestigious Colleges and Universities were near the average in occupational status, they averaged about 11 points lower than expected on the Duncan SEI.

In comparing these findings about educational attainment, occupational status, and earnings, it is a striking fact that the adjusted deviations for the 12 college categories are not consistent across outcome variables. For example, after controlling input variables, men who attended Wisconsin County Teachers Colleges obtained more schooling and held higher status jobs than the average, but they also had lower than average earnings. Conversely, men from Marquette University or the Technological Colleges and Institutes were close to the average in years of schooling, but they obtained higher status jobs and higher earnings than the average.

To measure the degree of consistency in the net effects of the college categories, we computed the correlations of adjusted deviations in schooling, occupational status, and 1967 earnings across the 12 categories. These were $r = .109$ between educational attainment and occupational status, $r = .505$ between occupational status and earnings, and $r = -.337$ between educational attainment and earnings. Clearly, these results do not suggest the existence of a single dimension of college quality along which one could array the several institutional types represented in our classification of colleges and universities. On the contrary our findings seem to imply that the diversity of institutions of collegiate education is partly manifested in a diversity of effects on the several outcomes of schooling.

Summary and Conclusions

In this chapter, we have described and analyzed college differences in earnings. Most of the analysis pertains to earnings in 1967 in the subsample of male Wisconsin high school graduates of 1957 who had some college experience between 1957 and 1964 and who were neither in school nor in military service in 1964. Our interest in the effects of colleges stems from the argument that, in higher education, specific institutional qualities, and not merely the fact of college attendance, have an important bearing on an individual's socioeconomic life chances. While this argument has a long history, its importance has grown along with college enrollments.

We have attempted to answer five questions about the earnings of men who attend different types of colleges or universities. How large are the variations in earnings from one school to the next, and how do these compare to institutional differences in the chances of graduating from college or entering a high-status occupation? Do institutional environments change the way in which background, ability, or high school experiences affect earnings? To what extent do college differences in earnings represent institutional effects by way of socialization or certification, and to what extent are they artifacts of the differential selection and recruitment of students with respect to factors affecting earnings? Is the decision as to which college or university to attend a mechanism by which some families pass on economic advantage to their offspring? Finally, what are the mechanisms by which colleges affect earnings, and to what extent do the effects of colleges on earnings reflect differences in institutional quality?

Only about one-twentieth of the variance in earnings occurs among the dozen categories of colleges and universities treated in our analysis. This is about the same as the percentage of variance in occupational status that occurs among colleges, but it is less than that which occur in educational attainment. Since the variance in earnings among persons is quite large, so in some cases are the differences in earnings among men who attended different colleges. For example, in 1967, mean earnings were about $8000, and a gap of more than $3500 separated the average earnings of men in the most and least remunerative types of colleges.

In earlier chapters, we developed a social psychological model of achievement that estimates and interprets the effects of socioeconomic background, ability, and selected high school experiences on educational attainment, occupational status, and earnings. If college environments have distinct effects on the process of socioeconomic achievement, these might be partly manifested in changing relationships among background variables and achievements across the college categories. However, in a large number of tests we found no statistical interaction between colleges and prior variables. Thus, among college-goers the process of socioeconomic achievement appears to work in essentially the same way, no matter what college or university a young man attends.

Slightly more than half of the variance in earnings among colleges in our sample was explained by the fact that colleges select or recruit men with varying prospects for earnings. After controlling relevant input variables, only about one-fortieth of the variance in earnings occurred among college categories, and the difference between the highest- and lowest-earning college categories was reduced by more than $1000. Still, there remained differences in earnings among the college categories that were unrelated to social origins, ability, or high school experiences. Men who attended Marquette University or a Technological College or Institute earned $1000 more than the average in 1967, while men earned at least $600 less than the average if they attended Prestigious Colleges and Universities, Liberal Arts Colleges, Wisconsin County Teachers Colleges, or the marginal institutions included in the Other Colleges category.

In the sample of men who attended college, relatively few of the variables in our model of achievement affected earnings. Most of our measures were not designed to tap propensities to earn; some variables probably exhausted their effects in the process of selecting college attenders; and men in the sample were not well along in their careers. As in the more inclusive sample, we found a substantial effect of family economic status on 1967 earnings, $125 for each $1000 of father's average income in the period 1957–

1960. None of the other measures of socioeconomic background affected earnings. Less than 15% of the effect of father's income on son's earnings could be attributed to the different colleges attended by the sons of rich and poor families. Thus, "the old school tie" is not the connecting link between father's income and son's earnings.

Even among college-going men, high school academic performance had a large effect on 1967 earnings, about $500 for each change of a standard deviation (15 points in the total population of high school graduates). About one-fourth of this effect could be attributed to the different colleges attended by men with high and low grades. Each 10 points on the Duncan SEI of occupational aspiration in 1957 was worth about $250 in 1967 earnings, but only one-sixth of this was explained by attendance at different colleges. In all, while colleges do have modest independent effects on earnings in the early career, they do not seem to account for the effects on earnings of background or high school experiences.

Colleges differ in the likelihood their matriculants will graduate and also in the types of jobs their graduates obtain. The influence of colleges on years of schooling and on occupational status is about as large as on earnings, but it does not begin to account for the effects of colleges on earnings. Indeed, the effects of colleges on years of schooling, occupational status, and earnings in the early career are not highly correlated across the college categories, and there is even a slight inverse relationship between the effects of colleges on years of schooling and on earnings. This lack of consistency in the effects of colleges on education, occupation, and earnings suggests that no single dimension of institutional quality defines the effectiveness of institutions of higher education.

6

Post-High School Earnings: When and for Whom Does "Ability" Seem to Matter?[1]

Recent and ongoing studies of investment in human capital claim their proximate origins in the field of economic growth. Spurred by the discovery that a substantial proportion of previously unaccounted-for variance in growth could be accounted for by improvements in quality of the labor force, a great deal of talent has since been devoted to unraveling relationships between education, training, health, and other input factors and a variety of output measures. With the bold and ambitious foundation building by Schultz (1960, 1961a,b), Becker (1964), and others, studies in this field have expanded rapidly and in diverse directions. Among these have been investigations to unearth and exploit all extant sources of data that include some measure of ability. Such data would then be used to estimate functions that might, once "properly specified," reveal what proportion of economic growth apparently due to increased educational level should hang its true coefficient on another variable called "ability." But ability is not the only fly in this ointment. Other correlates of education are suspected of influencing its estimated effects if these, too, are not appropriately taken into account.

[1] This chapter was prepared by Janet A. Fisher, Kenneth G. Lutterman, and Dorothy M. Ellegaard.

Parallel inquiries have been made to find an adjustment factor for estimates of the private rates of return to education per se. Again the proposed list of associated variables includes ability along with such others as motivation, educational quality, and components of socioeconomic background.

There is a difference between the questions related to economic growth and the ones related to estimating private rates of return. The latter involves members of a specific cohort or, at most, members of that cohort and the particular cohort mix of its parents. The former refer to the generations in the period over which growth is measured. Thus, our study of the relationships between earnings and ability for different educational attainment levels is but one aspect of these larger problems.

Estimates of the proportion by which zero-order relations between income and education require adjustment cover a wide range. These results depend, in part, upon the number of years of schooling represented, the education-related variables selected, and the manner in which these variables have been measured (Denison, 1962; Becker, 1964; Weisbrod and Karpoff, 1968; Hansen and Weisbrod, 1969; Griliches and Mason, 1972; and Chapters 3 and 4 of this volume).

The capital analogue for human resources has brought economics back into the age-old heredity–environment controversy. Genetic endowment is what we would measure if we could. Then we would proceed to quantify each of the value-modifying factors sequentially. In the interim, for analytical purposes, it has been useful to separate the index-number question from the causal one (Griliches, 1970). This is so, even though the dividing line is arbitrary. Their marriage should come about with both increased knowledge and understanding of the underlying processes.

At this juncture, we feel that evidence developed in previous studies provides a plausible case for the study of interaction effects. One of the most interesting in our view is the interaction between education and ability in relation to income or, preferably, earnings. The evidence for this interaction rather consistently shows income to be positively related to ability at the higher levels of educational attainment and the steepness of the slope for the regression of income on ability to be positively related to the level of educational attainment (Wolfle and Smith, 1956; Husen, 1969; Rogers, 1969). If, with a given additional investment in education, the marginal increment to marginal productivity is greater for those of high ability than for those of low ability, then we should expect to find this kind of interaction. Therefore, this interrelationship provides a focus for the analysis presented here. We attempt to trace its development during the early post-high school years. We also investigate some of its implications with respect to investment in college education; more specifically, we examine several dimensions of earnings foregone by those who went to college.

Properly to pursue this investigation, we must first sort out the varieties of post-high school experience. For some, formal education ends with high school. For others, it continues without interruption through college and graduate or professional school. For still others, there are a number of variations on the educational theme. These include delayed college entry and/or one or more years in and out of college. Military service may intervene at any stage, and such service may alter both the timing and the extent of higher education as well as the date of entry into the civilian labor force. All of these dimensions of post-high school investment complicate both the estimation of its major private component, earnings foregone, as well as the analysis of earnings profiles as they begin to take shape with full participation in the civilian labor force at different points in time.

The Data for 1957 Wisconsin High School Seniors

For the analysis reported in this chapter, we have a set of data for a sample of more than 4000 young men who were seniors in the high schools of Wisconsin in 1957.[2] These data begin with information gathered in the spring of 1957 and include measures on

[2] The initial one-third sample of 1957 high school seniors included 4994 males. In 1964 information about educational and occupational attainment, military service, and marital status was collected for 4388 of this group. With the cooperation of the Wisconsin Department of Revenue, information on income and occupation of sample members and their parents was added from State tax records. Finally, annual earnings data were supplied by the Social Security Administration for 4316 of the 4388 cases. Of the 4316 cases with earnings records, 56 deceased by December of 1967 have not been included in this analysis. This leaves a total of 4260 cases, from which specific subgroups have been selected for the study of early earnings histories. For a discussion of the nature of Social Security earnings data, see Appendix C.

a unique collection of variables relevant to an understanding of the higher education investment process. In addition to full information on educational attainment as of 1964, limited information on military service, and a series of annual earnings data from Social Security Administration reports through 1967, there are percentile-ranked scores for the Henmon–Nelson test of mental ability (Henmon and Nelson, 1954). This test, which was administered during the junior year in high school, is one designed primarily to measure the kinds of ability required for academic work. Such a test of scholastic ability undoubtedly has certain limitations when applied to performance in the workaday world (see Chapter 2 for a more complete discussion of this sample and of data used in this analysis).

Nearly 60% of these young men attended some school or college between 1957 and 1964. About the same proportion served in the armed forces. One-third did both, while less than one-half of that proportion (about 15%) did neither. One-fourth attended either college or vocational and technical schools and had no military service. About 28% served in the armed forces and had no further education.

The figures in Table 6-1 not only summarize the interrelations among levels of educational attainment and military service; they also serve as a preface to the difficulties faced in selection of appropriate subgroups for investigation. Although few cases are not ascertained with respect to military service, we have almost no direct information on the specific years so spent. Likewise, we have less than full information on the dating of college enrollment and even less on the specific years devoted to technical and vocational training. The information we have facilitates the selection of subgroups for which the analysis plan is feasible. It also indicates that there is so much temporal heterogeneity of behavior within other subgroups that the plan is not feasible for them. The principal losses are those who failed to complete college by 1964 and those who attended vocational and technical schools.[3]

[3] We found great diversity in the timing of school attendance among those who attended vocational and technical schools, those who attended college but failed to graduate by 1964, and college graduates who continued their education thereafter. Not only is there considerable variation in dates of entrance and departure from educational institutions, there are also frequent cases with one or more years out of school between the first and last years of attendance. In some

TABLE 6-1

Military Service by Education beyond High School 1957–1964 (N = 4260)[a]

Military service	Education beyond high school						All levels
	None	Vocational or technical school	College: no degree		College graduate		
			Not enrolled in 1964	Enrolled in 1964	Bachelor's degree	Graduate or professional school	
None	33	28	34	21	48	79	37
Served between 1957 and 1964	54	58	45	66	25	10	46
Serving in 1964:							
Reserves or National Guard	3	6	6	5	4	3	4
On active duty	8	7	13	5	22	6	11
Not ascertained	2	1	2	3	2	2	2
Total	100	100	100	100	100	100	100
Percentage of sample	43	14	17	5	14	7	100

[a] In percentages.

147

The earnings data cover a period of almost continuous economic expansion. While high school graduates of 1957 did emerge to face the contraction that began in July of that year and ended in April of 1958, those who finished college in 1961 celebrated their graduation in more favorable times. The mild contraction of May 1960 to February 1961 was the only other to occur in the period 1957–1968. The trend in early earnings profiles for the entire cohort sample reflects the second contraction. The rate of increase in average earnings falls from 1960 to 1961. However, the average level of earnings rises throughout the entire period covered.

Analysis Plan

To determine, for a given year, if the earnings foregone by college students are related to their ability involves estimating the regression of annual earnings on the ability measure, both for those attending college and for members of the same cohort (with the same number of years of schooling up to that year) in the civilian labor force.[4] Ideally, we might examine the slopes of the simple regression for perfectly matched groups. If neither differed significantly from zero, or if the two were of equal size and direction, we would conclude that earnings foregone were unrelated to ability. The difference between intercepts would be the measure of earnings foregone at all levels of ability. This comparison would have to be made for each college year. Then, to determine total earnings foregone by a particular group of college students, both the number of years and their dates would have to be reckoned with.

Our data come closer to meeting some attributes of this ideal than do many other sets of data. Almost all members of the sample were born between 1938 and 1940. We have data for annual earnings rather than total income. However, classification by education beyond high school cannot produce perfectly

---

of these cases the intervening period was spent in the armed forces; in others it was spent in civilian employment. Unfortunately, we do not have information for dating these experiences. A further complication is that the earnings data are for calendar years, while school attendance is not.

[4] The question of an appropriate reference group for this comparison is discussed more fully on page 175.

matched groups. Mostly for substantive reasons discussed below, and partly for methodological ones, we have not attempted to reach the closest possible approximation to perfect matching. We have taken a middle course, relying on the classification of cases by certain attributes prior to estimating the equations for some subgroups; we have used dummy regressors to represent these same attributes in regression equations that are estimated for other subgroups.

In their analysis of "Education and Income," Morgan and David (1963:423–426) present a nicely reasoned exposition of the problems related to measuring the *true* effects of education on earnings. Although the problems involved in measuring the *true* effects of ability are not exactly analogous, they have a number of elements in common.

The information in Table 6-1 and the accompanying discussion of educational attainment in relation to military service indicate a few of the problems in locating the nearest approximation to groups that meet the desired criteria. Clearly there are more. Classification by educational attainment is classification by a major correlate of ability. However, as anyone interested in the talent loss problem is painfully aware, this correlation is far from perfect (Sewell and Shah, 1967; Taubman and Wales, 1972). Thus, although the distributions by ability differ by level of educational attainment and are, in fact, skewed in opposite directions for those with the least and those with the most education, from 90% to 100% of the measured range is represented in the groups we analyze (Table 6-3).

Socioeconomic Background Variables and the Earnings Data

With the exception of farm background, socioeconomic variables do not directly affect the choice of groups analyzed and are not entered in the equations estimated. Although this exception is necessary for the proper treatment of Social Security covered earnings data in the period up to 1961 (see Appendix C), it is also of central importance to an understanding of post-high school career patterns of Wisconsin youth. The 1950s and 1960s belong to a long period of dramatic decline in the number and proportion of persons engaged in agriculture. During the years under consideration, the transition out of agriculture was in large part an intergenerational one. More than one-fifth of the fathers of 1957 male Wisconsin high school seniors were farmers. Less than one-twentieth of their sons had entered that occupation by 1964.

Farm youth also differ from their nonfarm contemporaries in both the size and kind of investment made in education beyond high school. Fifty-seven percent of the former and 38% of the latter made no such investment. Among farm youth with further education, 36% attended vocational or technical schools. Of nonfarm youth with further education, 22% attended such institutions.

Correlated with these differences in educational attainment are a number of social and economic factors including money income. From Wisconsin state tax return data, we estimate the 1957–1960 average annual parental income for farm youth ($3726) to be little more than half that of nonfarm youth ($7161). In addition, in the nonfarm sector, although sons' educational attainment exhibits a clear and systematic relation to parental income, the dollar and even the percentage differences are small between successive levels of attainment for farm youth (Table 6-2). Clearly the few farm youth who did get to graduate or professional school did not achieve that advanced education by virtue of familial economic circumstances, if the figures presented can be assumed to be reasonably good measures thereof.

As noted earlier, we focus the analysis upon questions concerning investment in and returns to schooling as they affect the role of education in economic growth and estimates of the private rate of return to higher education. In this context, we argue that the zero-order relationship between earnings and ability for specific educational attainment groups is a relevant one. To the extent that socioeconomic variables capture certain dimensions of ability not represented in the Henmon–Nelson test, we should include them if they did that and no more. To the extent that they represent indicators of other variables, we argue for their omission (Griliches, 1970). This does not mean that we assume that labor markets are perfect, nor that the ability measure itself is uncontaminated by socioeconomic status. However, just as we cannot untangle the labeling or certification effects of education on earnings, so too we do not attempt to unravel those of family status. Questions concerning intergenerational status transmission and the equality of educational opportunity, in which socioeconomic back-

TABLE 6-2

1957–1960 Average Parental Income and Sample Proportions by Educational Attainment and Family Background

Education beyond high school	1957–1960 average parental income				Percentage			N^a
	Nonfarm background	Farm background	All		Nonfarm background	Farm background	All	
None	5671[b] (3416)[c]	3467 (1772)	5004 (3180)		70	30	100	1632
Vocational or technical school	6391 (3589)	3667 (1839)	5723 (3453)		75	25	100	538
College: All	8528 (6669)	4316 (2444)	7957 (6429)		86	14	100	1699
No degree	7821 (5813)	4238 (2490)	7314 (5607)		86	14	100	848
Bachelor's degree	9015 (7608)	4571 (2392)	8387 (7274)		86	14	100	566
Graduate or professional school	9614 (6794)	3950 (2280)	9018 (6699)		89	11	100	285
All levels	7161 (5444)	3726 (2016)	6401 (5100)		78	22	100	3869

[a] Does not include 391 cases for which average parental income was not ascertained.
[b] Mean.
[c] Standard deviation.

ground variables have a central role, are beyond the scope of this chapter. (For evidence on these matters, see Chapters 3, 4, and 5.)

Social Security earnings reports have special characteristics that have been taken into account in this analysis. These are more fully discussed in Appendix C. Perhaps the most important in terms of research strategy is the treatment of zero-earnings reports. For, while some of these reflect true zero earnings, others occur because of earnings from employment that is not covered by Social Security. The latter appear to be numerically very few in this sample.[5] Assuming that among persons in the civilian labor force most, if not all, of such cases are in the latter category, we omitted them from regression computations. Assuming that most of the zero-earnings reports for college students represent true zero earnings, we included them in computations for the college years. However, for these years, in order to give proper weight to zero earnings, estimations were made with the Limited Dependent Variable, or Probit Regression Program (Tobin, 1958; Goldberger, 1964:251–255). Other important characteristics of these earnings data that require special consideration include: (1) the ceiling on covered earnings that necessitated the estimation of figures above that level; (2) the limitation of military service earnings coverage to basic pay. It should also be noted that these are before-tax earnings.

Analysis Groups

In the next section we examine the earnings of those with no education beyond high school. These are classified into four subgroups on the basis of farm background and of military service. In the following section, we turn to those who went to college and examine earnings histories of a group that graduated by 1962 and did not undertake graduate study.

A somewhat different strategy is used in each of these sections. With more than 1500 cases in the group with no education beyond high school, it was possible to estimate separate regression equa-

[5] Occupational data for 1964 show very few cases in those categories of employment such as U.S. civil service and railroad and protective services that are not covered by Social Security.

tions for the indicated subgroups. It was also desirable to do this because of the kinds of differences there are between both the incidence and the apparent consequences of military service by farm background. With fewer cases in the college graduate group analyzed, a much smaller proportion of these from farm background, and less difference by background with respect to measured ability, only one set of regression equations was estimated for the college group. However, a dummy regressor was used to take into account the early post-high school differences in earnings or earnings coverage or both of these, for farm youth. Likewise, for the postcollege years, no separate regression equations were estimated for subgroups classified by military service. Again dummy regressors and also some interaction terms were introduced to handle such differences. In general, wherever possible, we have coordinated information collected in the initial 1957 questionnaires and in the 1964 follow-up study with what we know of earnings coverage and earnings correlates.

As indicated earlier, our purpose is primarily an exploratory one. We do not use Social Security earnings data as the basis for new dollar estimates of earnings foregone by college students nor of the early returns to higher education. Instead, we use them to raise and reexamine certain questions that pertain to the kinds of assumptions made in that estimation process.

HIGH SCHOOL EDUCATION ONLY

More than 40% of the 1957 Wisconsin male high school seniors had no further formal education.[6] For this group, the incidence of military service was much higher than it was for those who completed college by 1964 and about the same as for college dropouts (although that group apparently served later). Among those with no education beyond high school, the incidence of military service was somewhat lower than it was among men who attended vocational and technical schools (Table 6-1).

[6] The phrase, "1957 high school seniors," accurately describes the initial population chosen for study. As noted, the first questionnaires were administered to these young men in the spring of their senior year in high school. It is possible that a few left school before graduation. Most, if not all, of these probably belong to the group with no further education. Where the term "high school graduate" is used, especially for those with no further education, ease of expression is the benefit of a small cost in accuracy.

TABLE 6-3

Henmon–Nelson Percentile Rank and Sample Proportion by Educational Attainment and Family Background

Education beyond high school	Henmon–Nelson percentile rank			Percentage			N
	Nonfarm background	Farm background	All	Nonfarm background	Farm background	All	
None	39[a] (26)[b]	35 (26)	38 (26)	71	29	100	1809
Vocational or technical school	44 (27)	51 (28)	46 (27)	76	24	100	589
College: All	67 (25)	64 (27)	66 (25)	86	14	100	1862
No degree	59 (26)	58 (29)	59 (26)	86	14	100	935
Bachelor's degree	72 (22)	69 (23)	71 (22)	85	15	100	612
Graduate or professional school	79 (20)	75 (20)	78 (20)	89	11	100	315
All levels	53 (29)	45 (29)	51 (29)	78	22	100	4260

[a] Mean.
[b] Standard deviation.

In terms of background, the group with no further education differs markedly from other members of the sample. Thirty percent of them came from farm families. That is twice the proportion of persons with farm background among these two entered college and is also twice the proportion among those who graduated from college (Table 6-3).

To facilitate the analysis of earnings for those with no further schooling, we have excluded the ones who were still serving in the armed forces in 1964 and the few for whom we have no information concerning military service. We classify the remaining 87% of these 1957 high school seniors by both family background and military service. (See Table 6-4). In the regression of annual earnings on ability for those who served prior to 1964, then, we can focus upon these relationships in their postservice years.

The Relation of Average Earnings to Family Background and Military Service. Before analyzing the relationship between earnings and ability, we first sort out the ways in which earnings profiles differ by background and service in the armed forces. Thereby we find certain consequences of military service by family background with implications that might well affect the interpretation of much research designed to estimate earnings foregone by college or vocational school students.

TABLE 6-4

Military Service by Family Background for Males with No Education beyond High School (N = 1575[a])

	Family background		
Military service by 1964	Nonfarm	Farm	Total
Served	64%	57%	62%
Did not serve	36%	43%	38%
Total	100%	100%	100%
Percentage	70%	30%	100%

[a] Does not include 192 males still serving in the armed forces in 1964 and 42 for whom military service was not ascertained.

The coverage of earnings under Social Security is remarkably high for those with no education beyond high school. In fact, it is little short of 100% for most of the four subgroups in most of the years 1957–1967. Two qualifications should be noted. First, farm youths under 21 who worked on their parents' farms were not covered. This is evident in the relatively small number of them (not in military service) with earnings reports prior to 1961 (Table 6-7). Second, the coverage of earnings received by members of the armed forces is restricted to basic pay, and, within the group that served, we are unable to identify those individuals in service in any given year (see Appendix C).

Among those with no further education from farm families, occupational choice is related to military service. Responses to the 1964 questionnaires show that one-fourth of all those with a farm background had themselves become farmers. However, while one-third of the farm youth who did not have military service followed their fathers' occupation, only one-sixth of the ones with military service did so. Even some of these may have farmed but briefly.

Among those with no military service, average earnings of the entire farm background group are well below earnings of the non-farm group throughout the period 1957–1967 (Table 6-5, column 10). By contrast, there is little or no difference by background among those who served in the armed forces during most of the years prior to 1962. Even the differences thereafter are quite small (Table 6-5, column 11).

These comparisons reflect not only the service-related difference in proportions of farm youth who became farmers, but apparently also some military-related differences in farm earnings (Table 6-5, column 12). On these points our evidence is limited by sample size. Although both the estimated dollar and the estimated percentage differences appear to be large for both 1964 and 1965, with relatively few cases, conventional criteria for statistical significance are not met. The still greater differences for 1966 and 1967 do meet such criteria. However, for these years we hesitate to assume that this result is not a function of occupational mobility. Some of the farm youth who had been through military service and returned to farm thereafter may have entered other occupations within the next few years.

Earnings data for the nonfarm males contain equally interesting differences when classified by military service (Table 6-5, column

13). Remembering that service-connected earnings are limited to basic pay, we can infer that 1957 through 1960 were the years with the highest proportions in service. These are the years of greatest percentage difference in mean earnings. Thereafter, these series converge, until by 1964 the earnings of those who had served approach 95% of the mean earnings of those who had not. This difference of several hundred dollars persists through 1967. For reasons given above, we cannot estimate service-connected earnings foregone (a knotty problem at best).[7] However, we can estimate postservice earnings differences in 1965, 1966, and 1967. For these differences, our findings are consistent with the position that private costs of military service will be understated if only the period in service is taken into account (Willett, 1968). This statement is qualified with a reminder that two sets of information are incomplete. First, we cannot date the military service period exactly. Therefore, these averages may well reflect some differences in the length of continuous labor force participation. Second, we do not know whether any of the young men in either group returned to school after 1964.

The postservice earnings differences just described are found only in the earnings of young men with nonfarm backgrounds.[8] Quite the opposite relationship seems to characterize those from farm families (Table 6-5, columns 3 and 7). In fact, for farm youth after 1963, the negative association of earnings with military service persists neither for those who became farmers nor for those

[7] The difficulties involved in comparing compensation in the armed forces with compensation in civilian employment are more fully described in Moskos (1970: 44–45), Oi (1967b), and Hansen and Weisbrod (1967).

[8] Among those from nonfarm families, some of the possible reasons for earnings differences between those who had and those who had not served in the armed forces have been investigated. Whether considering the distributions of father's occupation, father's education, or average parental income, as estimated from Wisconsin tax returns for 1957–1960, none of these provides any clues. All three are remarkably similar for these two groups. However, the relationship between these background variables and earnings may differ by military service. We found some evidence for this in the regression of annual earnings, 1964–1967, on parental income. These regressions show a consistently higher slope in each of these years for the group that had not served in the armed forces.

One standard correlate of earnings does differ by military service. That is marital status. More than one-third of those who did not serve had married before 1960 and about 80% of them by mid-1964. By contrast, but one-sixth of those who served had married by 1960 and 70% by mid-1964.

TABLE 6-5

Average Annual Earnings, 1957–1967, by Military Service, Family Background, and Son's Occupation in 1964: Nonzero Earners among 1575 Males with No Education beyond High School

Year 1	No military service				Had military service[a]				Difference between indicated columns and standard error of the difference			
	Father: nonfarm	Father: farm			Father: nonfarm	Father: farm						
		Son's occupation in 1964				Son's occupation in 1964						
	All 2	All 3	Nonfarm 4	Farm 5	All 6	All 7	Nonfarm 8	Farm 9	(2–3) 10	(6–7) 11	(5–9) 12	(2–6) 13
1957	1486[b] (749)[c]	1063 (656)	1143 (648)	768 (583)	1069 (638)	796 (616)	843 (595)	583 (656)	423[d] (74)	273[d] (48)	186 (155)	417[d] (44)
1958	2672 (1229)	2133 (1314)	2336 (1290)	1402 (1099)	1775 (1078)	1483 (982)	1565 (619)	1069 (947)	539[d] (123)	292[d] (78)	333 (244)	897[d] (73)
1959	3538 (1359)	2780 (1503)	3165 (1380)	1553 (1162)	2286 (1356)	2134 (1300)	2253 (1249)	1562 (1368)	758[d] (132)	152 (98)	−9 (283)	1252[d] (87)
1960	3945 (1573)	3157 (1670)	3769 (1467)	1742 (1162)	2750 (1505)	2580 (1434)	2714 (1422)	1921 (1290)	787[d] (146)	170 (108)	−179 (251)	1195[d] (98)
1961	4120 (1629)	3201 (1635)	3850 (1431)	1925 (1186)	3121 (1524)	2974 (1635)	3174 (1649)	2032 (1155)	919[d] (145)	147 (113)	−107 (229)	999[d] (100)
1962	4725 (1554)	3697 (1852)	4481 (1536)	2212 (1428)	3687 (1782)	3310 (1916)	3545 (1948)	2184 (1204)	1028[d] (147)	377[d] (131)	28 (259)	1038[d] (109)
1963	5211 (1801)	4148 (2055)	5099 (1595)	2182 (1374)	4493 (1894)	4078 (2541)	4424 (2599)	2436 (1282)	1062[d] (169)	415[d] (152)	−253 (263)	717[d] (119)

(Continued)

TABLE 6-5 (Continued)

Year	No military service				Had military service[a]				Difference between indicated columns and standard error of the difference			
1	Father: nonfarm	Father: farm			Father: nonfarm	Father: farm						
		Son's occupation in 1964				Son's occupation in 1964						
	All	All	Nonfarm	Farm	All	All	Nonfarm	Farm	(2–3)	(6–7)	(5–9)	(2–6)
	2	3	4	5	6	7	8	9	10	11	12	13
1964	5616[b] (1890)[c]	4458 (2340)	5474 (1822)	2409 (1858)	5284 (1931)	4796 (1953)	5182 (1782)	2925 (1612)	1158[d] (182)	488[d] (141)	−516 (347)	332[d] (123)
1965	6110 (2172)	5139 (3024)	6235 (3005)	3048 (1599)	5838 (2036)	5462 (2451)	5871 (2332)	3470 (1969)	971[d] (221)	376[d] (157)	−422 (343)	272[d] (134)
1966	6820 (2531)	5516 (2318)	6483 (1760)	3778 (2148)	6468 (2215)	6307 (2436)	6640 (2347)	4763 (2211)	1303[d] (217)	161 (165)	−985[d] (417)	352[d] (149)
1967	7249 (2519)	5960 (2510)	7017 (1908)	4033 (2324)	6932 (2449)	6555 (2452)	6905 (2349)	4897 (2214)	1289[d] (223)	377[d] (178)	−864[d] (437)	317[d] (159)
N[e]	398	201	128	73	705	268	220	48	599	973	121	1103

[a] The earnings figures for those who had military service between high school graduation and 1964 are understated in those years. In-service earnings include basic pay only.
[b] Mean.
[c] Standard deviation.
[d] Significant at the .05 level.
[e] Total number of cases including those with no reported earnings in some year or years.

who did not (Table 6-5, columns 5 and 9, 4 and 8). Thus, in terms of relation both to occupational choice and to earnings regardless of occupation, the apparent effects of military service upon earnings interact with family background.

These differences in earnings history between high school graduates of farm and nonfarm background by military service demonstrate the importance of both factors to the appropriate estimation of earnings foregone by college students and also to the appropriate estimation of at least the early returns to higher education. During the past two decades, the actual choices faced by young men at the point of high school graduation have involved a complex of timing elements with respect to the potential "taxation effects" of military service along with the potential investment costs and benefits of higher education. Nevertheless, of the subgroups dealt with here, the *nonfarm* one with *no military service* comes closest to satisfying the criteria for determining what college students might have earned had they been working full time.[9] In addition, we can compare the 1962–1967 earnings patterns of this same group with the patterns of those who graduated from college in the early 1960s and who had no military service. We can also compare the 1964–1967 patterns of the nonfarm high school graduates who had military service with those of the college graduates who served in the armed forces some time during the 1961–1964 period.

The Relation of Annual Earnings to Ability. The mean Henmon–Nelson percentile rank was 35 for farm youth and 39 for nonfarm youth with no further schooling. This compares with a mean of 51 for the total male sample and of 66 for all of those who went to college (Table 6-3). Within the different educational attainment categories, we have found that Henmon–Nelson test rankings do not vary by military service. The full Henmon–Nelson range is represented in each of the four military services by background subgroups. The distribution for each, however, is positively skewed.

Prior to 1960, the estimated coefficient in the linear regression of annual earnings on Henmon–Nelson percentile rank is not significantly different from zero. In 1960, the estimated coefficient is $72 per Henmon–Nelson decile, and, by 1967, it is more than $100

---

[9] This question is more fully discussed later, page 175.

per decile. In both instances the coefficient is statistically significant at a level better than .02. In every one of the intervening years the coefficient is positive. In all but 1965 the coefficient has a significance level of about .10 or better. However, there is no systematic pattern of increase between 1960 and 1967. Only four of seven year-to-year changes are nonnegative. The estimated coefficients have approximately the same dollar value of just under $90 per decile in 1961, 1963, and 1966 (Table 6-6).

We made another set of estimates for these equations. In the second set, the linearity assumption is relaxed, and dummy regressors are used for each of the three bottom Henmon–Nelson quintiles separately (with the lowest as intercept) and for the top two combined. In the first full year out of high school (1958), earnings of men in the next to lowest Henmon–Nelson quintile are significantly above those of men in the bottom group. In five of the nine years thereafter, the difference between these two groups is significant at the .05 level or better. In the rest, its sign is positive, and its magnitude ranges from around $300 to as much as $600. For the two top groups with Henmon–Nelson percentile rank of 40–59 and 60–99, the pattern is somewhat more variable. For neither of them do earnings exceed those of the second lowest quintile except at the end of the period covered. Only by 1967 do we actually find the suggestion of a systematic increase from the lowest through the highest ability group. From the variability revealed in these estimates, one might speculate that on-the-job training or the successful search for better job placements or both of these factors delay the attainment of relatively high earnings among the more able. Such investment in human capital is certainly consistent with analyses made elsewhere (Becker, 1964; Mincer, 1962). That on-the-job training may be positively related to ability does not seem unreasonable. Therefore, without adjustment for these investment factors, estimates of earnings foregone by college students, especially for those of very high ability, would probably be overstated.

Another suggested interpretation of these estimates is that, for most of the years 1958–1966, they exhibit a reasonably consistent one-step function; namely, earnings tend to be lowest for those in the bottom Henmon–Nelson quintile and tend not to vary in any systematic fashion by ability among those above that level.

All of the estimates just discussed are for the young men of

TABLE 6-6

Regression of Annual Earnings, 1957–1967, on Henmon–Nelson Percentile Rank

Year	Linear regression			Henmon–Nelson percentile rank intervals					N
	Constant	Henmon–Nelson percentile rank	Significance level	00–19	20–39	40–59	60–99	Significance level	
Part 1: Nonzero Earners among 389 Nonfarm Background Males with No Education beyond High School, No Military Service by 1964									
1957	$1535 (69)	$−1.29 (1.50)	.39	$1452 (70)	$189 (107)	$ 17 (110)	$−65 (108)	.14	361
1958	2562 (111)	2.91 (2.41)	.23	2496 (111)	370 (173)	197 (177)	213 (174)	.19	371
1959	3532 (121)	0.16 (2.64)	.95	3375 (121)	548 (188)	102 (193)	60 (190)	.02	377
1960	3676 (139)	7.24 (3.05)	.02	3652 (140)	469 (216)	388 (223)	451 (222)	.09	379
1961	3792 (143)	8.84 (3.14)	.01	3742 (144)	609 (223)	472 (230)	612 (228)	.01	379
1962	4538 (138)	5.04 (3.03)	.10	4516 (139)	333 (214)	323 (222)	280 (221)	.33	379
1963	4882 (158)	8.86 (3.49)	.01	4844 (159)	571 (248)	550 (255)	529 (254)	.05	378
1964	5397 (169)	5.88 (3.69)	.11	5299 (170)	517 (261)	552 (269)	341 (267)	.12	377

(Continued)

TABLE 6-6 (Continued)

| | Linear regression | | | Henmon–Nelson percentile rank intervals | | | | | |
Year	Constant	Henmon–Nelson percentile rank	Significance level	00–19	20–39	40–59	60–99	Significance level	N
1965	6002 (194)	2.89 (4.23)	.50	5893 (195)	400 (301)	410 (311)	156 (306)	.46	380
1966	6484 (224)	8.96 (4.88)	.07	6404 (226)	619 (349)	546 (361)	687 (354)	.16	381
1967	6814 (224)	11.58 (4.86)	.02	6844 (226)	443 (348)	569 (359)	788 (353)	.14	380
N^a				127	91	82	89		

Part 2: Nonzero Earners among 705 Nonfarm Background Males with No Education beyond High School, Who Had Military Service by 1964

1964	$5168 (131)	$2.95 (2.76)	.29	$5274 (137)	$–150 (199)	$ 45 (218)	$160 (200)	.51	684
1965	5683 (139)	3.95 (2.91)	.18	5788 (144)	–134 (210)	178 (232)	205 (211)	.38	679
1966	6409 (151)	1.49 (3.16)	.64	6547 (157)	–265 (229)	–156 (252)	74 (228)	.47	682
1967	6714 (168)	5.50 (3.51)	.12	6890 (175)	–117 (253)	–202 (279)	423 (254)	.10	675
N^a				203	183	136	183		

[a] Total number of cases, including those with no reported earnings in one or more years.

163

nonfarm background who entered civilian employment after leaving high school and did not serve in the armed forces. For the other *nonfarm* group, the one that *had military service,* the linear regression of annual earnings on Henmon–Nelson percentile rank does show a small positive relationship beginning with 1964. However, not even by 1967 is the estimated coefficient more than $55 per decile, nor is it then significant at the .10 level.

Earlier, we noted that military service is associated with relatively low average earnings during the postservice years (1964–1967) in civilian employment. Now we see that military service may have consequences in terms of the relation of earnings to ability during these same years. Results of the estimates for the regression of 1964–1967 annual earnings on Henmon–Nelson quintile groups for the men who had military service reinforces this impression. These estimates again show almost no indication of a positive association between earnings and ability. In fact, only in 1967 does the coefficient for the top Henmon–Nelson group (60–99) seem to be significantly different from the coefficient for any of the lower ones. It is also quite interesting to compare average earnings of the bottom quintile groups across military service. For those of low ability (0–19), there is no difference in any of the years 1964–1967 by military service.

To investigate the relation between earnings and ability for the groups from farm background, we adopted a somewhat different approach—one that seemed more appropriate for them. In all of these equations we introduced a dummy variable to represent those who themselves became farmers, according to the information gathered in 1964. The expected negative coefficient for this regressor is relatively large and significant in every year from 1957 through 1967, both for those who served in the armed forces and for those who did not (Table 6-7). For the group with no military service, this regressor accounts for more than 20% of the earnings variance in every year after 1958, as much as 44% in 1963, and 38% in 1964. The proportion drops to one-fourth in 1965 but is close to one-third in the two following years.

Among farm youth with military service, not only did a smaller proportion become farmers, but also the earnings differences are smaller between those who took up farming and those who did not. For both of these reasons the proportion of variance associated with farming is much less in equations for the group with

TABLE 6-7

Regression of Annual Earnings, 1957–1967, on Henmon–Nelson Percentile Rank with a Dummy Regressor for Farmers

Year	Constant	1964 occupa- tion: farmer	Henmon– Nelson percentile rank	Significance level of Henmon–Nelson percentile rank	N
Part 1: Nonzero Earners among 201 Males of Farm Background with No Education beyond High School, No Military Service by 1964					
1957	$1055 (94)	$ −378 (136)	$3.01 (2.37)	.21	131
1958	2295 (178)	−932 (257)	1.30 (4.23)	.76	143
1959	3141 (176)	−1614 (247)	0.81 (4.28)	.85	163
1960	3676 (178)	−2034 (227)	3.10 (4.26)	.47	179
1961	3747 (168)	−1945 (210)	3.43 (3.89)	.38	190
1962	4368 (185)	−2286 (229)	3.76 (4.26)	.38	194
1963	4943 (189)	−2951 (241)	5.25 (4.39)	.23	187
1964	5329 (228)	−3101 (287)	4.86 (5.31)	.36	190
1965	6035 (324)	−3226 (401)	6.76 (7.56)	.37	192
1966	6235 (238)	−2745 (289)	8.35 (5.50)	.13	193
1967	6725 (255)	−3041 (312)	9.82 (5.90)	.10	192
Part 2: Nonzero Earners among 268 Males of Farm Background with No Education beyond High School, Who Had Military Service by 1964					
1964	$5460 (188)	$−2221 (287)	$ −7.98 (4.18)	.06	263
1965	6353 (243)	−2345 (370)	−13.88 (5.44)	.01	264
1966	7160 (247)	−1798 (372)	−15.03 (5.53)	.01	265
1967	7508 (246)	−1928 (373)	−17.43 (5.53)	.00	264

military service. The highest coefficients of determination for this group are .19 in 1964 and .13 in 1965. Thereafter, they drop to .08 and .09 in the final years. Again for the group that had military service, the rather high average earnings of 1964 farmers invite the speculation that some of them entered more lucrative occupations in 1965 or 1966 (Table 6-5). The regression equations, with their large and increasing negative coefficients for Henmon–Nelson percentile rank, invite the further speculation that other members of this same group of farmers, in particular those of high ability, resumed their education within a year or two after military service (Table 6-7, Part 2). Estimation of separate regression coefficients for those who did and for those who did not become farmers give results consistent with this statement. The coefficients for farmers are −$20 per Henmon–Nelson percentile with a standard error of about $6 in each of the years 1965–1967.

For those with *no military service*, again, as in the case of their nonfarm counterparts, we find no relationship between earnings and the measure of mental ability during the early post-high school period (Table 6-7). The estimated regression coefficients are positive for all years and generally below those for the nonfarm group with no military service. Only in 1966 and 1967 does the relationship approach a statistically significant level.

During the period under consideration, the incidence of military service was greater for young men whose education ended with high school graduation than for those who earned a college degree. While for purposes of estimating potential total earnings of college students, the nonfarm high school graduates with no military service may provide the best possible choice, it must be emphasized that they constitute a little less than one-fourth of the entire group without education beyond high school. It is likely that some of those who chose to go on to college and were qualified and able to do so viewed that choice not only in the context of earnings foregone in civilian labor force employment, but also in terms of the military service alternative. The opportunity costs of a college education, both monetary and nonmonetary, might be assessed quite differently if proper account of a taxation coefficient for military service could be included. This would involve estimation of earnings foregone under a variety of different timing patterns for both military service and advanced education, with appropriate weights to represent the probabilities of military service, given different levels of educational attainment.

For those with a farm background, the elements involved in the post-high school decision were apparently different from those faced by their urban contemporaries. For them, too, the opportunity costs of a college education depend upon how the various alternatives are evaluated. The pressures and incentives under which farm youth make these decisions have included agricultural deferments of military service as well as military service as a potential means for entry into nonagricultural occupations.

In conclusion, although we present the estimated mean earnings figures of nonfarm background males with no education beyond high school as a first approximation from which to measure the earnings foregone by college students, we also suggest that the mechanical application of these figures requires important qualifications.

COLLEGE GRADUATES

There are 398 young men in the group of 1957 Wisconsin high school graduates chosen for intensive analysis of earnings in relation to ability during and immediately after their years in college. The selection criteria were (1) college entrance by the fall of 1958, (2) graduation by 1962, (3) no year out of college between entrance and graduation, and (4) no formal education beyond that for a bachelor's degree. Thus, we have a group that entered college immediately after completing high school, or at latest one year thereafter, attended continuously, and completed their formal education with graduation from college four or five years after they had left high school. These criteria minimize a number of possible ambiguities in the interpretation of annual earnings. They were established only after intensive exploration of college and university attendance patterns. (The first stage of that exploration is represented in Table 6-1.) The group so selected is less than one-fourth of the total who were enrolled in college at any time between 1957 and 1964, less than one-half of those who earned a college degree during that period, and only 80% of those who entered college before 1959, graduated by 1964, and did not undertake graduate study.

The selection process is informative. It illustrates how the members of a cohort of high school graduates who attended college became members of a number of cohorts of college entrants; how

TABLE 6-8

Educational Attainment in 1964 by First Year in College (N = 1862)[a]

Educational attainment	First year in college					All years
	1957	1958	1959	1960–1964	Not ascertained	
No degree:	36	52	70	92	69	50
Attended, not in school in 1964	30	45	62	41	61	39
Attending in 1964	6	7	8	51	8	11
College graduates:	64	48	30	8	31	50
Bachelor's degree	40	35	—[b]	—[b]	25	33
Attended or attending graduate or professional school in 1964	24	13	—[b]	—[b]	6	17
All levels	100	100	100	100	100	100
Percentage	57	15	5	11	12	100

[a] In percentages.

[b] Those who entered college in 1959 and 1960–1964, earned a bachelor's degree, and went to graduate school are not shown separately because, under the agreement with the Social Security Administration, no information was available to us for cells of less than five cases.

a cohort of college entrants divided into those who earned degrees and those who did not; how those who earned degrees, first differentiated by entrance date, were then further differentiated by date of graduation; and, finally, how members of all these groups can be characterized by the continuity or discontinuity in college attendance. Just a part of this picture is summarized in the distributions presented in Table 6-8, in which educational attainment, as of 1964, is related to date of entrance. Both date of entrance and attainment level are in turn positively correlated with ability (Table 6-9).[10] Thus, we hypothesize that timing is one dimension of in-

[10] Using data collected some years ago, Bridgman (1960:182) took age of college entry as a proxy for ability and found earnings after graduation, especially 20 and 30 years thereafter, to be positively related to that measure.

TABLE 6-9

Henmon–Nelson Percentile Rank by Educational Attainment by 1964 and First Year in College (N = 1862)

Educational attainment	First year in college					All years
	1957	1958	1959	1960–1964	Not ascertained	
No degree: All	61[a]	59	58	58	56	59
	(26)[b]	(26)	(27)	(25)	(26)	(26)
Attended, not in school in 1964	60	57	57	55	55	58
	(27)	(26)	(27)	(24)	(26)	(26)
Attending in 1964	70	71	64	60	62	64
	(22)	(23)	(27)	(25)	(26)	(24)
College graduate: All	76	71	62	58	68	74
	(21)	(21)	(26)	(28)	(25)	(22)
Bachelor's degree	74	69	62	57	66	71
	(21)	(22)	(27)	(24)	(25)	(22)
Attended or attending graduate or professional school in 1964	79	78	—[c]	—[c]	77	78
	(20)	(17)	—[c]	—[c]	(25)	(20)
All levels	70	65	59	58	60	66
	(24)	(25)	(27)	(25)	(26)	(25)

[a] Mean.
[b] Standard deviation.
[c] Those who entered college in 1959 and 1960–1964, earned a bachelor's degree, and went to graduate school are not shown separately because under the agreement with the Social Security Administration, no information was available to us for cells of less than five cases.

vestment in higher education whereby ability and the size of that investment are related. To test this hypothesis, however, would require information on the comparative earnings foregone by entrants in each year, by ability, and on the timing and duration of their advanced education. Such a test could only be made with a larger sample and with more detailed information on the timing of military service.

All of the problems outlined above also apply to the analysis of earnings profiles for the 315 men who earned not only a bachelor's

degree but also attended graduate or professional school thereafter. For this group as well, we found differences in dates of entry,
interruptions for military service and/or civilian employment, and
differences in the total number of years spent in school. In addition, 34% of this group were still pursuing advanced degrees in
1964 (the last year for which we have such information). Nevertheless, of these 315, 261 met all the rest of the criteria used in selecting the 398 college graduates who had completed their education
by 1962. We combined these two groups and reestimated the regression equations of annual earnings on ability up to 1961 for all
659 cases. Thus, we were able to find out if results obtained for the
"college only" group could be generalized for all undergraduates
who entered by 1958 and earned degrees by 1962, regardless of
whether or not they went on to graduate school.

Earnings during the Years in College. The college graduate
group of 398 men selected for regression of annual earnings on
Henmon–Nelson percentile rank throughout the entire period has
the following characteristics. Of the group, 15% are from farm
families; 46% served in the armed forces after graduating from college; of this last group, more than half were still in service in 1964;
86% entered college in 1957; 58% graduated in 1961; and nearly
one-third spent five years to earn a degree.

As noted earlier, for the college years, we make the assumption
that reports of no earnings for Social Security purposes represent
true zero earnings, and we include such cases in the analysis (see
Appendix C). However, because of the concentration of cases at
zero, these equations have been estimated with the Limited Dependent Variable, or Probit Regression Program (Tobin, 1958).
The proportion with zero earnings is just over 20% in 1957, 17%
in 1958, and just over 10% in 1959 and 1960. It is down to 8% in
1961 and 5% in 1962.

In the equations for earnings 1957–1961, we included a dummy
regressor to represent farm background and another for late entrance or early graduation. We did investigate other possible categories, such as five versus four years in college. We present only
that equation for each year that seemed most appropriate. For example, farm background no longer shows a significant difference
by 1961, the year by which earnings of most of those still working
on family farms would have been covered by Social Security.

The estimated relationship between earnings and Henmon–Nelson percentile rank is positive, small, and not significantly different from zero in each of the years 1957–1962 (Table 6-10). However, the regression coefficient does increase systematically from one year to the next and also increases in relation to its standard error.[11] It might be argued that this subgroup of early college graduates does not adequately represent the total that also includes the young men who subsequently attended graduate or professional schools. Therefore, as mentioned earlier, we did re-estimate the equations for 1957–1960 for that entire group. The results (not presented) differ little. Once again, all coefficients are small, and all are less than their standard errors. In sum, we find no strong evidence that the earnings of those college students who earn at least a bachelor's degree vary with their measured ability.

Now, to return to the question, "Do earnings foregone vary with ability?" We must compare the relationships for college students with those for full-time labor force participants among high school graduates (Table 6-6). From the linear coefficients for Henmon–Nelson percentile rank, we might infer that earnings foregone are positively related to ability, but only after the first two years. However, the coefficients for Henmon–Nelson quintile groups show little variation in either 1960 or 1961, by ability, for those above the twentieth percentile in Henmon–Nelson test scores. Almost all of the 398 college students are above that level. Therefore, this would seem to be the crucial one for comparison. However, although we find little evidence of a difference in earnings foregone, by ability, for these college students, the key to such a difference may yet be found in the timing of college attendance. With a posi-

---

[11] The estimates obtained from ordinary regression for the relation of earnings to ability differ little from the ones obtained by probit regression (Table 6-10). The coefficients for Henmon–Nelson percentile rank and their standard errors for the indicated years are:

1957	1958	1959	1960	1961	1962
$0.48	$1.02	$0.92	$1.58	$2.03	$7.76
(1.13)	(1.32)	(1.53)	(1.87)	(2.50)	(4.33)

However, somewhat greater differences in estimates do occur in some of the dummy regressors, especially those for farm background, which has a higher negative value when estimated by probit regression.

TABLE 6-10

Regression of Annual Earnings 1957–1962 on Henmon–Nelson Percentile Rank with Dummy Regressors for Farm Background, Entered College in 1958, Graduated in 1961, and Military Service after Graduation: Limited Dependent Variable Program Estimates for 398 Males Who Graduated from College by 1962

Year	Constant	Farm background	Entered in 1958	Graduated in 1961	Military service (1961 graduates)		Henmon–Nelson percentile rank	Significance level of Henmon–Nelson percentile rank	Number of zero earners
					Served before 1964	Still serving in 1964			
1957	$ 551 (116)	$−523 (101)	$298 (83)	—	—	—	$ .47 (1.43)	.74	69
1958	543 (131)	−389 (115)	341 (98)	—	—	—	1.00 (1.65)	.55	68
1959	1014 (157)	−350 (116)	—	$−241 (77)	—	—	1.13 (1.81)	.53	48
1960	1089 (130)	−412 (99)	—	−353 (66)	—	—	1.50 (1.53)	.33	45
1961	904 (235)	—	—	657 (121)	—	—	2.57 (2.80)	.36	31
1962	2055 (396)	—	—	1708 (243)	$−1635 (324)	$−1842 (325)	8.64 (4.69)	.06	20

tive relation between ability and early attendance, earnings foregone may in turn be inversely related to ability.

Earnings after Graduation from College. To estimate the regression of annual earnings on Henmon–Nelson percentile rank
for the postcollege years, we revert to ordinary regression. We assume that the zero-earnings reports for these years are mostly, if
not entirely, for persons in uncovered employment, just as we did
for those who entered the labor force immediately after high
school. (See pp. 150–152 and Appendix C.) Therefore, we exclude
the cases with reported zero earnings (in this instance, they number between 20 and 30).

In these equations, we introduce dummy regressors to capture
the effects of military service for the postcollege years, 1963–1967.
For college graduates, as for those with no education beyond high
school, we cannot measure exactly the size of earnings foregone
attributable to military service (*1*) because our measure of service-
covered earnings is limited to basic pay and (2) because we cannot identify the individuals who were in the service in a particular
year. But we can draw some inferences about how having served
in the armed forces is related to earnings during early civilian labor
force participation. For young men with no education beyond high
school who did not come from farms, it will be remembered that
the postservice earnings of those who had been in the armed
forces remained about 5% below the 1964–1967 earnings of those
with no military service (Table 6-5 and pp. 156–157). On the contrary, for college graduates we find little indication that *having*
served in the armed forces depresses earnings thereafter (Table
6-13). Perhaps college certification protects these young men from
the kind of earnings loss experienced by the ones with no education beyond high school. Likewise, for the college graduates who
served in the armed forces and entered civilian employment by
1964, the positive relation of earnings to ability does not appear to
have been depressed as it appeared to be in the case of those with
less education (see Table 6-6 and pp. 161–164). We estimated equations to test both of these hypotheses for the college graduates. We
then reestimated the equations for the years 1963–1967 with the
results presented in Table 6-11.

The coefficients for Henmon–Nelson percentile rank for those
in civilian employment during this brief period suggest an increas-

TABLE 6-11

Regression of Annual Earnings, 1963–1967, on Henmon–Nelson Percentile Rank with Dummy Regressors for Military Service by 1964: Nonzero Earners Each Year among 398 Who Graduated from College by 1962

Year	Constant	Military service		Henmon–Nelson percentile rank[a]	Significance level of Henmon–Nelson percentile rank	N
		Served before 1964	Still serving in 1964			
1963	$4601 (445)	$—305 (485)	$—1819 (482)	$13.21 (5.79)	.02	378
1964	4808 (441)	—	—10ᴀ0 (493)	16.68 (5.80)	.00	379
1965	5907 (480)	—	—621 (537)	11.49 (6.32)	.07	368
1966	7485 (629)	—	—1306 (704)	3.27 (8.26)	.69	370
1967	7176 (658)	—	316 (739)	17.82 (8.68)	.04	369

[a] The coefficient for each year is estimated for those cases not in the armed forces in that year.

ingly positive relationship. All but one of the point estimates for the period 1962–1967 are above those for the earlier years. However, the systematic increase is interrupted with a decline in the years 1964–1966 that is followed by an increase to $17.82 per Henmon–Nelson percentile in 1967. We can merely speculate about reasons for the two low regression coefficients for 1965 and 1966. First, some college graduates of exceptional ability may have resumed their studies in the fall of 1965. Second, others who had not served in the armed forces may have gone into service when this country became deeply involved in the war in Southeast Asia.

Previously, we examined characteristics of earnings foregone by college students by comparing the set of regression estimates for their 1957–1962 annual earnings with a set of estimates for a group whose formal education ended with high school. Now, returning to the initial focus of this investigation, we make similar comparisons for the later years. For all of the postcollege years except 1966, point estimates of the earnings ability relationship for college graduates are above those for the high school group with continuous civilian labor force participation (Tables 6-6 and 6-7). By 1967, there is an earnings difference of $180 per Henmon–Nelson decile for college graduates, and that is approximately 55% above the estimated $116 (Table 6-6) for high school graduates of nonfarm background and no military service. This comparison of the relation between earnings and ability at two levels of educational attainment is consistent with the results of other research done at other times in other places with samples from different populations and even differences in measurement and model specification. In addition, unlike Wolfle and Smith (1956), Husen (1969), or Rogers (1969), we do not yet have earnings data for the peak earnings period of members of our sample. By 1967 their modal age was 28.

Average Earnings before and after College Graduation. In order to get meaningful figures for average earnings we have sorted the college group, first by dates of attendance and then by military service. For the college years only, we present an additional set of figures for the students with a nonfarm background.

To estimate earnings foregone, Becker (1964:75) has suggested that the earnings of college freshmen be compared with those of high school graduates in full-time employment, that earnings of sophomores be compared with those of persons who had spent one year in college, and so on. Neither the data available to him nor those we have for the 1957 Wisconsin sample are amenable to such comparisons. Perhaps viewing the total four- to five-year capital investment for graduation from college reveals certain merits of the comparison that is possible, namely, the comparison between in-college earnings with earnings of age-equivalent high school graduates. Results of a recent study add weight to this position. The study shows that year-round employment among college students tends to be higher among those who fail to graduate than among those who earn a degree. It indicates that the opportunity costs differ between these two groups (Astin, 1972:37).

All of these considerations lend support to Becker's simpler assumption that the earnings of undergraduates who do finish college approximate one-fourth of what they might have earned from year-round employment (Becker, 1964:169–170). It is interesting to see how some of the figures in Table 6-12, especially mean earn-

TABLE 6-12

Annual Earnings, 1957–1962, of 398 College Students by Dates of College Attendance

| | Dates of college attendance | | | | | |
| | 1957–1961 | | 1957–1962 | | 1958–1962 | |
Year	All	Nonfarm	All	Nonfarm	All	Nonfarm
Part 1: All Students and Those from Nonfarm Background						
1957	558[a] (453)[b]	617 (451)	623 (529)	669 (531)	821 (543)	892 (529)
1958	611 (498)	654 (496)	683 (625)	733 (631)	928 (610)	915 (554)
1959	859 (576)	891 (565)	1079 (762)	1145 (757)	1080 (664)	1107 (576)
1960	854 (730)	893 (746)	1154 (924)	1213 (939)	1223 (746)	1310 (725)
1961	1769 (1117)	1768 (1123)	1153 (939)	1193 (958)	1253 (941)	1271 (993)
N[c]	226	193	115	104	52	40

(Continued)

TABLE 6-12 (*Continued*)

| | Dates of college attendance | | | | | |
| | 1957–1961 | | 1957–1962 | | 1958–1962 | |
Year	Did not serve in the Armed Forces	Served in the Armed Forces	Did not serve in the Armed Forces	Served in the Armed Forces	Did not serve in the Armed Forces	Served in the Armed Forces
Part 2: Military Service after Graduation						
1962	$4467 (2133)	$2661 (1358)	$3192 (2003)	$2087 (1445)	$3082 (1591)	$2616 (1522)
N ^{c}	123	103	65	50	23	29

[a] Mean.
[b] Standard deviation.
[c] Does not include five cases with attendance dates 1958–1961.

ings of the nonfarm group that graduated in 1961, conform with this assumption when compared with mean earnings of high school graduates of similar background (Table 6-5, column 2). It is equally interesting to speculate about deviations from the "one-fourth rule" in the earnings of others who earn a bachelor's degree, not only the two other groups represented here in Table 6-12 but later entrants as well.

In Table 6-13 we observe that the average earnings of 1961–1962 college graduates, most of whom probably had continuous civilian labor force participation, rise rapidly through 1967. By 1963, the graduates earn more than those who did not go to college (Table 6-5), and the gap between these earnings series increases each year thereafter.

TABLE 6-13

Annual Earnings of College Graduates, 1963–1967, by Military Service (Non-zero Earners Only)

Year	Military service					
	Did not serve	N	Served be-fore 1964	N	Still serving in 1964	N
1963	$5576[a] (1945)[b]	199	$4296 (2027)	86	$2783 (1070)	93
1964	6208 (2151)	197	5617 (2655)	88	3768 (1404)	94
1965	6890 (2484)	194	6409 (2536)	85	5286 (1353)	89
1966	7780 (3090)	196	7595 (3395)	84	6179 (2236)	90
1967	8486 (3418)	196	8438 (3352)	85	7492 (2222)	88

[a] Mean.
[b] Standard deviation.

Summary and Conclusions

The relation of earnings to ability at different levels of educational attainment is important for an understanding of investment in human resources and in assessing the returns to such investment. Although that relation has provided the focus for this chapter, two other elements in the contemporary United States scene have played so large a role in the opportunity structure and decision process that they have been incorporated into the analysis scheme. To ignore the interrelationships between both farm background and military service with ability and educational attainment would invite serious misspecification.

The principal and tentative findings of this research can be summarized under two headings: (1) the relation of earnings foregone to the ability of college students (late graduates and nongraduates excepted) and (2) postcollege earnings and the interaction of education with ability. The findings are all based upon information about young men belonging to a cohort sample of 1957 Wisconsin high school graduates.

1. The relation of earnings foregone to ability. We have found little evidence that earnings foregone, the major component of private investment in higher education, are related to ability. That tentative conclusion is qualified (1) by the fact that it could be affected by incomplete earnings coverage for college students and (2) by the evidence we have presented on the relation between ability and the timing of higher education for the entire group that went to college (all late attenders included).

2. Postcollege earnings and the interaction of education with ability. Our analysis supports the hypothesis that the relationship between earnings and ability has a steeper slope for college graduates than for those whose education ends with high school. However, although the Henmon–Nelson measure of ability ranks high among the correlates of educational attainment, neither within nor across the attainment levels beyond high school does this ability measure account for any substantial proportion of the total variance in annual earnings. The reason for not presenting figures for that proportion here is that neither for high school nor for college graduates does it reach 5% in any of the years for which we have data.

Of equal or perhaps greater importance are the questions raised with respect to the interrelationships among military service, farm background, educational attainment, and both the level of earnings and the ways in which earnings vary with ability. Both military service and farm background are inversely related to educational attainment. The relationship of earnings during military service to postservice earnings varies both by background and by educational attainment. Nearly two-thirds of the men with no education beyond high school had military service. One-half of the early college graduates went into the armed forces thereafter. Graduate study is associated with the very lowest incidence of military service. Thus, the choices before these young men cannot be evaluated solely in terms of immediate post-high school participation in the civilian labor force versus additional investment in human capital.

7

Summary and Conclusions[1]

Our research has been stimulated by the pioneering work of Peter M. Blau and Otis Dudley Duncan (1967) and by subsequent elaborations of it (Duncan, Featherman, and Duncan, 1972). By virtue of that research, the basic features of processes linking the socioeconomic achievements of fathers and sons in the United States and the role of formal schooling in those processes are now widely understood within the academic community and, to a lesser degree, among the public (Jencks et al., 1972). Within the framework of concepts, measures, and methods introduced by these studies, we have tried to exploit a territorially and temporally limited set of longitudinal data to enrich the social and psychological detail of our understanding of processes of achievement in the United States.

In the present volume we have traced the educational, occupational, and earning histories of a large sample of young men who graduated from Wisconsin high schools in 1957 through their first 10 years of post-secondary schooling, military service, and labor force experience. In carrying out our longitudinal analysis we have benefited from the advantages of a response rate which assures

[1] This chapter was prepared by William H. Sewell and Robert M. Hauser.

that our data are highly representative of the population from which our sample was drawn and, also, of the high quality of our data on the economic circumstances of our respondents at the time they left high school and in the years that followed. Further, because our data include measures of academic ability and performance in high school and of educational and occupational aspirations, we have been able to obtain new insights into the social psychological processes linking socioeconomic background, educational attainment, and occupational and financial achievement.

Background and Ability

We began our analysis by looking at various components of a four-equation structural model that links socioeconomic background and ability with educational, occupational, and financial achievement. The model postulates that socioeconomic background (father's and mother's educational attainment, father's occupational status, and parents' income) affects a son's measured mental ability; that background and ability affect the level of postsecondary schooling he completes; that background, ability, and schooling affect the socioeconomic status of the son's occupation; and that all of the foregoing variables affect the son's earnings. Although our sample represents a somewhat larger and more heterogeneous population, we thought it appropriate to estimate and interpret the parameters of this model for young men who were of nonfarm background, and who were in the labor force but not in school or in military service in 1964. While it is not possible to estimate all of the parameters of this basic model in any cross-section sample of men in the United States, we were able to estimate modified versions of each equation of the model in one or more national samples. Comparisons between parameter estimates in the national samples and in our own sample suggested that processes of achievement were similar in our sample and among young men in the United States.

Our analysis of our basic model of socioeconomic achievement left us impressed with the complexity of the achievement process, with the large role played in that process by factors which vary randomly with respect to socioeconomic origins, and with the persistence over the early career of certain effects of socioeconomic background. These points may appear mutually contradictory, so they require some elaboration.

The complexity of the process of socioeconomic achievement is reflected in the differentially persistent effects of parents' educational attainment, occupational status, and income on corresponding achievements of sons. All four components of socioeconomic background affect measured ability and post-secondary schooling. Net of measured ability, a year of father's or mother's education, $1000 in parents' average income, or 10 points of father's occupational status are each worth .04 to .08 years of son's schooling beyond high school. At the same time, even when socioeconomic background is well specified, a 10-point difference in measured mental ability is worth about .4 years of schooling, and less than one-fifth of the association between ability and schooling can be attributed to the mutual dependence of these variables on socioeconomic background.

When we look at son's occupational status, there is a small effect of father's occupational status, even after the effects of ability and schooling have been taken into account, such that a 10-point shift in father's occupational status is worth about .6 points of son's occupational status. However, except for their effects via ability and schooling, none of the other three measures of socioeconomic background affects occupational status. As in the case of schooling, there are substantial effects of measured ability on occupational status, both directly and by way of schooling, and there is a very large effect of educational attainment on occupational status even after controlling socioeconomic background and ability.

When we control ability, schooling, and occupational status, a dollar of parents' annual income (averaged over the years 1957–1960) is still worth more than 13 cents in son's earnings 8 to 10 years after high school graduation, but the effects on son's earnings of parents' education and father's occupational status are entirely indirect. Finally, each of the mediating variables: ability, schooling, and occupational status, enters the final equation for earnings, so none of their effects is wholly spurious.

In our view these results imply that it is fundamentally inaccurate to view the inheritance of socioeconomic position across generations in terms of the persistence of rankings on some global dimension of socioeconomic background or of social class. Rather, the persistence of social position across generations ought to be

treated separately for each of the several dimensions of social inequality, and references to global constructs of social inequality
ought to be recognized as having only summary or heuristic value.
Moreover, our finding of the distinct mediating and direct effects
of ability, schooling, and occupational status adds to the prepon-
derance of evidence that factors of achievement as well as of social background enter importantly in the processes by which social
goods are distributed in the United States. However sophisticated
our notions about social origins, it is not possible to give an accounting of the distribution of education, occupation, and income
in the United States that excludes individual achievement and
ability.

If almost all of the measured variables in our model figure directly or indirectly in the determination of educational attainment,
occupational status, and earnings, it is also true that the largest
component of the variation in each of our achievement measures
is entirely independent of its measured causes. Thus, our basic
model accounts for no more than 9% of the variance in measured
ability, 28% of the variance in educational attainment, 41% of the
variance in occupational status, and 8% of the variance in average
earnings in the period 1965–1967. If we restrict our model to a
simple accounting of the inheritance of status positions across generations, we explain no more than 16% of the variance in educational attainment, 12% of the variance in occupational status, and
4% of the variance in earnings. This modest degree of determi-
nacy in our model should not be counted as a defect in any sense.
Rather, it reflects the fundamental importance of factors other than
socioeconomic background, ability, and schooling in the allocation
of social positions and attendant rewards.

We are arguing that our model is basic not only because it is
relatively uncomplicated, but because it exhausts the influence of
fundamental conditions of ascription and achievement (at least
within the population treated herein). Consequently, factors of
luck or chance are implicated in the process of achievement to the
extent of indeterminacy in the outcomes of our basic model. These
observations are not contradicted by our later efforts to add explanatory variables to the basic model, even though those efforts
add substantially to the explained variance in education. On the
contrary, it is only because our new explanatory variables are
largely independent of factors of socioeconomic background and

ability that they add to the proportions of variance explained. By elaborating our model, we are able to specify what we mean by luck or chance, but this in no way lessens the role of luck or chance relative to the circumstances of an individual's upbringing.

Finally, though the process of achievement is factorially complex and is subject to important components of luck or chance, these facts in no way contradict our finding that there are important effects of socioeconomic origins on achievements in school and in the labor market, and these effects are not fully compatible with expressed national goals of equal opportunity. We have already noted the extent to which socioeconomic background affects educational attainment, occupational status, and earnings, even when we control academic ability and intervening achievements. Moreover, we find that socioeconomic background accounts for significant components of the association of measured ability, schooling, and occupational status with each subsequent variable. For example, our findings suggest the naiveté of efforts to measure the economic returns to education without controlling socioeconomic background and ability. Finally, except in the case of earnings (which are only affected by parents' income), every measure of socioeconomic background affects each measure of son's achievement. The fact that influences of socioeconomic background on educational attainment, occupational status, or earnings are partly mediated by measured ability or intervening achievements scarcely lessens their role in restricting opportunity.

Social Psychological Factors

In order to explain more fully the ways in which socioeconomic origins affect post-high school achievements, we elaborated our basic model by adding three sets of social psychological intervening variables: high school rank, perceived expectations of significant others, and educational and occupational aspirations. We believe these variables intervene in the order indicated and help to mediate the effects of socioeconomic origins and academic ability on educational attainment, occupational status, and earnings. In this regard, our expectations proved to have a stronger basis in fact in respect to educational attainment than in relation to occupational status or earnings.

The social psychological variables increased substantially the explained variance in schooling; with these variables added to our basic model, we are able to account for 54% of the variance in post-secondary education. Further, because they also depend to a moderate degree on socioeconomic background and ability, the social psychological variables account for a substantial share of the effects of background and ability on schooling. The intervening social psychological variables account for 60% to 80% of the effects of the background variables on schooling and about 85% of the effect of ability on schooling.

The social psychological variables are of less direct importance in the equations for occupational status and earnings; with them added to our basic model, we are able to explain 42.6% of the variance in occupational status in 1964 and 7.6% of the variance in 1967 earnings. Only high school rank and occupational aspiration have statistically significant effects in the final equation for occupational status, and only occupational status has a significant coefficient in the final equation for 1967 earnings. We draw three lessons from these seemingly unimpressive results. First, as before, the differential importance of our explanatory variables in the equations for educational attainment, occupational status, and earnings leaves us impressed with the factorial complexity of the achievement process. Second, our results, to the extent they are negative, may also reflect the specific reference of four of the social psychological measures to educational attainment rather than to the more strictly economic dimensions of achievement. In this respect, it is instructive that occupational aspiration appears in the equations for both occupational status and earnings. Thus, rather than implying the irrelevance of youthful aspirations for achievements beyond schooling, we believe it would be desirable to ascertain economic as well as educational aspirations and expectations, and to learn more about the youth's perception of the extent of encouragement that significant others provide for occupational and economic as well as educational aspirations. Third, the fact that the social psychological variables do not all appear in the final equations for occupational status and earnings does not lessen their importance, already implicit in the discussion above, in mediating effects of background and ability on later achievements by way of schooling.

College Effects

We have also examined the effects of the colleges attended on earnings in the early years after graduation. Only about one-twentieth of the variance in earnings of men with college experience occurs among the dozen categories of colleges and universities treated in our analysis. This is about the same as the percentage of variance in occupational status that occurs among colleges, but less than that in educational attainment. Since the variance in earnings among persons is quite large, so in some cases are the differences in earnings among men who attended different colleges. For example, in 1967, mean earnings were about $8000, and a gap of more than $3500 separated the average earnings of men in the most and least remunerative types of colleges.

If college environments have distinct effects on the process of socioeconomic achievement, these might be partly manifested in changing relationships among background variables and achievements across the college categories. However, in a large number of tests, we found no statistical interaction between colleges and prior variables. Thus, among college-goers the process of socio-economic achievement appears to work in essentially the same way, no matter what college or university a young man attends.

Slightly more than half of the variance in earnings among colleges in our sample was explained by the fact that colleges select or recruit men with varying prospects for earnings. After controlling relevant input variables, only about one-fortieth of the variance in earnings occurred among college categories, and the difference between the highest- and lowest-earning college categories was reduced by more than $1000. Still, there remained differences in earnings among the college categories which were unrelated to the social origins, ability, or high school experiences of the students who attended them.

In the sample of men who attended college, relatively few of the variables in our model of achievement affected earnings. Most of our measures were not designed to tap propensities to earn; some variables probably exhausted their effects in the process of selecting college attenders; and men in the sample were not well along in their earning careers. As in the more inclusive sample, we found a substantial effect of family economic status on 1967 earnings, $125 for each $1000 of father's average income in the period 1957–1960. None of the other measures of socioeconomic background affected earnings. Less than 10% of the effect of father's income on son's earnings could be attributed to the different colleges attended by sons of rich and poor families. Thus, the old school tie is not the connecting link between father's income and son's earnings.

Even among college-going men, high school academic performance had a large effect on 1967 earnings, about $500 for each change of a standard deviation (15 points in the total population of high school graduates). About one-fourth of this effect could be attributed to the different colleges attended by men with high and low grades. Each 10 points on the Duncan SEI scale of occupational aspiration in 1957 was worth about $250 in 1967 earnings, but only one-sixth of this was explained by attendance at different colleges. In all, while colleges do have modest independent effects on earnings in the early career, they do not seem to account for the effects of background or high school experiences on earnings.

Colleges differ in the likelihood their matriculants will graduate and also in the jobs their graduates obtain. The influence of colleges on years of schooling and on occupational status is about as large as on earnings, but it does not begin to account for the effects of colleges on earnings. Indeed, the effects of colleges on years of schooling, occupational status, and earnings in the early career are not highly correlated across the college categories, and there is even a slight inverse relationship between the effects of colleges on years of schooling and on earnings. This lack of consistency in the effects of colleges on education, occupation, and earnings suggests that no single dimension of institutional quality defines the effectiveness of institutions of higher education.

Ability–Schooling Interactions

The relation of earnings to ability, at different levels of educational attainment, is important for an understanding of investment in human resources and for assessing the returns to such investment. Further, two other elements in the contemporary American scene have played so large a role in the opportunity structure and decision process that they have been incorporated into the analysis scheme. To ignore the interrelationships between either farm background or military service and either ability or educational attainment would invite serious misspecification. The principal and tentative findings of this part of our research can be summarized under two headings: (1) the relation of earnings foregone to the ability of college students (late graduates and nongraduates excepted) and (2) postcollege earnings and the interaction of education with ability.

We have found little evidence that earnings foregone, the major component of private investment in higher education, is related to ability. That tentative conclusion is qualified (1) by the fact that it could be affected by incomplete earnings coverage for college students and (2) by the evidence we have presented on the relation between ability and the timing of higher education for the entire group that went to college (all late attenders included).

Our analysis supports the hypothesis that the relationship between earnings and ability has a steeper slope for college graduates than for those whose education ends with high school. However, although the Henmon–Nelson measure of ability ranks high among the correlates of educational attainment, neither within nor across the attainment levels beyond high school does this ability measure account for any substantial proportion of the total variance in annual earnings.

Of equal or perhaps greater importance are the questions raised with respect to the interrelationships among military service, farm background, educational attainment, and both the level of earnings and the ways in which earnings vary with ability. Both military service and farm background are inversely related to educational attainment. The relationship of military to postservice earnings varies both by background and by educational attainment. Nearly two-thirds of the men with no education beyond high school had military service. One-half of the early college graduates went into the armed forces thereafter. Graduate study is associated with the very lowest incidence of military service. Thus, the choices before these young men cannot be evaluated solely in terms of immediate post-high school participation in the civilian labor force versus additional investment in human capital.

Implications for Further Research

We believe that the work we have reported in this volume makes a solid contribution to the measurement and understanding of socioeconomic achievement in American society. Although our results are based on data from only one state and on a single co-hort of high school seniors, we believe that the pattern of the achievement process that we have elaborated can be generalized to other areas, and probably to the nation as a whole. We say this not because we believe that Wisconsin is particularly representative of the United States—although it is not atypical in its population and economic and social structure—but because we believe that the process of socioeconomic achievement is not greatly different in its major details in the various states and regions of the country. We are struck by the extent of convergence between our findings and those from national samples, in every instance in which it has been possible to make close comparisons. In our future research we expect to continue to describe and analyze the socioeconomic life history of our cohort and to increase the complementarity of our findings with those from national samples.

Although we are greatly impressed by the extent to which our models account for educational and occupational attainments, and by the extent to which we are able to elaborate the social processes leading to these attainments, we are also impressed by the lack of effectiveness of our models in explaining earnings. We interpret this less as a reflection of any defect in our models than as an indication of the complexity of social achievement in American society. Further, we believe that their weaker showing for earnings is in part due to the fact that all our information on earnings applies to an early period in the careers of the young men in our sample. At one extreme, those whose educational careers ended with high school graduation could have been in full-time employment for at most 10 years—and many of these young men had significant interruptions in their working careers, mainly because of military service. At the other extreme, those who pursued professional studies, such as medicine, dentistry, or law, and those who entered graduate schools for advanced training in the sciences, humanities, or education, either were still in training or were at a low point in their earnings careers even by 1967, the latest year for which we have earnings information. Consequently, we believe that our present models will be more effective in explaining earnings in later years.

Another weakness of our current models for the explication of earnings achievements is that most of the variables in the models refer to experiences during high school or in the years immediately following high school graduation. These experiences are powerful factors in explaining educational achievement and early occupational status but become much less important, with the passage of time, for the explanation of later achievements. Even our information on occupational achievement is based on reports obtained in 1964. We would like to have information about jobs and other factors which are more pertinent and proximate to current earnings.

During the next few years we plan to obtain such information. We intend, with the cooperation of the Social Security Administration, to continue obtaining data on the earnings of the young men in our sample. In addition, we plan in the near future to conduct a survey to obtain information about more recent experiences in such areas as family formation, marital stability, migration, graduate and adult education, on-the-job training, and occupation. Following leads from the present analyses, we shall obtain further data on the timing of schooling, military service, marriage, and family formation. We shall seek a few items of basic background information that were not available from the earlier surveys—especially on race, ethnic identification, religion, and the size and structure of the family of orientation. We shall attempt to measure the implications of social psychological variables such as job satisfaction and aspirations for the future; this, when taken in conjunction with our earlier measurements, should shed further light on the role of motivations in socioeconomic achievement. Following the example of Duncan, Featherman, and Duncan (1972) and of Jencks *et al.* (1972), we shall ascertain selected items of socioeconomic data about our respondents' siblings; these can be used to estimate the total effects of family origins and not merely their socioeconomic components. We plan to include females as well as males in the new round of data collection and analysis. In so doing, we expect to come up with important evidence and interpretations of inequality of opportunity between the sexes as well as among persons of differing socioeconomic origins. Finally, the new field operations are intended to use concepts and measurement procedures that will be strictly comparable to those of the 1962 and 1973 national surveys of occupational and educational mobility in the United States (Blau and Duncan, 1967; Featherman and Hauser, 1974). We expect that the analysis of both state and national data will be complemented by the virtues of social psychological detail and of national representation within a common conceptual and procedural framework.

We shall not attempt here to detail the course of our future analyses of occupational status and earnings. Perhaps it is sufficient to say that, with data resources like those outlined above, we shall be able to continue the socioeconomic life history of our cohort, and, more important, to evaluate and extend our present understanding of the processes of socioeconomic achievement in American society.

Appendix A

1957 Questionnaire

MY PLANS BEYOND HIGH SCHOOL

Name _____ Age _____ M _____
                                                                                                F _____

School _____ Home address _____

_____ Father's name _____
                                                                        (or other parent or guardian)

1. I plan: (Place a cross (x) before the statement which describes what you plan to do next year)

   _____ To continue going to school   _____ To go into military service
   _____ To get a job   _____ To work at my home
   _____ To become an apprentice   _____ I have no definite plans
   _____ (Other, specify) _____

       If the plan you have checked is not what you would really like to do, place an (L) in front of the statement above which described what you would most like to do, then state what circumstances prevent you from doing what you would most like to do. _____

       How sure are you that you will be doing what you plan? _____ certain   _____ uncertain

2. If you checked that you plan to go to school next year, what kind of school do you plan to attend?

   Public   Private
   _____ Vocational school   _____ Liberal arts college
   _____ County teachers college   _____ University
   _____ State college   _____ Business or trade school
   _____ University   _____ Other _____
                                                              (Specify)

   Do you plan to attend school outside Wisconsin? _____ yes   _____ no

   I plan to attend school _____ full-time   _____ part-time

3. If you plan to continue your schooling or training, answer the items below. If not, go to question 4.

   I plan to enter the following courses or fields:

   In trade or vocational school _____
                                                  Specify field or training

   Apprenticeship _____
                              Specify field or trade

   College or university: (check the field of your interest)

   _____ Agriculture   _____ Engineering   _____ Liberal Arts
   _____ Architecture   _____ Fine Arts   _____ Medicine
   _____ Aeronautics   _____ Forestry   _____ Nursing
   _____ Business   _____ Home Economics   _____ Pharmacy
   _____ Chemistry   _____ Journalism   _____ Social Work
   _____ Dentistry   _____ Law   _____ Teaching
   _____ Undecided   _____ _____   _____ Veterinary
                                          (Other)

4. If you plan to get a job next year, check the statement below which applies to you.

   _____ I have applied, but do not yet have a job
   _____ I have applied and have been accepted
   _____ I have not applied
   _____ I will continue in a job I now have
   _____ Other _____

   My job will be: (describe) _____

       (Name of firm) _____

   It will pay about _____ per week

5. To what extent have you discussed your plans with your teachers or school counselors?

   _____ not at all   _____ some   _____ very much

   How much did they influence your plans?

   _____ not at all   _____ some   _____ very much

Do not write in this col.
1-6 _____
7-8 _____
9-10 _____
11 _____
12 _____
13 _____
14 _____
15 _____
16 _____
17 _____
18 _____
19 _____
20-21 _____
22-23 _____
24 _____
25 _____

194

6. To what extent have you discussed your plans with your parents?
   _____ not at all   _____ some   _____ very much

   How much did they influence your plans?
   _____ not at all   _____ some   _____ very much

7. Education of father and mother (check highest level attained)

High School	Father	Mother
did not attend	_____	_____
attended	_____	_____
graduated from	_____	_____
Trade or business school:		
attended	_____	_____
College:		
attended	_____	_____
graduated from	_____	_____
has master's or Ph.D. degree	_____	_____
Do not know	_____	_____

8. Education of older brother and sister who have had most schooling. (Check the highest level reached; if more than one, show number at each level.)

	Brother	Sister
Some high school	_____	_____
High school graduate	_____	_____
Some college	_____	_____
Attending college	_____	_____
College graduate	_____	_____
Attending graduate school (or attended)	_____	_____
None older	_____	_____

9. (a) My father is engaged in the type of occupation checked in the left hand column below.

   (b) I hope eventually to enter the type of occupation checked in the right hand column below.

   Father   Me

   _____ Office work (cashier, clerk, secretary, bookkeeper, etc.)   _____
   _____ Professional (doctor, lawyer, minister, teacher, etc.)   _____
   _____ Executive (manages large business, industry, firm)   _____
   _____ Factory worker (laborer, janitor, farm hand, etc.)   _____
   _____ Salesman (insurance, real estate, auto, store, etc.)   _____
   _____ Owns, rents, manages small business (store, station, newspaper, cafe, etc.)   _____
   _____ Owns, rents, manages farm   _____
   _____ Other occupation (be specific) _____   _____

   (c) If your mother has a job outside the home, place an (M) before the type of occupation in which she works.

10. How much do you think it costs per school year to attend college away from home?
   _____ Less than $1000   _____ Between $1500 and $2000
   _____ Between $1000 and $1500   _____ More than $2000

11. How do you estimate the ability of your parents to help you go to college, if you desire to go?
   _____ can easily afford it   _____ cannot afford it
   _____ can afford it, but with much sacrifice   _____ I must work to help support the family

12. In terms of income or wealth of families in my community, I think my family is:
   _____ considerably above average   _____ average
   _____ somewhat above average   _____ somewhat below average
                                            _____ considerably below average

13. (a) Have you ever considered attending college?   _____ yes   _____ no
    (b) If no, would you consider it if you had the money   _____ yes   _____ no
    (c) Would you borrow money for college expenses if you
        could pay it back on the installment plan after
        leaving college   _____ yes   _____ no
    (d) About how much could you or your family contribute to your college expenses next year (if you were going)?
        _____ none   _____ less than $500   _____ Between $500 and $1000
        _____ between $1000 and $1500   _____ all my expenses

26 _____
27 _____
28 _____
29 _____
30 _____
31 _____
32 _____
33 _____
34 _____
35 _____
36 _____
37 _____
38 _____
39 _____

195

14. Did you apply for admission to a school or college? (Check the statements which apply to you)

_____ I have not applied   _____ I have applied, but have not heard
_____ I have not applied, but plan to   _____ I plan to apply
I have applied but was refused because: _____ I have been tentatively admitted, and expect to
     _____ I did not rank high enough   attend:
     _____ I did not take the right subjects
     _____ The school could not take more students

_____   _____ |40_____
          (Name of School(s))   (Name of School)

I sent applications to _____ schools |41_____
               (number)

15. Did you take the National Merit Scholarship Examinations?   _____ yes   _____ no |42_____

16. Did you take the College Entrance Board Examinations: _____ yes   _____ no

         _____ Scholastic Aptitude Test

         _____ Subject matter in (fields) _____ |43_____

17. Have you applied for a scholarship?

_____ I did not apply
_____ I have applied, but have not yet heard
_____ I have applied, but was not successful
I have received a scholarship from:

     _____ a college _____
                             (Name)

     _____ company or corporation _____
                                     (Name)

     _____ organization or society _____
                                 (Name)

     _____ other _____ |44_____

18. The scholarship or awards I have will pay the following part of my college expenses next year:

     _____ tuition, one semester   _____ tuition, plus $ _____

     _____ tuition, both semesters   _____ $ _____
                                         (cash)

                               _____ all expenses |45_____

19. If you are going to school next year what part of your school or college expenses do you expect to provide from summer earnings or part-time work at school?

     _____ Less than $250   _____ Between $500 and $750

     _____ Between $250 and $500   _____ More than $750 |46_____

20. Has marriage or the early prospect of marriage influenced your plan for next year? _____ yes _____ no |47_____

21. Place a circle around the number of semesters in which you studied the following subjects?

Algebra	0 1 2 3 4	English	0 2 4 6 8	48-53_____
Geometry	0 1 2 3 4	History	0 2 4 6 8	
Trigonometry	0 1 2 3 4	Social Studies	0 2 4 6 8	
Biology	0 1 2 3 4	Foreign Language	0 2 4 6 8	54-57_____
Chemistry	0 1 2 3 4	Specify Language (s) _____		
Physics	0 1 2 3 4			

Did you take a college preparatory course?   _____ yes   _____ no   58_____

22. Did your high school give you practice in the following college-type experiences? (Check those in which you had considerable experience)

_____ Taking notes from lectures
_____ Writing term reports
_____ Taking final semester examinations during a scheduled period
_____ Making individual studies with oral reports
_____ Long-term assignments
_____ Planning own use of study time rather than required study period
_____ (If other, describe) _____ 59_____

196

23. For the work I want to do, a college education is:
    ____ necessary   ____ desirable   ____ unnecessary   60_____

24. My teachers in high school have:
    ____ encouraged me to go to college
    ____ discouraged me from going to college
    ____ have had no effect on my decision   61_____

25. My parents:
    ____ want me to go to college   ____ do not care whether I go
    ____ do not want me to go   ____ will not let me go   62_____

26. Most of my friends are:
    ____ going to college   ____ going into military service
    ____ getting jobs   ____ other _____ 63_____

27. High school studies:
    ____ have been interesting; I want to learn more
    ____ have been uninteresting; I would rather work than study
    ____ have had no especial influence upon my plans   64_____

28. The prospect of military service: (boys only)
    ____ has influenced me to attend college and join the ROTC
    ____ has made me uncertain about my future plans
    ____ has caused me to plan a military career
    ____ has had no influence upon my plans

29. The fact that boys must go into military service: (girls only)
    ____ has caused me to be unsettled in my plans
    ____ has had no influence upon my decisions
    ____ has caused me to plan to enter military service too   65_____

30. Which of the following statements best describe your opinion of the value of going to college? (Answer
    whether you plan to go to college or not. Check the 3 statements which seem most important to you.)

    ____ I would rather start earning money quickly, and learn on the job
    ____ I (am) would be greatly dissatisfied to stop at my present level of knowledge
    ____ College life and activities (like athletics) attract me very much
    ____ College graduates get jobs with better pay
    ____ The country needs more people who have highly developed skills and knowledge
    ____ College is a good place to meet a worthy life-mate
    ____ Skilled laborers get paid as much as most college graduates
    ____ Going to college enables you to study more lines of work before deciding on a career
    ____ A college education helps you live a happier, more complete life
    ____ Going to college costs more than it is worth
    ____ College studies will make you work at a high intellectual level, and I like that
    ____ College graduates usually have the leadership positions
    ____ Learning on a job is more practical than most school learning
    ____ Persons who do not have college educations often make better leaders
    ____ College life broadens you socially, and developes your personality
    ____ Success in life depends upon ability and effort, not amount of education
    ____ Going to college would be a waste of time for me
    ____ Going to college has just been accepted; I have never thought of anything else   66+ _____

WISCONSIN STATE DEPARTMENT OF PUBLIC INSTRUCTION
AND
SCHOOL OF EDUCATION, UNIVERSITY OF WISCONSIN

April, 1957

Appendix B

Follow-up Questionnaire

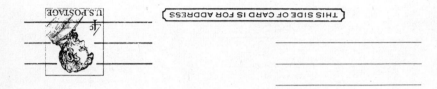

(THIS SIDE OF CARD IS FOR ADDRESS)

U.S. POSTAGE

THE UNIVERSITY OF WISCONSIN

Dear Parent:

In 1957 your son took part in a survey of the post-high school plans of Wisconsin high school seniors. The Department of Sociology of The University of Wisconsin is conducting a study of the educational and work experiences of these students since leaving high school.

The information we are seeking concerning your son will be used in the state-wide Study of Wisconsin High School Students and will be of great help in planning for future educational developments in Wisconsin. Please fill out and return the attached post card immediately. Be sure to include your return address in the upper left-hand corner of the card.

Only with your help can we get complete information about what has happened to your son's high school class. THANK YOU FOR YOUR COOPERATION.

Sincerely,

William H. Sewell
Professor of Sociology

200

To the parents of _____

SCHOOL OR COLLEGE

1. Since high school, has your son attended any school or college? YES____ NO____
2. If YES:

Name Of School	Years From	To	Graduated
_____	____	____	YES____ NO____
_____	____	____	YES____ NO____
_____	____	____	YES____ NO____

EMPLOYMENT

3. What is his present occupation? _____
Name of firm: _____ Job title: _____

OTHER

4. Is your son married? YES____ NO____ If YES, year married _____
5. Military Service: now serving _____ has served _____ has not served _____
6. What is YOUR SON'S present mailing address?

_____
street

_____
city   state

Appendix C

Characteristics of Social Security Earnings Data[1]

The arrangement we have worked out with the Social Security Administration to insure the anonymity of individual earnings involves the following procedure. We send a tape to the Social Security Administration that includes all of the information we have on the men in our sample. By matching Social Security numbers, they are able to add earnings information to the tape; they then eradicate all identification information (including the Social Security numbers), scramble the order of the cases, and return the resulting tape to a senior member of the staff of the Madison Academic Computing Center. This person has been designated as the representative of the Social Security Administration, and is under instructions to insure the security of the tape and the information it contains. He keeps the tape in locked storage, mounting it only on orders from the project staff. (No member of the project staff has direct access to the tape.) He is instructed not to duplicate the tape, make any listing of cases, or provide any cross-tabulation with fewer than five cases in any cell. The tape may not be put into a data bank and must be returned to the Social Security Administration when the research is completed. No one other than certified members of the project staff can obtain runs from the tape without the express written authorization of the Director of the Social Security Administration or his deputy. This scheme, though cumbersome in some respects, has worked quite satisfactorily and, we believe, fully meets all legal and ethical requirements for the security of individual records. Members of the project staff have been scrupulous in following the agreement.

The proportion of the sample of 1957 Wisconsin male high school seniors with

1 This appendix was prepared by Janet A. Fisher and William H. Sewell.

earnings from employment covered by Social Security is remarkably high through-out the period 1957 through 1967.[2] It is almost 90% for 1957. It reaches 95% by 1960 and remains at that level throughout the rest of the period. That com-pares with a national average for employed males of 90%. Nevertheless, there are some characteristics of these earnings data that must be taken into account in the interpretation of any research in which they play a central role. The re-search strategy for this project was designed with the specific measurement problems of these earnings data in mind. A more detailed account of the earn-ings data is presented here.

The principal characteristics of Social Security coverage are as follows. (1) Not everyone with earnings is engaged in covered employment. Clearly, most are. (2) Some of those with covered earnings in a given year may also have additional earnings from uncovered employment in that same year. (3) Earnings of persons under 21 years of age are not covered if these earnings are from employment by members of that person's family. (4) Earnings of persons serving in the armed forces have been covered since 1 January 1957, but coverage has been limited to basic pay. (5) There is a ceiling on the size of earnings covered, and for most persons whose earnings exceed that ceiling, total earnings have to be estimated.

The treatment of zero-earnings reports posed some problems. True zero earn-ings and earnings from employment not covered by Social Security are indistin-guishable in the Social Security records. Therefore, we made the following deci-sions, based upon the indicated assumptions. (1) For nonstudents, the compara-tively few zero earners in each year are excluded from all computations, on the assumption that they are most likely to be persons in uncovered employment. Classification is used to handle the important exception to this: farm youth under age 21. (2) For students, zero earners are included, but in estimating relationships between earnings and ability in Chapter 6 we used the Limited Dependent Varia-ble Program rather than ordinary regression (see Chapter 6 for explanation). The assumption behind this approach is that there are more likely to be true zero earners among students than among nonstudents. However, this assumption is qualified for students of farm background by introduction of a dummy regressor to allow for the separate effect of their limited coverage while under age 21.

Earnings of students employed by the institutions in which they are enrolled are not covered by Social Security. If that happens to have been the sole source of support for some students, then our assumption is wrong for them. Likewise, any student so employed with additional earnings from at least one job in cov-ered employment will have earnings that are understated.[3]

[2] All of the information in this section on the coverage of earnings under Social Security laws can be found in the *Social Security Handbook,* 1969.

[3] Without earnings from college and university employment, we estimate that average student earnings may be understated by about 5%, and that the earnings figures for approximately 10% of the students would be altered by their inclu-sion. The figures for resident males at the University of Wisconsin during the 1960–1961 academic year are somewhat higher (Lins, 1961:40). However, for the total sample, we make allowance for the probable difference between all under-graduates and those who earn a degree, and also for differences in economic resources between those who attended the University of Wisconsin—Madison and other institutions, including private and out-of-state schools.

Military service raises additional problems. Although basic pay has been covered by Social Security since 1 January 1957, all other service-connected compensation has not. Oi (1967a) has estimated that basic pay represents between 55% and 66% of total compensation for enlisted men, depending upon number of years of service. His estimates include all cash payments, income in kind, and tax advantages.

For the sample data, treatment of service-connected earnings is complicated by limited information on the period of service. We can only distinguish between those who served prior to 1964 and those still serving in that year. Therefore, for the group with no education beyond high school, we can at best classify by military service. However, for those who entered college soon after high school graduation and graduated within 4 or 5 years, we can infer that any of them who served did so upon completion of college. For this group, the best strategy seemed to be to capture the attendant covered earnings differences with dummy regressors.

The ceiling for earnings covered by Social Security payments was $4200 in 1957. It increased to $4800 in 1959 and $6600 in 1966. Not only have these ceilings failed to meet the initial intent of Social Security legislation to cover total wages, but both the lag in ceiling increases and their limited size have been accompanied by higher and higher proportions of wage earners with above-ceiling earnings. With the single exception of self-employed persons whose total earnings are reported to the Social Security Administration by the Internal Revenue Service, all above-ceiling earnings must be estimated.

For young men just out of high school, very few are affected by this situation. Whereas half or more of all males in the civilian labor force earned more than $4200 in 1958 and more than $4800 in 1959, less than 5% of 1957 Wisconsin high school graduates had such high earnings in those years. However, by 1962 the sample proportion with above-ceiling earnings was almost one-fourth, by 1965 nearly two-thirds, and with the increased ceiling in 1966, little under one-half. Therefore, all above-ceiling earnings with the exception of those for the self-employed were estimated. The Social Security Administration provided the set of estimating equations developed for this purpose in their own research (Resnick, 1966:42–43).

Appendix D

Coverage of Male Wisconsin Youth in the 1957 Survey[1]

The cohort of 1957 Wisconsin high school graduates is sufficiently large and representative to warrant extensive analyses of its members' post-high school achievements. The vast majority of United States youth complete high school, and the transition from high school to college is both the point of greatest attrition in the schooling process and the point at which socioeconomic factors most affect continuation in school. Hence, one need not be apologetic about an interest in the socioeconomic life chances of a cohort of high school graduates. At the same time, it should be kept in mind that a cohort of high school graduates is not a birth cohort, while the latter is the population unit to which we ultimately want to refer our findings about the process of socioeconomic achievement.

The published documentation of the quality of representation in the Wisconsin sample is less than satisfactory, although it is not essentially misleading (Sewell and Shah, 1967:4–5):

> The use of Wisconsin students for a study of this kind is, of course, less ideal than would be a large, randomly selected cohort of the nation's students chosen at some point earlier in the educational process than graduation from high school. Wisconsin, however, is in many ways a good state for a study of the educational attainment of high school youth. Its holding power over its school children is very high; more than 88 percent of its 16–17 year olds were in school in 1960. Thus, the high school senior class retains a more representative body of students of all

1 This appendix was prepared by Robert M. Hauser.

207

ability and socioeconomic levels than would be true in states where the dropout rate is higher.

The source of these figures just cited is 1960 United States Census data, as reported in Marshall (1963:29).

Age-Specific Enrollment Rates

While the comparison between rates of enrollment in Wisconsin and in the total United States is not essentially misleading, the rates of enrollment for 16- and 17-year-olds tell us little about the probability that a youth might appear in a sample of high school graduates. This is a consequence of the fact that a cohort of high school graduates cuts across several birth cohorts, and, more specifically, a consequence of the fact that 16- and 17-year-olds are typically not old enough to appear in a cohort of high school seniors. Unfortunately, we cannot document these assertions with age-specific, grade-specific enrollment rates for 1957, but such data are available for the 1960 census year (see Table D-1). In April 1960, 91.8% of 16-year-old men and 84.6% of 17-year-old men were enrolled in school, but 89.4% of the 16-year-olds and 42.9% of the 17-year-olds were en-

TABLE D-1

Enrollment Status and Grade Level of Enrolled Males by Age: Wisconsin, 1960

Age	Not enrolled	Enrolled			Total
		11 or lower	12	13 or higher	
Frequencies					
16	2,606	28,439	731	23	31,799
17	4,937	13,760	13,084	317	32,098
18	10,228	2,221	8,115	4,989	25,553
19	13,069	624	1,559	6,048	21,300
Percentages					
16	8.2	89.4	2.3	.1	100.0
17	15.4	42.9	40.8	1.0	100.0
18	40.0	8.7	31.8	19.5	100.0
19	61.4	2.9	7.3	28.4	100.0

Source: U.S. Bureau of the Census, *U.S. Census of Population, 1960,* Vol. 1, *Characteristics of the Population,* Part 51, Wisconsin, Tables 101, 102.

rolled *below* the twelfth grade level. Even at age 17, the modal age for enroll-ment in grade 12, only 40.8% of 17-year-olds were enrolled at that grade level. The age-specific enrollment data are no more informative at ages 18 or 19, be-cause large numbers of youth at these ages have completed their education. In 1960, 40% of 18-year-old Wisconsin men were not enrolled in school, 8.7% were enrolled below the twelfth grade level, 19.5% were enrolled in college, and only 31.8% were enrolled in grade 12.

Of persons not enrolled, even at the younger ages, many have already had the opportunity to appear in a sample of high school graduates (see Table D-2). Among nonenrolled Wisconsin men, 4.8% of the 16-year-olds, 24.5% of the 17-year-olds, 58.6% of the 18-year-olds, and 66.4% of the 19-year-olds had com-pleted at least four years of high school and might have appeared in a sample of high school graduates.

Insofar as school enrollment data by age do bear on the point at issue, it is clear that conditions are more favorable in Wisconsin than in the nation as a whole (see Table D-3). In 1960, age-specific enrollment rates for 15- to 20-year-olds were uniformly higher in Wisconsin than in the total United States. Not-withstanding the favorable character of such comparisons, it is clear that they do not tell us what we want to know. Indeed, if schooling took place at later than average ages in Wisconsin, high age-specific enrollment rates in the late teens could be indicative of lower than average attainment levels. Our interest lies in the probability during the late 1950s that a Wisconsin youth might appear in a sample of high school graduates.

TABLE D-2

Educational Attainment of Nonenrolled 16–19-Year-Old Males by Age: Wiscon-sin, 1960

Age	11 or less	12	13 or more	Total
Frequencies				
16	2,483	119	4	2,606
17	3,729	1,193	15	4,937
18	4,234	5,835	159	10,228
19	4,382	8,017	670	13,069
Percentages				
16	95.3	4.6	.2	100.0
17	75.5	24.2	.3	100.0
18	41.4	57.0	1.6	100.0
19	33.5	61.3	5.1	100.0

Source: U.S. Bureau of the Census, *U.S. Census of Population, 1960,* Vol. 1, *Characteristics of the Population,* Part 51, Wisconsin, Table 102.

TABLE D-3

School Enrollment Rates of Males by Age: United States and Wisconsin, 1960

Age	United States	Wisconsin
15	93.12	95.99
16	86.56	91.80
17	76.33	84.62
18	54.64	59.97
19	37.27	38.64
20	27.91	28.46

Source: U.S. Bureau of the Census, *U.S. Census of Population, 1960,* Vol. 1, *Characteristics of the Population,* Part 1, U.S. Summary, Tables 168, 172; Part 51, Wisconsin, Tables 101, 102.

Educational Attainment

Though not without their disadvantages, rates of educational attainment by age are more appropriate for our purpose, since they express the cumulative exposure of a cohort to the educational system (see Table D-4). In the United States

TABLE D-4

Percentage of Males Completing at Least Four Years of High School, by Age: United States and Wisconsin, 1960

Age	United States	Wisconsin
15	0.28	0.26
16	0.72	0.45
17	5.58	4.75
18	38.55	42.98
19	58.25	69.17
20	61.76	72.62
21	62.66	71.36
22	62.53	70.61
23	61.41	69.59
24	60.97	69.27
20–24	61.88	70.67
25–29	59.65	65.99
30–34	53.39	58.35

Source: U.S. Bureau of the Census, *U.S. Census of Population, 1960,* Vol. 1, *Characteristics of the Population,* Part 1, U.S. Summary, Tables 173, 174; Part 51, Wisconsin, Tables 101, 102.

and in Wisconsin, there is a rapid increase in the proportion completing four years of high school from age 15 to age 20–21, followed by a slight decline for each subsequent year of age. This age pattern reflects the combined effects of the cumulative exposure of the members of each cohort to the last year of high school and the secular increase in levels of educational attainment. At ages 18 and over, the attainments of Wisconsin men are clearly superior to those in the total United States. Among men between 20 and 24 years of age, 71% of Wisconsin males had completed at least four years of high school, while only 62% of United States men had attained that much schooling.

Interpretation of the Wisconsin–United States comparisons is complicated by the fact that Wisconsin is a net importer of young persons, who go there for the purpose of obtaining a college education. For example, in the fall of 1963, there were 10,889 Wisconsin residents (of both sexes) enrolled in out-of-state undergraduate institutions, while 16,332 out-of-state residents were enrolled in Wisconsin undergraduate schools. That is, there was a net in-migration of 5443 undergraduate students (Rice and Mason, 1965:43). Unfortunately, there is no way to eliminate the college level in-migrants from the Wisconsin data, or for that matter to eliminate the effects of in- or out-migration for any other reason, because there are no state-level tabulations of educational attainment by mobility status by single years of age.

TABLE D-5

Rate of High School Completion (or Current Grade 12 Enrollment) among All Males and for Those without College Experience, by Age: United States and Wisconsin, April 1960

Age	All	No college
United States		
15	0.78	0.71
16	4.38	4.14
17	40.91	39.78
18	62.24	53.08
19	65.49	51.80
20	64.74	50.44
Wisconsin		
15	0.52	0.45
16	2.76	2.68
17	45.51	44.94
18	74.74	68.36
19	76.50	65.67
20	74.74	62.98

Source: U.S. Bureau of the Census, *U.S. Census of Population, 1960,* Vol. I, *Characteristics of the Population,* Part 1, U.S. Summary, Tables 168, 172; Part 51, Wisconsin, Tables 101, 102.

As a crude way of avoiding this problem, it was assumed that net migration would not affect United States–Wisconsin comparisons of educational attainment for persons with no schooling beyond the high school level, and rates of high school completion were calculated for persons who had not completed at least a year of college (see Table D-5). One other effort was made to represent the concept of potential inclusion in a sample of high school seniors. Persons currently enrolled in grade 12, as well as high school graduates, were included In the numerators of these rates. This change of concept has the effect of raising the rates for 17- and 18-year-olds well above those reported in Table D-4, but it has little effect on the rates at older ages. The elimination of persons with college experience does not reduce the educational advantage of Wisconsin residents and if anything it increases their apparent educational advantage. For example, among 19-year-old United States men 65.5% had completed high school or were currently enrolled in the twelfth grade, while 76.5% of 19-year-old Wisconsin men were in that position; thus, there was a Wisconsin advantage of 11 percentage points. At the same time, for 19-year-old men with no college experience, the United States rate of high school completion was 51.8%, while the Wisconsin rate was 65.7%; thus, the Wisconsin advantage in the second comparison was 13.9 percentage points.

Grade Progress Ratios

We can make another crude comparison of United States and Wisconsin school retention patterns using annual data on enrollment by grade level as reported by the Wisconsin State Department of Public Instruction. Table D-6 shows estimated grade progress ratios (for both sexes) in Wisconsin for grades 7–12 in the period 1950–1961. The ratios are defined as the number of enrollees at each grade level in one year divided by the number of enrollees one grade lower in the previous year. The state reports of enrollment by grade by year pertain only to public schools, and the time referent is the close of the academic year. The share of total enrollment that is in public school varies markedly with grade level, while the census enrollment data, which report both private and public school enrollment, pertain to the time of the census in early April. Consequently, in order to obtain grade progress ratios for total school enrollment, the ratio of total census enrollment to state-reported public school enrollment in 1960 was calculated for each grade in school, and the ratios were multiplied by the annual state reports of school enrollment at each grade level before the grade progress ratios were calculated. That is, we assumed that public schools had the same share of total enrollment at each grade level in earlier years as in 1960. If one has faith in these calculations, he must conclude that school retention in Wisconsin was rather high in the period under consideration for the seven cohorts that were followed from the 7th–12th grades. The grade 7 to grade 12 progress ratio ranged from 78.2 to 86.8, and the value was 79.8 for the 1957 cohort of high school seniors.

The preceding calculations are conceptually deficient because they are not true cohort continuation rates. Persons who complete one grade may not enter the

TABLE D-6

Estimated Grade Progress Ratios by Grade: Wisconsin, 1950–1960

Year completed grade 7	7–8	8–9	9–10	10–11	11–12	7–12
1946	—	—	—	—	97.8	—
1947	—	—	—	89.4	98.8	—
1948	—	—	93.4	88.6	98.7	—
1949	—	94.1	93.3	90.2	99.2	—
1950	97.2	95.2	93.6	90.9	99.4	78.2
1951	97.8	95.0	95.7	91.6	98.1	79.9
1952	97.0	95.9	95.9	91.0	98.3	79.8[a]
1953	98.4	96.4	95.6	91.1	99.3	82.0
1954	97.8	96.9	96.7	92.8	98.1	83.4
1955	98.0	98.4	97.6	91.9	99.1	85.6
1956	98.1	98.5	97.3	92.9	99.4	86.8
1957	99.2	97.0	97.7	93.2	—	—
1958	98.5	98.4	98.1	—	—	—
1959	99.3	99.4	—	—	—	—
1960	98.7	—	—	—	—	—

[a] Ratio of the 1957 cohort of Wisconsin graduates.

Sources: Wisconsin State Department of Public Instruction, Biennial Reports, 1949–51 to 1959–61; U.S. Bureau of the Census, *U.S. Census of Population, 1960,* Vol. I, *Characteristics of the Population.*

next grade for a variety of reasons (death, migration, grade retardation, grade acceleration), and, similarly, persons who enter a given grade in a given year may not have completed the next lower grade in the preceding year within the same territorial unit. These calculations were produced only because they may be compared with a similarly deficient statistical series produced by the United States Office of Education, which is reproduced in Table D-7. The Office of Education enrollment data pertain to fall enrollment, i.e., entry into a given grade level. Consequently, a comparison of grade 8 entrants with grade 12 entrants four years later should show greater retention than a comparison of those completing the 7th grade with those completing the 12th grade five years later. Despite this conservative bias, it is apparent from a comparison of Table 6 and Table 7 that retention in Wisconsin is substantially better than that in the United States as a whole for comparable cohorts. For the cohorts graduating in 1956 and 1958, the United States grade 8–12 retention rates, based on Office of Education data, are 66.6 and 68.6, which may be compared with the grade 7–12 progress ratio for the 1957 cohort of 79.8.

TABLE D-7

Estimated "Retention Rates," Entrance to Grade 8 to Entry to Grade 12: United States Grade 8 Entrants, 1949–1957

Year entered grade 8	Retention rate, grade 5–grade 8 A	Retention rate, grade 5–grade 12 B	B/A
1949	919	583	63.4
1951	929	619	66.6[a]
1953	921	632	68.6[a]
1955	939	667	71.3
1957	948	684	72.2

[a] Ratios for the 1956 and 1958 cohorts of United States graduates.

Source: National Center for Educational Statistics, *Digest of Educational Statistics,* 1969, Table 8.

Synthetic Cohort Rates

Age-grade-specific enrollment data from the 1960 census were used in one other effort to assess the risk of exposure to the end of the senior year in high school in Wisconsin. If no individual could enroll in a single grade more than once, if there were no intercohort shifts in grade-specific enrollment rates, and if there were no mortality or migration, then the sum of period rates of enrollment in grade 12 over the relevant ages would express the cumulative exposure of a cohort to twelfth grade enrollment. The last of these three conditions may be assumed to hold approximately true for the total United States, but not for an individual state. The first two assumptions are clearly inaccurate. A student may be enrolled in the same grade in school for more than one year, and there have been regular and substantial upward intercohort shifts in educational attainment that suggest (though they do not require) there will be upward shifts in age-specific enrollment rates for the higher grades in school. To the extent that either of these assumptions is violated, we may expect that the sum across ages of period age-grade-specific enrollment rates will be greater than the true cohort rate of cumulative exposure for a cohort recently completing its exposure to the educational system.

These suggestions are supported when synthetic rates are constructed by summing the 1960 age-specific grade 12 enrollment rates for 15- to 20-year-olds. These may be compared with the true cohort rates of exposure to the twelfth grade for 20-year-old United States males in 1960 (see Table D-8). The synthetic rates are uniformly higher than the observed exposure rates for 20-year-olds, and for synthetic rates, as for the observed cohort rates, exposure to the senior year in high school is markedly more prevalent in Wisconsin than in the total United States. Examination of the synthetic rates is particularly instructive because net

TABLE D-8

Male Synthetic Cohort Grade 12 Exposure Rates and Percentage of 20-Year-Old Males Completing or Exposed to Grade 12: United States and Wisconsin, 1960

	Synthetic rate	Observed 20-year-old rate
United States	73.39	64.70
Wisconsin	84.50	74.74

Source: U.S. Bureau of the Census, *U.S. Census of Population, 1960,* Vol. I, *Characteristics of the Population,* Part 1, U.S. Summary, Tables 168, 173; Part 51, Wisconsin, Tables 101, 102.

in-migration of highly educated young persons to Wisconsin would tend to depress rates of twelfth grade enrollment and thereby lower the synthetic rate.

Conclusion

None of these manipulations of available data is particularly conclusive when taken by itself. This may follow as much from our inability to pose an appropriate question as from erroneous or incomplete data. Nonetheless, it seems reasonable to conclude that, in the late 1950s, school retention to grade 12 was markedly higher in Wisconsin than in the total United States and that from 75% to 80% of the Wisconsin men of high school age at about that time might have appeared in a sample of high school graduates.

References

Alexander, Karl, and Bruce K. Eckland
  1973   Effects of education on the social mobility of high school sophomores fifteen years later (1955–1970). Final report on project no. 10202, National Institute of Education Grant #OEG–4–71–0037.
Alwin, Duane F.
  1972   College effects on educational and socioeconomic achievements. Unpublished Ph.D. dissertation, University of Wisconsin, Madison.
  1974   College effects on educational and occupational attainments. *American Sociological Review* **39** (Apr.):210–230.
Arrow, Kenneth J.
  1972   Higher education as a filter. Technical Report No. 71, The Economic Series, Institute for Mathematical Studies in the Social Sciences, Stanford University.
Ashenfelter, Orley A., and Joseph D. Mooney
  1968   Graduate education, ability and earnings. *Review of Economics and Statistics* **50** (Feb.):78–86.
Astin, Alexander W.
  1965   *Who goes where to college?* Chicago: Science Research Associates, Inc.
  1972   *College dropouts: A national profile.* ACE Research Reports, Vol. 7. Washington, D.C.: American Council on Education.
Astin, Alexander W., and Calvin B. T. Lee
  1972   *The invisible colleges.* New York: McGraw-Hill.
Astin, Alexander W., and Robert J. Panos
  1969   *The educational and vocational development of college students.* Washington, D.C.: American Council on Education.

Babcock, F. Lawrence
    1941   *The U. S. college graduate.* New York: Macmillan.
Bailey, D., and T. F. Cargill
    1969   The military draft and future income. *Western Economics Journal* **7** (Dec.):365–370.
Baur, E. Jackson
    1947   Response bias in a mail survey. *Public Opinion Quarterly* **10** (Winter): 594–600.
Becker, Gary S.
    1964   *Human capital.* New York: National Bureau of Economic Research.
Beilin, Harry, and Emmy E. Werner
    1957   Interviewing availability of a follow-up sample of rural youth. *Public Opinion Quarterly* **21** (Fall):380–384.
Berdie, Ralph F.
    1954   *After high school what?* Minneapolis: Univ. of Minnesota Press.
Berdie, Ralph F., and Albert B. Hood
    1965   *Decisions for tomorrow.* Minneapolis: Univ. of Minnesota Press.
Blau, Peter M., and Otis Dudley Duncan
    1967   *The American occupational structure.* New York: John Wiley and Sons.
Blaug, Mark B.
    1967   The private and the social returns on investment in education: Some results for Great Britain. *Journal of Human Resources* **2** (Summer):330–346.
Blum, Zahava D.
    1971   Family structure and occupational achievement. Mimeograph (April).
    1972   White and black careers during the first decade of labor force experience. Part II: Income differences. *Social Science Research* **1** (Sept.):271–292.
Blum, Zahava D., and James S. Coleman
    1970   *Longitudinal effects of education on the incomes and occupational prestige of blacks and whites.* Report No. 70, Center for the Study of Social Organization of Schools, Johns Hopkins University (June).
Borus, M. E., and G. Nestel
    1973   Response bias in reports of father's education and socioeconomic status. *Journal of American Statistical Association* **68**:816–820.
Bowles, Samuel
    1972   Schooling and inequality from generation to generation. *Journal of Political Economy* **80** (May/June, Part II):S219–S251.
Bowles, Samuel, and Herbert Gintis
    1972   IQ in the U.S. class structure. *Social Policy* **3** (Nov.):65–96.
Bowman, Mary Jean
    1969   Economics of education. *Review of Educational Research* **39** (Dec.): 641–670.
Boyle, Richard P.
    1966   On neighborhood context and college plans (III). *American Sociological Review* **31** (Oct.):706–707.
Bridgman, D. S.
    1960   Problems in estimating the monetary value of college education. *Review of Economics and Statistics* **42** (Aug.):180–184.

Brim, Orville G., Jr., and Stanton Wheeler
1966 *Socialization after childhood: Two essays*. New York: John Wiley and Sons.
Burgess, M. Elaine, and Daniel O. Price
1963 *An American dependency challenge*. Chicago: American Public Welfare Association.
Campbell, Richard T.
1973 Social class and college graduation: A replication and extension. Unpublished Ph.D. dissertation, University of Wisconsin, Madison.
Cochran, William G.
1953 *Sampling techniques*. New York: John Wiley and Sons.
Cohen, Jacob
1968 Multiple regression as a general data-analytic system. *Psychological Bulletin* **70** (Dec.):426–443.
Coleman, James S., Charles C. Berry, and Zahava D. Blum
1972 White and black careers during the first decade of labor force experience. Part III: Occupational status and income together. *Social Science Research* **1** (Sept.):293–304.
Coleman, James S., Ernest Q. Campbell, Carol J. Hobson, James McPartland, Alexander M. Mood, Frederick D. Weinfeld, and Robert L. York
1966 *Equality of educational opportunity*. Washington, D.C.: U.S. Government Printing Office.
Cooley, William W., and Susan J. Becker
1966 The junior college student. *Personnel and Guidance Journal* **44** (Jan.): 464–469.
Cooley, William W., and Paul R. Lohnes
1963 *Multivariate procedures for the behavioral sciences*. New York: John Wiley and Sons.
Cutwright, Phillips
1969 *Achievement, military service and earnings*. Social Security Administration, Contract No. SSA 67–2031 (May).
Daniere, Andre, and Jerry Mechling
1970 Direct and marginal productivity of college education in relation to college aptitude of students and production costs of institutions. *Journal of Human Resources* **5** (Winter):51–70.
Deming, W. Edwards
1960 *Sample design in business research*. New York: John Wiley and Sons.
Denison, Edward F.
1962 *The sources of growth in the United States and the alternatives before us*. Supplementary Paper No. 13. New York: Committee on Economic Development.
1964 Measuring the contribution of education. In *The residual factor and economic growth organization for economic cooperation and development*. Paris: Organization for Economic Cooperation and Development. Pp. 13–102.
Donald, Marjorie N.
1960 Implications of nonresponse for the interpretation of mail questionnaire data. *Public Opinion Quarterly* **24** (Spring): 99–114.

Duncan, Beverly, and Otis D. Duncan
1968   Minorities and the process of stratification. *American Sociological Review* **33** (June):356–364.

Duncan, Otis Dudley
1961   A socioeconomic index for all occupations. In *Occupations and social status*, by Albert J. Reiss, Jr., New York: Free Press. Pp. 109–138.
1966   Path analysis: Sociological examples. *American Journal of Sociology* **72** (July):3–16.
1968a   Ability and achievement. *Eugenics Quarterly* **15** (Mar.):1–11.
1968b   Inheritance of poverty or inheritance of race. In *On understanding poverty*, edited by Daniel P. Moynihan. New York: Basic Books. Pp. 85–110.
1969   Contingencies in constructing causal models. In *Sociological methodology*, edited by Edgar F. Borgatta. San Francisco: Jossey–Bass. Pp. 74–112.
1970   Partials, partitions and paths. In *Sociological methodology*, edited by Edgar F. Borgatta and George W. Bohrnstedt. San Francisco: Jossey–Bass. Pp. 38–47.
1971   Path analysis: Sociological examples. In *Causal models in the social sciences*, edited by Hubert M. Blalock, Jr. Chicago: Aldine–Atherton. Pp. 115–138.

Duncan, Otis D., and David L. Featherman
1972   Psychological and cultural factors in the process of occupational achievement. *Social Science Research* **1** (June):121–145.

Duncan, Otis Dudley, David L. Featherman, and Beverly Duncan
1972   *Socioeconomic background and achievements*. New York: Seminar Press.

Duncan, Otis Dudley, and Robert W. Hodge
1963   Education and occupational mobility: A regression analysis. *American Journal of Sociology* **68** (May):629–644.

Eckland, Bruce K.
1965   Academic ability, higher education and occupational mobility. *American Sociological Review* **30** (Oct.):735–746.

Edgerton, Harold A., Steuart H. Britt, and Ralph D. Norman
1947   Objective differences among various types of respondents to a mailed questionnaire. *American Sociological Review* **12** (Aug.):435–444.

Ellis, Robert A., Calvin M. Endo, and J. Michael Armer
1970   The use of potential nonrespondents for studying nonresponse bias. *Pacific Sociological Review* **13**, No. 2 (Spring):103–109.

Featherman, David L.
1969   The socioeconomic achievement of white married males in the United States:1957–67. Unpublished Ph.D. dissertation, University of Michigan.
1971   The socioeconomic achievement of white religio–ethnic subgroups: Social and psychological explanations. *American Sociological Review* **36** (Apr.): 207–222.

Featherman, David L., and Robert M. Hauser
1974   Design for a replicated study of social mobility in the United States. In *Social indicator models*, edited by K. C. Land and S. Spilerman. New York: Russell Sage Foundation.

Flanagan, John C., and William W. Cooley

1966   Project talent—One year follow-up studies. Pittsburgh: Univ. of Pittsburgh.

Flanagan, John C., Marion F. Shaycoft, James M. Richards, Jr., and John G. Claudy
1971   Project talent: Five years after high school. Pittsburgh: Univ. of Pittsburgh.

Folger, John K., Helen S. Astin, and Alan E. Bayer
1970   Human resources and higher education. New York: Russell Sage Foundation.

Gasson, Ruth M., Archibald O. Haller, and William H. Sewell
1972   Attitudes and facilitation in status attainment. Washington, D.C.: Rose Monograph Series, American Sociological Association.

Gintis, Herbert
1971   Education, technology and the characteristics of worker productivity. American Economic Review 61 (May):266–279.

Goldberger, Arthur S.
1964   Econometric theory. New York: John Wiley and Sons.

Goodman, Leo A.
1968   The analysis of cross-classified data: Independence, quasi-independence and interactions in contingency tables with or without missing entries. Journal of the American Statistical Association 63 (Dec.):1091–1131.
1971   The analysis of multidimensional contingency tables: Stepwise procedures and direct estimation methods for building models for multiple classifications. Technometrics 13 (Feb.):33–61.

Griliches, Zvi
1970   Notes on the role of education in production functions and growth accounting. In Education, income and human capital, edited by W. Lee Hansen. New York: National Bureau of Economic Research. Pp. 71–127.

Griliches, Zvi, and William M. Mason
1972   Education, income and ability. Journal of Political Economy 80 (May/June):S74–S103.

Gujarati, Damodar
1970   Use of dummy variables in testing for equality between sets of coefficients in linear regressions: A generalization. American Statistician 24 (Dec.): 18–22.

Haller, Archibald O., and Alejandro Portes
1973   Status attainment process. Sociology of Education 46 (Winter):51–91.

Haller, Archibald O., and William H. Sewell
1967   Occupational choices of Wisconsin farm boys. Rural Sociology 32 (Mar.):37–55.

Hanoch, Giora H.
1967   An economic analysis of earnings and schooling. Journal of Human Resources 2 (Summer):310–329.

Hansen, W. Lee (Ed.)
1970   Education, income and human capital. New York: Columbia Univ. Press.

Hansen, W. Lee, and Burton A. Weisbrod
1967   Economics of the military draft. Quarterly Journal of Economics 81 (Aug.):395–421.

1969 *Benefits, costs and finance of public higher education.* Chicago: Markham.

Hansen, W. Lee, Burton A. Weisbrod, and William J. Scanlon
1970 Schooling and earnings of low achievers. *American Economics Review* **60** (June):409–418.

Hanushek, Eric A.
1971 Regional differences in the structure of earnings. Discussion Paper No. 66, Program on Regional and Urban Economics, Harvard University.

Hause, John C.
1971 Ability and schooling as determinants of lifetime earnings or if you're so smart, why aren't you rich? *American Economics Review* **61** (May):289–298.
1972 Earnings profile: Ability and schooling. *Journal of Political Economy* **80** (May/June, Part II):S108–S138.

Hauser, Robert M.
1969 Schools and the stratification process. *American Journal of Sociology* **74** (May):598–611.
1970a Context and consex: A cautionary tale. *American Journal of Sociology* **75** (Jan.):645–664.
1970b Educational stratification in the United States. *Sociological Inquiry* **40** (Spring):102–129.
1971 *Socioeconomic background and educational performance.* Washington, D.C.: Rose Monograph Series, American Sociological Association.
1972 Disaggregating a social–psychological model of educational attainment. *Social Science Research* **1** (June):159–188.

Hauser, Robert M., and Arthur S. Goldberger
1971 The treatment of unobservable variables in path analysis. In *Sociological methodology*, edited by Herbert L. Costner. San Francisco: Jossey–Bass. Pp. 81–117.

Hauser, Robert M., K. G. Lutterman, and William H. Sewell
1971 Socioeconomic background and the earnings of high school graduates. Mimeograph, (August).

Havemann, Ernest, and Patricia Salter West
1952 *They went to college.* New York: Harcourt.

Heise, David R.
1969 Problems in path analysis and causal inference. In *Sociological methodology*, edited by Edgar F. Borgatta. San Francisco: Jossey–Bass. Pp. 38–73.

Henmon, V. A. C., and M. J. Nelson
1954 *The Henmon–Nelson test of mental ability: Manual for administration.* Chicago: Houghton–Mifflin.

Hodge, Robert W.
1970 Social integration, psychological well-being and their socioeconomic correlates. *Sociological Inquiry* **40** (Spring):182–206.

Hunt, Shane
1963 Income determinants for college graduates and the return to educational investment. Unpublished Ph.D. dissertation, Yale University.

Husen, Torsten
   1969   *Talent, opportunity and career*. Stockholm: Almqvest and Wiksell.
Jencks, Christopher
   1968   Social stratification and higher education. *Harvard Educational Review* **38** (Spring):277–316.
Jencks, Christopher, and David Riesman
   1968   *The academic revolution*. New York: Doubleday.
Jencks, Christopher S., Marshall Smith, Henry Acland, Mary Jo Bane, David Cohen, Herbert Gintis, Barbara Heyns, and Stephan Michelson
   1972   *Inequality: A reassessment of the effect of family and schooling in America*. New York: Basic Books.
Johnson, Thomas
   1970   Returns from investment in human capital. *American Economic Review* **60** (Sept.):546–560.
Joint Economic Committee, Congress of the United States
   1969   *The economics and financing of higher education in the United States*. Washington, D.C.: U.S. Government Printing Office.
Jorgenson, D. W., and Z. Griliches
   1967   The explanation of productivity change. *Review of Economic Studies* **34** (July):249–283.
Karabel, Jerome, and Alexander W. Astin
   1972   Social class, academic ability and college quality. Mimeograph, American Council in Education.
Kerckhoff, Alan C., William M. Mason, and Sharon Sandomirsky Poss
   1973   On the accuracy of children's reports of family social status. *Sociology of Education* **46** (Spring):219–247.
Kiker, B. F. (Ed.)
   1971   *Investment in human capital*. Columbia: Univ. of South Carolina Press.
Kinloch, Graham C., and Robert Perrucci
   1969   Social origins, academic achievement, and mobility channels: Sponsored and contest mobility among college graduates. *Social Forces* **48** (Sept.): 36–45.
Kish, Leslie
   1965   *Survey sampling*. New York: John Wiley and Sons.
Kivlin, Joseph E.
   1965   Contributions to the study of mail-back bias. *Rural Sociology* **30** (Sept.):322–326.
Kohen, Andrew I.
   1971   Determinants of early labor market success among young men: Ability, quantity, and quality of schooling. Paper presented at the meeting of the American Educational Research Association, New York (February).
Land, Kenneth C.
   1969   Principles of path analysis. In *Sociological methodology*, edited by Edgar F. Borgatta. San Francisco: Jossey–Bass. Pp. 3–37.
Larson, Richard F., and William R. Catton, Jr.
   1959   Can the mail-back bias contribute to a study's validity? *American Sociological Review* **24** (Apr.):243–245.

Laumann, Edward O., and Robert N. Rapoport
    1968   The institutional effect on career achievement of technologists. *Human Relations* **21** (Aug.):222–239.
Lehman, Edward C., Jr.
    1963   Tests of significance and partial returns to mail questionnaires. *Rural Sociology* **28** (Sept.):284–289.
Lenski, Gerhard
    1963   *The religious factor.* Garden City, N.Y.: Anchor Books.
Lins, L. J.
    1961   *Student expenses and sources of income 1960–61 academic year, the University of Wisconsin—Madison campus.* Madison: Univ. of Wisconsin.
Little, J. Kenneth
    1958   *A statewide inquiry into decisions of youth about education beyond high school.* Madison: School of Education, Univ. of Wisconsin.
    1959   *Explorations into the college plans and experiences of high school graduates.* Madison: School of Education, Univ. of Wisconsin.
Marshall, Douglas G.
    1963   *Wisconsin's population: Changes and prospects.* Bulletin No. 241, Wisconsin Agricultural Experimentation Station, Madison.
Mason, William M.
    1970   On the socioeconomic effects of military service. Unpublished Ph.D. dissertation, Department of Sociology, Univ. of Chicago.
Mayer, Charles S., and Robert W. Pratt, Jr.
    1966   A note on nonresponse in a mail survey. *Public Opinion Quarterly* **30** (Winter):637–646.
Michael, John A.
    1966   On neighborhood context and college plans (II). *American Sociological Review* **31** (Oct.):702–706.
Mincer, J.
    1962   On-the-job training: Costs, returns, and some implications. *Journal of Political Economy* **70** (Oct.):S50–S79.
Morgan, J., and M. David
    1963   Education and income. *Quarterly Journal of Economics* **77** (Aug.):423–437.
Morgan, James M., Martin H. David, Wilbur J. Cohen, and Harvey E. Brazer
    1962   *Income and welfare in the United States.* New York: McGraw–Hill.
Moser, C. A.
    1959   *Survey methods in social investigation.* London: William Heinemann.
Moskos, Charles C.
    1970   *The American enlisted man.* New York: Russell Sage Foundation.
National Science Foundation, Bureau of Social Science Research, Inc.
    1963   *Two years after the college degree.* Washington, D.C.: U.S. Government Printing Office.
Oi, W. Y.
    1967a   The costs and implications of an all volunteer force. In *The draft,* edited by Sol Tax. Chicago: Univ. of Chicago Press. Pp. 221–251.
    1967b   The economic cost of the draft. *American Economics Review* **57** (May):39–62.

Orwig, M. D. (Ed.)
  1971   *Financing higher education: Alternatives for the federal government.*
  Iowa City: American College Testing Program.
Pan, Ju–Shu
  1950   Social characteristics of respondents and nonrespondents in a questionnaire study of the aged. *American Sociological Review* **15** (Dec.):780–781.
Parnes, Herbert S., Robert C. Miljus, Ruth S. Spitz, and associates
  1969   Career thresholds: A longitudinal study of the educational and labor
  market experience of male youth 14 to 24 years of age. Center for Human
  Resource Research, Ohio State University, Columbus (February).
Parsons, Talcott
  1959   The school class as a social system: Some of its functions in American
  society. *Harvard Educational Review* **29** (Fall):297–318.
Pavalko, Ronald M., and Kenneth G. Lutterman
  1973   Characteristics of willing and reluctant respondents. *Pacific Sociological Review* **16** (Oct.):463–476.
Portes, Alejandro, Archibald O. Haller, and William H. Sewell
  1968   Professional–executive vs. farming as unique occupational choices.
  Rural Sociology **2** (June):153–159.
Reed, Ritchie H., and Herman P. Miller
  1970   Some determinants of the variation in earnings for college men. *Journal of Human Resources* **5** (Spring):177–190.
Reiss, Albert J., Jr.
  1961   *Occupations and social status.* New York: Free Press of Glencoe.
Resnick, M.
  1966   Annual earnings and the taxable maximum for OASDHI. *Social Security Bulletin* **29** (Nov.):38–43, 59.
Reuss, Carl F.
  1943   Differences between persons responding and not responding to a
  mailed questionnaire. *American Sociological Review* **8** (Aug.):433–438.
Rice, Mabel C., and Paul L. Mason
  1965   *Resident and migration of college students, Fall 1963: State and
  regional data.* Circular 783, U.S. Office of Education. Washington, D.C.:
  U.S. Government Printing Office.
Robinson, E. A. G., and J. E. Vaizey (Eds.)
  1966   *The economics of education.* New York: St. Martins.
Rogers, Daniel C.
  1969   Private rates of return to education in the United States: A case study.
  Yale Economic Essays **9** (Spring):88–134.
Schiller, Bradley R.
  1970   Stratified opportunities: The essence of the "Vicious circle." *American
  Journal of Sociology* **76** (Nov.):426–442.
Schultz, Theodore W.
  1960   Capital formation by education. *Journal of Political Economy* **67**
  (Dec.):571–583.
  1961a   Investment in human capital. *American Economic Review* **51** (Mar.):
  1–17.

1961b   Education and economic growth. In *Social forces influencing higher education,* edited by Harry B. Nelson. Chicago: Univ. of Chicago Press.

1963   *The economic value of education.* New York: Columbia Univ. Press.

1972   Investment in education: The equity-efficiency quandary. *Journal of Political Economy* **80** (May/June, Part II):S1–S292.

Schuman, Howard

1971   The religious factor in Detroit: Review, replication, and reanalysis. *American Sociological Review* **36** (Feb.):30–48.

Schwirian, Kent P., and Harry R. Blaine

1966   Questionnaire-return bias in the study of blue-collar workers. *Public Opinion Quarterly* **30** (Winter):656–663.

Sewell, William H.

1963   *Educational and occupational perspectives of rural youth.* (mimeo.) Washington, D.C.: National Committee for Children and Youth.

1964   Community of residence and college plans. *American Sociological Review* **29** (Feb.):24–38.

1971   Inequality of opportunity for higher education. *American Sociological Review* **36** (Oct.):793–809.

Sewell, William H., and J. Michael Armer

1966a   Neighborhood context and college plans. *American Sociological Review* **31** (Apr.):159–168.

1966b   Response to Turner, Michael and Boyle. *American Sociological Review* **31** (Oct.):707–712.

Sewell, William H., and Archibald O. Haller

1965   Educational and occupational perspectives of farm and rural youth. In *Rural youth in crisis: Facts, myths, and social change,* edited by Lee G. Burchinal. Washington, D.C.: U.S. Government Printing Office. Pp. 149–169.

Sewell, William H., Archibald O. Haller, and George W. Ohlendorf

1970   The educational and early occupational status attainment process: Replication and revision. *American Sociological Review* **35** (Dec.):1014–1027.

Sewell, William H., Archibald O. Haller, and Alejandro Portes

1969   The educational and early occupational attainment process. *American Sociological Review* **34** (Feb.):82–92.

Sewell, William H., and Robert M. Hauser

1972   Causes and consequences of higher education: Models of the status attainment process. *American Journal of Agricultural Economics* **54** (Dec.): 851–861.

Sewell, William H., Robert M. Hauser, and Vimal P. Shah

Social status and higher education. Unpublished manuscript.

Sewell, William H., and Alan M. Orenstein

1965   Community of residence and occupational choice. *American Journal of Sociology* **70** (Mar.):551–563.

Sewell, William H., and Vimal P. Shah

1967   Socioeconomic status, intelligence, and the attainment of higher education. *Sociology of Education* **40** (Winter):1–23.

1968a   Social class, parental encouragement, and educational aspirations. *American Journal of Sociology* **73** (Mar.):559–572.

1968b Parents' education and children's educational aspirations and achievements. *American Sociological Review* **33** (Apr.):191–209.

Sharp, Laure M.
1965 *Five years after the college degree, part III*. Washington, D.C.: Bureau of Social Science Research, Inc. (October).
1970 *Education and employment*. Baltimore: Johns Hopkins Press.

Smith, Robert B.
1972 Neighborhood context and college plans: An ordinal path analysis. *Social Forces* **50** (Dec.):199–217.

Solmon, Lewis C.
1972a The definition and impact of college quality. Unpublished manuscript, National Bureau of Economic Research (June).
1972b Schooling and subsequent success: Influence of ability, background, and formal education. Paper prepared for the Woods Hole Conference, Panel on the Benefits of Higher Education, Board of Human Resources, National Research Council (July).

Solmon, Lewis C., and Paul Wachtel
1971 The effects on income of type of college attended. Unpublished manuscript, National Bureau of Economic Research (November).

Sorokin, Pitirim
1927 *Social mobility*. New York: Harper and Brothers.

Spaeth, Joe L.
1968a Occupational prestige expectations among male college graduates. *American Journal of Sociology* **73** (Mar.):548–558.
1968b The allocation of college graduates to graduate and professional schools. *Sociology of Education* **41** (Fall):342–349.

Spaeth, Joe L., and Richard A. Ellis
1969 Attrition and bias in the sample. NORC Working Paper, Chicago (Apr.).

Spaeth, Joe L., and Andrew M. Greeley
1970 *Recent alumni and higher education*. New York: McGraw–Hill.

Suchman, Edward A.
1962 An analysis of "bias" in survey research. *Public Opinion Quarterly* **27** (Spring):102–111.

Taubman, Paul, and Terence Wales
1972 *Mental ability and higher educational attainment in the twentieth century*. New York: McGraw-Hill.
1973 Higher education, mental ability, and screening. *Journal of Political Economy* **81** (Jan./Feb.):28–55.

Tobin, J.
1958 Estimation of relationships for limited dependent variables. *Econometrics* **26** (Jan.):24–36.

Treiman, Donald J., and Robert M. Hauser
1970 On the intergenerational transmission of income: An exercise in theory construction. Mimeograph (November).

Trent, James W., and Leland L. Medsker
1968 *Beyond high school*. San Francisco: Jossey–Bass.

Turner, Ralph H.
  1966   On neighborhood context and college plans (I). *American Sociological Review* **31** (Oct.):698–702.
U.S. Department of Health, Education, and Welfare
  1969   *Social Security handbook.* 4th ed. Washington, D.C.
Wales, Terence J.
  1973   The effect of college quality on earnings: Results from the NBER–Thorndike data. *Journal of Human Resources* **8** (Summer):306–317.
Wegner, Eldon L., and William H. Sewell
  1970   Selection and context as factors affecting the probability of graduation from college. *American Journal of Sociology* **75** (Jan.):665–679.
Weisbrod, B. A., and P. Karpoff
  1968   Monetary returns to college education, student ability and college quality. *Review of Economics and Statistics* **50** (Nov.):491–497.
Weiss, Randall D.
  1970   The effect of education on the earnings of blacks and whites. *Review of Economics and Statistics* **52** (May):150–159.
Wells, Donald E.
  1966   Adoption proneness and response to mail questionnaires. *Rural Sociology* **31** (Dec.):483–487.
Werts, Charles E.
  1968   The partitioning of variance in school effects studies. *American Educational Research Journal* **5** (May):311–318.
Willett, T. D.
  1968   Another cost of conscription. *Western Economics Journal* **6** (Dec.): 425–426.
Wilson, Alan B.
  1969   *The consequences of segregation: Academic achievement in a northern community.* Berkeley: Glendessary.
Wing, Cliff W., Jr., and Michael A. Wallach
  1971   *College admission and the psychology of talent.* Chicago: Holt.
Withey, Stephen B.
  1972   *A degree and what else?* New York: McGraw-Hill.
Wolfle, Dael L.
  1954   *America's resources of specialized talent.* Report of the Commission of Human Resources and Advanced Training. New York: Harper and Brothers.
Wolfle, D., and J. G. Smith
  1956   The occupational value of education for superior high school graduates. *Journal of Higher Education* **27** (Apr.):201–213.
Wood, W. D., and H. F. Campbell
  1970   *Cost-benefit analysis and the economics of investment in human resources: An annotated bibliography.* Kingston, Ont.: Industrial Relations Center, Queens University.

Author Index

Numbers in italics refer to the pages on which the complete references are listed.

A

Acland, Henry, 43, 57, 58, 181, 191, *221*
Alexander, Karl, 25, *215*
Alwin, Duane F., 19, 113, 119, 120, 126, 132, 136, *215*
Armer, J. Michael, 6, 7, 16, 27, *218, 224*
Arrow, Kenneth J., 44, *215*
Ashenfelter, Orley A., 44, *215*
Astin, Alexander W., 115, 116, 117, 175, *215, 221*
Astin, Helen S., 115, 116, *219*

B

Babcock, F. Lawrence, 113, *216*
Bailey, D., *216*
Bane, Mary Jo, 43, 57, 58, 181, 191, *221*
Baur, E. Jackson, 27, *216*
Bayer, Alan E., 115, 116, *219*
Becker, Gary S., 11, 44, 143, 144, 161, 175, *216*
Becker, Susan J., 115, *217*
Beilin, Harry, 27, *216*
Berdie, Ralph F., 25, *216*
Berry, Charles C., 44, 59, *217*
Blaine, Harry R., 27, 37, *224*
Blau, Peter M., 2, 3, 11, 57, 181, 192, *216*
Blaug, Mark B., 44, *216*
Blum, Zahava D., 44, 45, 59, *216, 217*
Borus, M. E., 18, *216*

Bowles, Samuel, 44, 77, 105, *216*
Bowman, Mary Jean, 11, 44, 67, *216*
Boyle, Richard P., 7, *216*
Brazer, Harvey E., 43, *222*
Bridgman, D. S., 168, *216*
Brim, Orville G., Jr., 117, *217*
Britt, Steuart H., 27, *218*
Burgess, M. Elaine, 74, *217*

C

Campbell, Ernest Q., 7, *217*
Campbell, H. F., 11, *226*
Campbell, Richard T., 127, *217*
Cargill, T. F., *216*
Catton, William R., Jr., 27, *221*
Claudy, John G., 25, *219*
Cochran, William G., 27, *217*
Cohen, David, 43, 57, 58, 181, 191, *221*
Cohen, Jacob, *217*
Cohen, Wilbur J., 43, *222*
Coleman, James S., 7, 44, 45, 59, *216, 217*
Cooley, William W., 25, 54, 115, *217, 218, 219*
Cutwright, Phillips, 44, *217*

D

Daniere, Andre, 44, 114, *217*
David, Martin H., 43, 149, *222*
Deming, W. Edwards, 27, *217*

229

Subject Index